The Chicano Experience

Other Titles in This Series

Affirmative Action and Equal Opportunity: Action, Inaction, Reaction, Nijole Benokraitis and Joe R. Feagin

Immigration and Public Policy: Human and Economic Dilemmas of the Alien Issue, David Trippe Garza and Marta Cehelsky

Westview Special Studies
in Contemporary Social Issues

The Chicano Experience
edited by Stanley A. West and June Macklin

The past decade has seen a renewed interest in ethnicity by people in search of their own identities, as well as by writers and scholars from every discipline. But despite the contagion of ethnic "fever," the Chicano culture is neither widely known nor appreciated in the United States. The authors of this book attempt to close the gap in current knowledge. Their purpose is fourfold: (1) to add to the knowledge of Chicano communities; (2) to add to the knowledge and understanding of how Mexican Americans have adapted in various urban areas; (3) to present descriptions and analyses of communities in the Midwest, where the presence of Mexican Americans has been more typically neglected; and (4) to bring an anthropological approach to the understanding of this second-largest minority group in the United States.

Stanley A. West, a research social scientist with the Army Corps of Engineers, has been assistant professor of anthropology at Western Michigan University and assistant professor of civil engineering at MIT. June Macklin is professor and chairman of the Department of Anthropology at Connecticut College.

Chicanos in Toledo, Ohio, against a barrio mural comprising symbols of their heritage: the profile of a Mexican Indian, with a brooding Our Lady of Guadalupe hovering protectively. *Miguel Covarrubias.*

Mexican American, a former resident of the Bethlehem Steel Corporation's labor camp. *Stanley A. West.*

The Chicano Experience

edited by Stanley A. West
and June Macklin

Westview Press / Boulder, Colorado

Westview Special Studies in Contemporary Social Issues

Published in 1979 in the United States of America by
  Westview Press, Inc.
  5500 Central Avenue
  Boulder, Colorado 80301
  Frederick A. Praeger, Publisher

Library of Congress Cataloging in Publication Data
Main entry under title:
The Chicano experience.
  (Westview special studies in contemporary social issues)
  Includes index.
  1. Mexican Americans—Addresses, essays, lectures. I. West, Stanley A. II. Macklin, June.
E184.M5C44   301.45'16'872073   79-4257
ISBN: 0-89158-489-7

We wish to dedicate this book
to all of those people of Mexican descent
who permitted us to work and learn with them.
¡Que Dios se lo pague!

Contents

ix

Part 3
Voluntary Associations and Leadership

Tables and Figures

xi

Figures

Photographs

Acknowledgments

We gratefully acknowledge the pioneering work of labor economist Paul S. Taylor, whose research over fifty years ago set the stage for this book by preserving experiences of Mexican immigrants in the Southwest, Midwest, and East, as well as in Mexico after their repatriation from the United States. Our special thanks go to Joan W. Moore, whose careful reading and incisive comments in the early preparation of this manuscript were invaluable. Without the editorial and other assistance of R. E. Kent, this book could not have been finished.

Stanley A. West
June Macklin

About the Contributors

Alfredo H. Benavides, born in Robstown, Texas, is an assistant professor in the division of Elementary and Early Childhood Education, University of Iowa. He received a B.A. from Texas A&I University (Spanish and history), an M.A. (curriculum) and a Ph.D. from Michigan State University (administration and higher education). He has done fieldwork in western Michigan, and his research interests include multicultural and bilingual education, and educational anthropology.

Gilbert Cardenas is an assistant professor in the Department of Sociology at the University of Texas at Austin.

Alvina Teniente de Costilla, born on the West Side of San Antonio, Texas, where she also finished business college, migrated with her family from "as long as I can remember" until she settled out in Toledo, Ohio, in 1948. She entered the Ohio Bureau of Employment Services in 1954, and currently is an employment counselor with the bureau, working in the English-as-a-Second-Language Program. Her Texas-born husband was a migrant worker who settled in Ohio in 1948.

Armando Gutiérrez is an assistant professor in the Department of Political Science at the University of Texas at Austin.

Jane B. Haney is a lecturer in anthropology at Eastern Michigan University. She has B.A., M.A., and Ph.D. degrees from Michigan State University (anthropology) and has studied at Florence State University, the University of Alabama, and Universidad Nacional in Mexico City. She has done fieldwork with migratory farmworkers and permanent resident Mexican Americans in Michigan. Her research interests are comparative urban structures, political and economic anthropology.

Nicolás Kanellos is director of the Teatro Desengaño del Pueblo at Indiana University Northwest, Gary. His research interests include

Chicano and Puerto Rican theaters throughout the United States.

June Macklin is professor and chairman of the Department of Anthropology, Connecticut College, New London. She has a B.S. from Purdue University, an M.A. from the University of Chicago, and a Ph.D. from the University of Pennsylvania (anthropology); she spent a postgraduate year on a research grant in the Department of Anthropology at the University of Manchester, England. She has done fieldwork in Indiana, Ohio, Texas, Mexico, and Argentina, and her research interests are folk medicine among Mexicans and Mexican Americans, Spiritism in Latin America, Mexican Americans in the urban North of the United States, and Spiritualism in the United States.

Ricardo Parra is executive director, Midwest Council of La Raza, University of Notre Dame. He has a B.A. from Northeastern Illinois University (sociology), and his research interests are *la raza* in the Midwest, community organization, public policy, immigration, farm labor, civil rights, and the media. He is editor of *Los Desarraigados*, a newsletter of the Midwest Council of La Raza.

Victor Rios is with the Department of Sociology, University of Notre Dame, Indiana.

Joseph Spielberg Benitez, born and raised in the lower Rio Grande Valley of Texas, is professor in the Department of Anthropology, Michigan State University. He has a B.A. and M.A. from the University of Texas (sociology), and a Ph.D. from Michigan State University (anthropology). He has served as director of the Migrant Education Center, Central Michigan University, and was a visiting professor of Chicano studies, Department of Chicano Studies, University of California, Santa Barbara. He has done fieldwork in Guatemala, Mexico, Peru, Michigan, and southern Texas; his research interests are social organization, cultural ecology, and ethnohistory.

María-Luisa Urdaneta, born in Cali, Colombia, is assistant professor in the Department of Anthropology, University of Texas at San Antonio. She has an R.N. degree from Methodist Hospital, Dallas; a Certified R.N. Anesthetist degree from Baylor University Hospital, Dallas; a B.A. from the University of Texas at Austin (psychology); an M.A. from the University of Texas at Austin (sociology); an M.A. from Southern Methodist University (anthropology); and a Ph.D. from Southern Methodist University (anthropology). She has done fieldwork in the Southwest; her research interests are sociocultural factors affecting health, ethnomedicine, cultural ecology, urban anthropology, applied anthropology theory and implementation in the United States and Latin America, and problems of Hispanic-American women.

Irene Sosa Vásquez is a research and teaching assistant in the Department of Religion, Duke University. She has a B.A. from Western Michigan University (anthropology and religion), an M.A. from the University of Chicago (history of religion), and is a Ph.D. candidate at Duke University (history of religion). Her research interests include pre-Columbian and Latin-American religious history, phenomenology of religion, history of the disciplines of anthropology, and history of religion.

John R. Weeks is an associate professor and chairman, Department of Sociology, San Diego State University. He has an A.B. (sociology), and an M.A. and a Ph.D. (demography), all from the University of California, Berkeley. His research interests are fertility in Latin America, natural family planning, and home health care.

Brett Williams is an assistant professor of American studies at American University. Previously she was assistant professor in the Department of Anthropology, Illinois State University. She has a B.A. from Tufts University (history) and a Ph.D. from the University of Illinois (anthropology). Her fieldwork has been done in Illinois and Washington, D.C., and her research interests are migrant farmworkers, women's studies, family studies, and the anthropology of urban life.

Stanley A. West is a research associate, Department of Civil Engineering, Massachusetts Institute of Technology, currently on assignment with the Army Corps of Engineers in Vicksburg, Mississippi. Previously he was assistant professor with the Department of Anthropology, Western Michigan University, and assistant professor with the Department of Civil Engineering, Massachusetts Institute of Technology. He has a B.S. (physics) and a Ph.D. (anthropology) from Syracuse University. His fieldwork has been done in Mexico and Bethlehem, Pennsylvania; his research interests are Chicanos, environmental impact assessment, applied anthropology, and cognitive anthropology.

Laura Zarrugh is a research anthropologist and lecturer in the Department of Psychiatry and Medical Anthropology Program, University of California, San Francisco. She has a B.A., M.A., and Ph.D. (anthropology) from the University of California, Berkeley. Her fieldwork has been done in the San Francisco Bay area and Jalisco, Mexico; her research interests are Mexican and Mexican-American ethnography, family studies, migration, urban anthropology, and medical anthropology.

Introduction

Stanley A. West
and June Macklin

The past decade has seen a renewed interest in ethnicity on the part of people in search of their own identities, as well as among writers and scholars from every discipline. This outbreak of ethnic "fever" (Steinberg 1977:130) had its origins in the black community but rapidly spread to other racial and ethnic minorities. However, in spite of the "contagion" of the fever, Ricardo Romo and Raymund Paredes, pointing toward "new directions in Chicano scholarship," could assert (1978:v) that "Chicano culture has been neither widely known nor appreciated in the United States. This . . . applies as much to scholars as to the general public."

The purpose of this volume is fourfold.

1. To add to the knowledge of Chicano communities and cultures in general, with special emphasis on the heterogeneity among and within these communities. This heterogeneity is reflected in the old Mexican saying, *"Donde hay tres mexicanos, siempre hay cuatro opiniones"* ("Where there are three Mexicans, there are always four opinions") (Benavides Chapter 12).

2. To add to the knowledge and understanding of how Mexican Americans have adapted in various urban areas. Ten of the papers in this volume examine the experiences of the Chicano urbanite, including life in small towns, medium-sized cities, and metropolitan areas such as Detroit and Toledo. Inasmuch as the Chicano urban population in the United States grew by 6 percent from 1960 to 1970, and "it is possible that by 1980 at least 90 percent of the Chicano population may be urban residents" (Romo

1978:201), we believe that these descriptions and analyses will contribute to an understanding of the present and future of Mexicans and Mexican Americans in this country.

3. Specifically, to add descriptions and analyses of urban communities in the Midwest, because if Mexican Americans in the Southwest—where 90 percent of an estimated ten million live—have been "forgotten and invisible," their presence in other parts of the United States has been and continues to be even more neglected. "The first and largest wave of Chicanos came [to the Midwest] at the start of the Mexican Revolution in 1910," we are told, but "judging by the published literature, one would hardly know that Chicanos . . . reside outside the Southwest," (Parra et al. Chapter 12) and as one scholar wrote recently, whatever happens in these other "arenas," it certainly "would not be a mere reproduction of the Southwest experience" (Cardenas 1976b:182). Moore (1976) characterized three cultural areas to be found among Mexican Americans—Texas, New Mexico, and California; to these we must add the Midwest, a fourth area showing related but distinctive social and cultural adaptations.

4. To bring an anthropological approach to the understanding of Chicanos, the neglected, second-largest minority group in the United States. We believe with political scientist Wayne Cornelius that "one of the major strengths of the anthropological approach grows out of its deep concern for what happens at the grassroots level of society." Most of the data presented here have been collected by time-honored anthropological techniques—especially participant observation and the collection of life histories—that are "especially appropriate to the study of change processes at the individual, neighborhood or city level" (Cornelius 1974:10). While the anthropologist may "also engage in macro-level analysis and theorizing . . . his work is based in the first instance upon micro-level data referring to individuals" (Cornelius 1974:10), and is therefore a very humanistic social science.

Anthropological interest in ethnic groups and their adaptations to new situations can be seen in a rash of recent surveys on the subject (Bennett 1975; Cohen 1974; Despres 1975; De Vos and Romanucci-Ross 1975a and b; Gulick 1973; Hannerz 1974, 1976; Henry 1976a and b; Hicks and Leis 1977; Kushner 1970; Macklin 1977; Silverman 1976). Some curious paradoxes and contradictions are as apparent among the views of ethnic groups themselves as among investigators: some assert that ethnicity persists, that distinctive cultural ideas, behaviors, and social groups—based on different historical experiences—do exist, and that Americans are not becoming and will not become a homogeneous bowl of Anglo-Saxon mush. Others contend that the rediscovered "new" ethnicity is *not* authentic; it has reemerged, they say, because genuine differences are in fact fading; or perhaps because it has become expedient—economically, politically, and socially—to define oneself as being ethnic (Stein and Hill 1977).

The authors in this volume indicate that ethnicity is not a simple matter of either one or the other, but that both positions have some validity; that what is needed is an examination of the specific situations and conditions in which ethnic behaviors sometimes persist, transmitted from generation to generation through socialization; are transformed through interaction with others in the new environments in which the group finds itself; are lost; or are revived (occasionally with new interpretations and functions).

Several common points emerge from these papers, either explicitly or implicitly.

1. All consider both historically transmitted culture and contemporary socioeconomic constraints to be important determinants of ethnic behavior.

2. All realize that "being a descendant of an immigrant does not necessarily make an individual an ethnic in America" (Yancey, Ericksen, and Juliani 1976:100), and regard ethnicity as a process, a matter of degree, and sometimes as a dependent variable that responds to changes in the social structure. Clearly, we are examining Chicano experiences, not *the* Chicano experience.

3. Seven of the chapters are comparative, and although others focus on Chicano experiences in just one community, they offer data and analyses that can be compared profitably with studies focusing on the Southwest.

4. The Mexican-American populations discussed in this volume cannot be regarded as "internal colonies." All emigrated to the United States, and with one exception, were funneled through Texas and then traveled on to other states. And as Peñalosa has observed, "immigration in itself ordinarily implies some desire for change, a desire not necessarily shared by a conquered

people." Mexican immigrants "acculturate more rapidly to dominant Anglo society than . . . members of ethnic enclaves of centuries' standing" such as the Mexican-descent populations of California and New Mexico (1969:452).

5. All of the papers lend support to the claim that "the American Mexican population probably is more diverse in social composition than any [other] immigrant minority group in American history" (Moore 1976:1). Part of that diversity results from the attitudes and behaviors characteristic of different social classes. Several of our contributors supply ethnographic details about these differences, a subject not yet much discussed in the literature on Mexican-American populations (Cardenas 1976a:143).

6. All of our authors struggle with what to call the people of Mexican descent with whom they have lived and worked. Because of the diverse experiences and points of view held by the people themselves, some say they are "Mexican Americans" or, in Spanish, *"mexicano americanos"*—these often reject strongly the label "Chicano." Others—usually younger and politically active—insist on being called "Chicanos," while still others have adopted the language of the census and refer to themselves as "Spanish-speaking" or "Spanish-surname" populations. Often the social context determines usage. When speaking among themselves about their own group, they may use the blanket term "Mexican" (*"mexicano,"* *"mexicana"*) but distinguish Mexican nationals (citizens of the United States of Mexico) from Mexicans born in the United States of America by adding *"del otro lado"* ("from the other side"); or *"de este lado"* ("from this side"). *"Tejano"* is used among the groups discussed to refer to a Texas-born person of Mexican descent. *"Hispano"* is not used in any of the papers that follow because we are not dealing with the people of Mexican descent from either New Mexico or Colorado who prefer that term. Only two of our authors use *"Latino,"* and both use it to include other groups of Spanish-speaking people such as Puerto Ricans and South Americans. "Hispanic" is used in one paper in the same sense. *"La raza"* is used by Spanish-speaking people originating in many countries to refer to a shared, indefinable quality including identification with a unique spirit, sensibility, history, and destiny. Most of our authors finally resolve the issue by indicating that they will use the terms

"Chicano," "Mexican," and "Mexican American" interchangeably, realizing that use varies according to region, state, generation, social class, and political position.

7. Several authors deal specifically with something called "Anglo" culture, realizing that it, too, has been given monolithic treatment in the literature about Chicanos, seldom having been defined or described carefully; as a context it usually is taken for granted as being homogeneous and something about which "everybody knows" and agrees. Several papers point out that Anglo culture—which shapes the local communities into which Mexican Americans have come—is as varied, constantly changing, and emergent as are Mexican-American cultures.

Part 1. Immigration and the Migrant Way of Life

The first four papers examine immigration, settlement patterns, and the immigrant experience. Stanley West and Irene Vásquez outline the cultural patterns characteristic of Mexican villagers who emigrated in the early 1900s in order to show the relevance of their special shared history. Using data from newspaper archives and popular folk songs (*corridos*), West and Vásquez document the anguish of such separations as well as the indignities, deceit, and exploitation to which the emigrants were subjected by North American industrial and agribusiness interests, as well as by their own enterprising but more experienced countrymen (as has been the case among other American immigrants) (cf. Vecoli 1978:123).

The emigrants began at once to adapt Spanish to their new environment. Emigrants, Mexican nationals, and those of us who have worked on both sides of the border recognize that in some ways *mexicanos* and Chicanos are a people "separated by a common language"[1] (*pace* A. Paredes 1978).

Gilbert Cardenas suggests that the experience of Mexican emigrants going into the Midwest can be compared profitably with those of earlier European immigrant laborers. He concludes that both comprise a substratum of the American working class that "even in times of general economic prosperity still experiences conditions similar to those suffered by the greater spectrum of the nonethnic working class during depression." He also provides a historical explanation for some of the different adjustments of

Mexican-descent populations in the Midwest. Mexican immigrants and their children constitute an unusually high proportion of these populations in large urban areas (such as Kansas City, Chicago, and Detroit), he tells us, while in "the small and medium-sized cities, agricultural migrants, particularly from Texas, and other interstate migrants stand out as the single most distinctive segment."

Cardenas also found that the "majority" of Midwest-bound Mexican immigrants had lived in the United States for more than three years before legal admission, a point recently corroborated by other research (Price 1971; Hirschman 1978), as well as by Weeks and Spielberg Benitez, and Zarrugh in this volume. Precisely how such prior residence bears on later adjustment of permanent immigrants is difficult to assess from the data now available, and the question begs for more research.

Both West and Brett Williams provide examples of the conditions under which ethnic behavior becomes more pronounced. When immigrants are prohibited from social interaction with members of their host communities, and therefore from learning new cultural patterns, their traditional meaning systems—their historical patterns for problem solving—are likely to be carried into situations where they would not have been necessary in the migrants' communities of origin. A miracle-filled folk religion thrives: images of the saints accompany, nurture, protect, and interact with the migrants. Resilient migrants manipulate their "informal resources" (cf. Moore 1971)—family, godparent, and friendship patterns—to create flexible networks of people who can fill whatever role is needed at any given moment. Thus control is exercised over barren surroundings and an unpredictable and dangerous way of life. Individual and group rituals—uniquely Mexican—reinforce the group's consciousness and increase the frequency of personal interaction. The migrants' common interests are intensified because they share common positions in the occupational structure. West also shows that male and female immigrants evaluate the migration experience differently. Such intragroup diversity in adjustment to change has frequently been glossed over in the literature.

Perhaps better than any other paper in the volume, Williams' sensitive, rich ethnography illustrates how anthropological methods can illuminate microcultural patterns of interaction—the grass-roots level of living where daily decisions are made. The information she provides could never have been elicited by survey questionnaires.

Part 2. Ethnicity: Boundary Maintenance and Adaptiveness

June Macklin and Alvina Teniente de Costilla offer a general discussion of the issues of ethnicity, based on empirical data they began collecting twenty years ago on the Mexican-American community in Toledo, Ohio. They find (with West, Williams, Zarrugh, and Benavides) that the nuclear and extended families are strong, perdurable, and adaptive, as is the system of fictive kinship. But the tension between the model for social and cultural change expressed in the American Dream and that symbolized by Our Lady of Guadalupe creates various strategies for successful management of the environment in which Toledo's Mexican Americans find themselves.

Laura Zarrugh's paper makes several original contributions to the field of Chicano community studies, as she describes how people transplanted from the same Mexican village in the state of Jalisco to the San Francisco Bay area go about maintaining and reaffirming their social and cultural boundaries. Such community "transposition" is rare among Mexican Americans, and Zarrugh has pursued this advantage by spending time in the village from which her bay area informants came. She finds that if members of an ethnic enclave such as this can reproduce their original social organization within the host community, they are able to adapt with little stress and with little social or cultural change (cf. Ablon 1971). Zarrugh also finds paradoxically that modern technology—telephones, automobiles, public transportation—makes it possible for her group to feel and behave like members of a traditional community, an "urban village," even though they do not all live in the same neighborhood. She, West, and Macklin also show that ethnic communities may create new economic niches for some of their own group because of the psychological, social, and material needs they bring with them; *petit entrepreneurs* appear (e.g., folk healers, midwives, and restauranteurs; in *botanicas* and in tortilla factories) who have a vested interest in the persistence of the ethnic community itself.

In the next two papers, María-Luisa Urdaneta and June Macklin

deal with different facets of persistence and change in health beliefs, values, and practices among Mexican Americans. Urdaneta
attacks the current cultural explanation of why Mexican-American
women either do not use or underutilize family planning clinics.
Specifically, she finds that it is not their reputedly conservative values—*machismo,* Catholicism, and the socialization of
women into maternal and wifely female roles—that keeps them
from seeking such services. Her careful case studies point out
the relevance of education, class culture, and economic resources to their behavior. She analyses the "macrosystem" in which
the culture and realities of both the Mexican-American women and
the clinic are considered, and concludes—in the most applied paper
in the volume—with a plan for action that will be useful to
practitioners in various health care delivery systems.

Macklin's comparison of a traditional folk healer (*curandera*) in
Indiana and a Spiritist cult in San Antonio, Texas, suggests that
traditional healers are not fading from the Mexican-American
scene. Instead, it appears, in urban areas they are transforming
themselves into practitioners who are able to deal with more
complex problems—whether health-related, personal, social, or
economic—than those treated by their rural counterparts. Thus, they
need a more complex collection of spirits to assist, advise, and
guide them. Further, the folk healer and his or her clients flexibly use both traditional and "scientific" medicine, while the
practitioner of modern medicine inflexibly rejects the former as
"quackery."

Part 3. Voluntary Associations and Leadership

All of the authors in this section address themselves to the
assertion often made by social scientists and Mexican Americans
alike, that Chicanos "just can't get together, just can't organize themselves." Such observers conclude that formal organizations among
this "atomistic" minority group are doomed to fail, the blame being
placed on the underlying "traditional or poverty-induced cultural
values [that] determine the behavior of Chicanos, their relations to each other, and consequently, the relative absence . . . of
formal organizational life" (Weeks and Benitez Chapter 10).
None of our authors denies that there is some validity to these

earlier descriptions; all contend, however, that explanations for organizational functioning must take into account many highly complex factors.

Demographer Weeks and anthropologist Spielberg Benitez offer a new approach to this old problem, one that weds demographic and sociocultural processes to produce an interactive system that can be observed on local levels. They propose that small, recent, homogeneous Chicano populations (characteristic of those found in midwestern towns) *do* organize themselves into atomizing, family-like groups that retard changes in other areas of culture. The larger, older, more heterogeneous Chicano populations usually found in metropolitan areas (cf. Cardenas Chapter 2), tend to foster even more heterogeneity as Chicanos proliferate and suburbanization takes place. They also make the important point that the student of migration behavior and adjustment must consider what was happening in both Mexico and the United States at the time that a given "subpart" of the population emigrated. Comparing Detroit, Michigan, with Fremont, Ohio, they also are particularly clear about the diversity to be found in "Anglo" cultures.

Jane Haney and Alfredo Benavides, both drawing on data from other Michigan cities, provide local data that flesh out the framework offered by Weeks and Spielberg Benitez. Haney, comparing the functioning of Chicano agencies in Flint and Lansing (Mexican and Mexican-American populations of comparable size in cities of approximately the same size) found that the Flint Chicanos cooperated very well, while those in Lansing competed fiercely, were constantly bickering, and saw themselves as suspicious, jealous, and constitutionally unable to organize effectively. Haney explains these different orientations as the result of complex interactions between the Chicano communities and the political economies of the two cities.

Alfredo Benavides's provocative analysis of leadership in the Chicano community of "Port City" tells us that the homogeneous leadership upon which they rely cannot solve the heterogeneous problems posed by their community. He offers new support for Arthur Rubel's classic analysis (1966) of the role of *compadrazgo* and *personalismo* in the political life of the border town he studied, but Benavides cautions us not to make the "assumption that these concepts are simple in nature and accurate predictors of all Mexican-American social and political behavior . . . they are extremely complex and involve several variables."

Ricardo Parra, Victor Rios, and Armando Gutiérrez catalogue the many organizations that have come, gone, or persisted in the Midwest. They classify Chicano institutions in two categories: "parallel"—(modeled after Anglo patterns and economically "unsuccessful" because they are designed to accommodate Anglo wishes)—and "alternative"—institutions that seek fundamental change in society, and that disappear because of oppression by the dominant and alienating Anglo culture.

In Summary

We believe that this collection of papers will help to close the gaps in our knowledge about people of Mexican descent living in the United States. Although John Burma could remind us in 1970 that "Samora's book bears the title *La Raza: Forgotten Americans*; Heller's study, *Mexican American Youth: Forgotten at the Crossroads*; Sanchez's major work is titled *Forgotten People*; and the National Education Association's (NEA) Tucson study, 'The Invisible Minority,'" many scholars have contributed to the field of Chicano studies since then, as the bibliography of this Introduction and those of our authors testify. Many questions remain, and hypotheses stand untested. We hope our efforts here will stimulate further research, whether to corroborate, challenge, or correct us.

Note

1. This particular quote originated as a description of the dialectical differences between English English and American English, and is, of course, characteristic of how languages tend to change.

References

Ablon, Joan
   1971   "Retention of Cultural Values and Differential Urban Adaptation: Samoan and American Indians in a West Coast City." *Social Forces* 49, no. 3:385-393.

Bennett, John W., ed.
1975   *The New Ethnicity: Perspectives from Ethnology.* St. Paul, Minn.: West Publishing Co.

Burma, John H., ed.
1970   *Mexican-Americans in the United States: A Reader.* Cambridge, Mass.: Schenkman Publishing Co.

Cardenas, Gilbert
1976a   "Introduction. Who Are the Midwestern Chicanos: Implications for Chicano Studies." *Aztlán: International Journal of Chicano Studies Research* 7:141-152.

1976b   *"Los Desarriagados:* Chicanos in the Midwestern Region of the United States."*Aztlán: International Journal of Chicano Studies Research* 7:153-186.

Cohen, Abner
1974   "Introduction: The Lesson of Ethnicity." In *Urban Ethnicity,* edited by Abner Cohen, pp. 9-24. London: Tavistock Publications.

Cornelius, Wayne A.
1974   "Introduction." In *Latin American Urban Research: Anthropological Perspectives on Latin American Urbanization,* edited by Wayne A. Cornelius and Felicity M. Trueblood, pp. 9-20. Beverly Hills, Calif.: Sage Publications.

Despres, Leo A.
1968   "Anthropological Theory, Cultural Pluralism, and the Study of Complex Societies." *Current Anthropology* 9:3-16.

Despres, Leo A., ed.
1975   *Ethnicity and Resource Competition in Plural Societies.* The Hague: Mouton Publishers.

De Vos, George, and Romanucci-Ross, Lola, eds.
1975a   *Ethnic Identity: Cultural Continuities and Change.* Palo Alto, Calif.: Mayfield Publishing Company.

1975b   "Ethnicity: Vessel of Meaning and Emblem of Contrast." In *Ethnic Identity: Cultural Continuities and Change,* edited by G. De Vos and L. Romanucci-Ross, pp. 363-390. Palo Alto, Calif.: Mayfield Publishing Company.

Glenn, Norval D.
1971   "Some Reflections on a Landmark Publication and the Literature on Mexican Americans." *Social Science Quarterly* 52:8-38.

Gulick, John
1973   "Urban Anthropology." In *Handbook of Social and Cultural Anthropology,* edited by J. J. Honigmann, pp. 979-1029. Chicago: Rand McNally & Co.

Hannerz, Ulf
  1974   "Ethnicity and Opportunity in Urban America." In *Urban
          Ethnicity*, edited by Abner Cohen, pp. 37-76. London: Tavistock
          Publications.
  1976   "Some Comments on the Anthropology of Ethnicity in the
          United States." In *Ethnicity in the Americas*, edited by F. Henry,
          pp. 429-438. The Hague: Mouton Publishers.
Henry, Frances, ed.
  1976a   *Ethnicity in the Americas*. The Hague: Mouton Publishers.
  1976b   "Introduction." In *Ethnicity in the Americas*, edited by Frances
          Henry, pp. 1-7. The Hague: Mouton Publishers.
Hicks, George L.
  1977   "Introduction: Problems in the Study of Ethnicity." In *Ethnic
          Encounters: Identities and Contexts*, edited by George L. Hicks
          and Philip E. Leis, pp. 1-20. North Scituate, Maine: Duxbury
          Press.
Hicks, George L., and Leis, Philip E., eds.
  1977   *Ethnic Encounters: Identities and Contexts*. North Scituate,
          Maine: Duxbury Press.
Hirschman, Charles
  1978   "Prior U.S. Residence among Mexican Immigrants." *Social
          Forces* 5:1179-1202.
Kushner, Gilbert
  1970   "The Anthropology of Complex Societies." In *Biennial Review
          of Anthropology*, edited by B. J. Siegel, pp. 80-131. Stanford,
          Calif.: Stanford University Press.
Macklin, June
  1977   "Ethnic Minorities in the United States: Perspectives from Cul-
          tural Anthropology." *International Journal of Group Tensions*
          7, nos. 3 and 4:98-119.
Martinez, Joe L., Jr., ed.
  1977   *Chicano Psychology*. New York: Academic Press.
Meier, Matt S., and Rivera, Feliciano
  1972   *The Chicanos: a History of Mexican Americans*. New York: Hill
          & Wang, American Century Series.
Moore, Joan W.
  1971   "Mexican Americans and Cities: A Study in Migration and the
          Use of Formal Resources." *International Migration Review*
          5:292-308.
  1976   *Mexican Americans*, 2d ed. Englewood Cliffs, N.J.: Prentice-Hall.
Pacific Historical Review
  1973   "The Chicano." Vol. 42:269-406 (seven articles).

Paredes, Américo
1978   "On Ethnographic Work among Minority Groups: A Folklorist's Perspective." In *New Perspectives in Chicano Scholarship*, edited by Ricardo Romo and Raymund Paredes, pp. 1-32. La Jolla: Chicano Studies Monograph Series, Chicano Studies Program, University of California, San Diego.

Parra, Ricardo; Rios, Victor; and Gutiérrez, Armando
1976   "Chicano Organizations in the Midwest: Past, Present, and Possibilities." *Aztlán: International Journal of Chicano Studies Research* 7:235-253.

Peñalosa, Fernando
1969   "Education-income Discrepancies between Second and Later-generation Mexican Americans in the Southwest." *Sociology and Social Research* 53:448-454.

Price, D. O.
1971   "Rural to Urban Migration of Mexican Americans, Negroes and Anglos." *International Migration Review* 5:281-291.

Romo, Ricardo
1978   "The Urbanization of Southwestern Chicanos in the Early 20th Century." In *New Directions in Chicano Scholarship*, edited by Ricardo Romo and Raymund Paredes, pp. 183-207. La Jolla: Chicano Studies Monograph Series, Chicano Studies Program, University of California, San Diego.

Romo, Ricardo, and Paredes, Raymund
1978   "Introduction." In *New Directions in Chicano Scholarship*, edited by Ricardo Romo and Raymund Paredes, pp. v-vii. La Jolla: Chicano Studies Monograph Series, Chicano Studies Program, University of California, San Diego.

Rubel, Arthur J.
1966   *Across the Tracks: Mexican Americans in a Texas City*. Austin: University of Texas Press.

Silverman, Sydel
1976   "Ethnicity as Adaptation: Strategies and Systems." *Reviews in Anthropology* 3:626-636.

Social Science Quarterly
1973   "The Chicano Experience in the United States." Vol. 53: 652-942 (twenty-two articles).

Stein, Howard F., and Hill, Robert F.
1977   *The Ethnic Imperative: Examining the New White Ethnic Movement*. University Park: The Pennsylvania State University Press.

Steinberg, Stephen
1977   "Ethnicity in the United States: a Sociological Perspective." *International Journal of Group Tensions* 7, nos. 3 and 4:130-147.

Vecoli, Rudolph J.
  1978   "The Coming of Age of the Italian Americans: 1945-1974."
           Ethnicity 5:119-147.
Yancey, William L.; Ericksen, Eugene P.; and Juliani, Richard N.
  1976   "Emergent Ethnicity: A Review and Reformulation." American
           Sociological Review 41:391-403.

Part 1
Immigration and the
Migrant Way of Life

1
Early Migration from Central Mexico to the Northern United States

Stanley A. West
and Irene S. Vásquez

Introduction

This chapter is a historical reconstruction of the experiences encountered by Mexican immigrants of a half century ago who founded the Mexican *colonias* ("colonies") that have become contemporary Chicano barrios. That the immigrants called their settlements *"colonias"* is somewhat surprising because colonies are usually established with the intent of permanence, and few founders of Mexican *colonias* ever intended to remain long in the United States, though remain they did. While journeying toward unfounded or young *colonias*, Mexican immigrants faced physical hardships, economic insecurities, and a variety of indignities that are briefly described in this chapter. The negative observations in this chapter predominate over positive aspects only because the primary data studied reveal that hardship in fact prevailed over fulfillment of dreams. Whatever their evaluation, these human dimensions of Mexican immigration during the 1920s form an integral part of the Chicano heritage that fundamentally lent character to the personalities of today's eldest Chicanos.

Although no brief account, especially one pieced together five decades later, can provide a total description of the immigrants' varied experiences, this chapter is intended to reveal at least the courage that must have sustained Mexican immigrants of the 1920s. That was a courage about which their Chicano grandchildren and great-grandchildren may have been told too little because part of each suffering mind always tries to forget its past dehumanizing circumstances. Accounts like the one that follows serve to give Chicanos and non-Chicanos alike a basis for pride in *la raza*. Whether drawing on well-documented and systematically prepared historic accounts or fragmentary and casually assembled popular ideas about history, the goals pursued by Chicano politicians and activists are influenced by their images of Chicano history as well as by their perceptions of the present. The authors hope that this chapter will serve as an empirically well-founded historical reconstruction whatever the reason readers may turn to it.

Because few biographic accounts have been published, the following description is synthesized from a variety of sources, including personal interviews of elderly immigrants, books, journal articles, folk songs (*corridos*), and especially Spanish-language newspapers of the 1920s such as *La Prensa* of San Antonio, Texas.

Although the following story describes migration from one particular Mexican village in two ways, it is really about many Mexicans migrating from many different locations. The hamlet chosen, Arandas, is typical of North Central Mexico, which was the largest single source of migrants to the United States prior to World War II. Also, emigrants of this larger region settled in all the areas covered by other chapters in this book. Therefore, Arandas is a fitting, though somewhat arbitrary, starting point for this reconstruction.

The words of the following story lead immigrants to but one destination: Bethlehem, Pennsylvania. However, this chapter is equally pertinent to migration to the Midwest during that era because the trains carrying Mexicans passed through this region on their way east. Furthermore, stories that reached San Antonio (the principal labor recruitment center) from both Pennsylvania and the Midwest bespoke comparable conditions for Mexicans working in both locations. Therefore, the following story is relevant to nearly all of the subsequent chapters, despite an overt focus upon Pennsylvania.

Migration from the State of Jalisco to the United States

During the 1920s it was expected that adult males in the village of Arandas, Jalisco, would migrate to the United States and later return. Indeed, men who had never migrated to the United States seemed to be rather exceptional. Paul Taylor purposely chose to study this particular village because of the large numbers of its men who had migrated at least briefly to the United States, and he judged that this migration was typical of migration from the Mexican republic as a whole (Taylor 1933; cf. Gamio 1969a). Taylor's careful study includes a detailed description of the preparations that emigrants made for their trek to the United States. He found that emigrants from Arandas usually needed about one hundred pesos (then about fifty dollars— which equates to far more in 1979 currency) for their journey. If this sum seems inconsequential to present-day readers, they should consider that Mexican laborers working for the average agricultural wage during the 1920s would have been obliged to save the earnings of four hundred days' work in order to amass this amount. In contrast, the typical American laborer in the 1920s could have earned fifty dollars by working for only thirty-two days (Tannenbaum 1930:149). A few rare individuals wanting to emigrate were able to obtain enough cash from their savings or from the sale of animals, house, or land, but the majority were obliged to seek loans from local merchants, owners of large *ranchos*, or the owners of small *haciendas*. In return for their help these financiers charged from 12 to 200 percent annual interest (Taylor 1933:45).

Manuel Gamio, the Mexican anthropologist, observed that most Mexicans in their homeland were truly sedentary, the period of revolution not excluded (Gamio 1969:148). Thus, for many, the first departure for the United States was their only prolonged separation from kin and home community, and it thus sparked genuine life crises. The poignancy in the *corrido* "An Emigrant's Farewell" reflects great apprehension about emigration:

> I go sad and heavy-hearted
> to suffer and endure;
> my Mother of Guadalupe,
> grant my safe return.
> (Taylor 1935:234-5.)

As the balladeer's train passed through each successive Mexican city en route, he uttered a new lament about departing from his homeland. Soon, however, these emotions were overshadowed by the often frustrating and time-consuming problems of effecting a border crossing.

Upon reaching a Mexican city located at the northern frontier of

his nation—such as Cuidad Juarez, which bounds El Paso, Texas—
the Mexican had to decide whether to cross legally or illegally. To
enter through legal channels, one was required to endure a waiting
period on each side of the border. These formalities might have
consumed a week or more, during which time the immigrant
typically purchased shoes and overalls to replace his traditional white
pants and collarless shirt, sandals, *sombrero,* and serape. This
expenditure, together with the necessary living expenses incurred
while waiting in Juarez or some other border town, depleted his
resources; the payment of the head tax and the application fee for a
visa, totaling eighteen dollars, imposed additional financial burdens.
Finally, at the hands of U.S. agents, he suffered the most demeaning
experience greeting the legal Mexican immigrant: he was "bathed,
sometimes with gasoline, while his clothing was disinfected" (Gamio
1969b:148).

Given these costs and indignities, many Mexicans preferred to
accept the offers of *coyotes,* agents who for five or ten dollars
promised to smuggle them into the United States more quickly and
more cheaply than was possible through legal channels[1] (Gamio
1969b:205-206). As a variant of this procedure, some Mexicans
purchased counterfeit immigration documents from the ever-
resourceful, ever-exploitative *coyotes* (Gamio 1969b:204). Given the
1600-mile-long border between the United States and Mexico and the
ruggedness of the terrain, casual and ill-prepared attempts at crossing
were usually successful even without the assistance of *coyotes.* Of
course, because of their precarious legal status while in the United
States, the *mojados,* or "wetbacks," who swam the Rio Grande and
the *aerialistas* who climbed the fence that separated the two nations
easily fell prey to the Americans who prospered by exploiting
undocumented aliens.

Having crossed the border by one of these means, many Mexicans
were unable to settle down because they had to depend on seasonal
work. As one of the largest employers of Mexicans, the railroad
industry was responsible for the location of many Chicano *barrios.*
From the older settlements of Spanish Americans and Mexicans in the
American Southwest, many Mexicans followed the railroad network,
serving as *traqueros* (laborers who built or maintained railroad
tracks); several large *colonias*—notably in Chicago, Detroit, Kansas
City, Toledo, and Watts—were outgrowths of boxcar camps built for

Mexicans (McWilliams 1949:168). Although the colonies became permanent, economic pressures dictated that the turnover of residents would be high.

Typically, Mexican immigrants who were not going directly to the Pacific or Rocky Mountain states passed through San Antonio, Texas, which served as a gigantic "magnet" and "funnel" for the migration of Mexicans because of its reputation as the primary center for recruitment of Mexican laborers. Moreover, this city was widely known as the center of Mexican culture in the United States and has been referred to as "the capital of the Mexico that lies within the United States" (McWilliams 1941:5).

San Antonio and Work in Texas

Upon arriving in San Antonio, Mexican immigrants discovered that strong Mexican cultural influences persisted within the new and strange world of the Anglos. For example, persons who from childhood had believed that miraculous cures were possible at Mexican Catholic shrines found that in San Antonio they could petition at the shrine of El Señor de los Milagros ("The Lord of Miracles"). This chapel had been the personal property of a Mexican family for several generations, continuing to function despite opposition from the Catholic Church. Thousands of pilgrims attested to the efficacy of the crucifix of El Señor de los Milagros by placing *retablos* (pictures of figures depicting the miracles or favors granted by the saint) upon the building's walls.

Carey McWilliams had the following impressions of that *colonia:*

> The Mexican district of San Antonio is an indolent and rather unattractive quarter. Unpainted shacks, in a state of perpetual ill-repair, rest on stilts and lean precariously in all directions; dogs bark, children yell, and radios blare in every hovel. But the windows are decorated with plants, feeble shrubs sprout in the dirt yards, and morning glories climb the fence posts. Every corner has its grocery store and beer hall (and above the beer hall the *bagnio* [brothel]). (McWilliams 1949:179.)

Mexicans from Arandas arriving in San Antonio for the first time were not likely to have perceived poverty in the city, accustomed as they were to little material wealth.

Many Mexicans who accepted work as contract laborers in the

Southwest found that they were poorly paid and their lives were humiliating. From the name alone, Mexican immigrants might have anticipated a bad outcome from entering into labor contracts. In Spanish the contract laborers are known as *enganches*, a word derived from *enganchar* ("to ensnare"; "to press into military service"). Because for centuries army recruits in Mexico had been recruited by force or deceit and the related word *engaño* means deceit, Mexican immigrants to the United States might have felt trepidation about becoming *enganches*. The closely related word *gancho* has a colloquial meaning of "pimp" or "procurer," which has negative connotations rather appropriate to many labor contractors. *Ganchos* are also the coupling mechanisms that interconnect railroad cars; *ganchos* couple cattle and other cars that are reluctantly joined together by unyielding cast iron, rolling through clatter, dust, and cinders to indeterminate destinies.

Numerous similar accounts in San Antonio's Spanish language daily, *La Prensa*, decry the guile of the labor contractors *(enganchistas)* who duped hundreds of Mexican laborers, and reports of *engaño* (deceit or fraud) by labor contractors appeared repeatedly in its pages during 1923.[2] At times these workers were marched under armed guard through the streets of San Antonio and locked up at night as if they were human chattel. One reason for these measures was to foil "man snatchers," labor contractors who would sell a crew to an employer only to return stealthily under cover of darkness to forcibly steal back the *mexicanos* for subsequent resale. But workers who attempted to break exploitative contracts were sometimes chained and put under armed guard. To put it mildly, the scales of justice were tipped greatly in favor of *enganchistas* and large employers (McWilliams 1949). However, Mexicans who had few resources and desperately needed work had little choice but to accept the employment that was offered to them.

Another common fradulent practice of labor contractors was overcontracting: advertising for a much larger number of laborers than was really required. With excess labor on hand, employers were able to depress wages, regardless of the financial needs of the Mexican laborers. As a result, in March of 1923, thousands of indigent Mexicans returned to Juarez after encountering extensive unemployment in Texas. A total of 1200 of these persons, some of whom were reportedly dying of hunger (*La Prensa* 1923c), were provided with transportation into Mexico's interior by the Mexican government.

La Prensa published an article describing a variant of the *enganchistas'* duplicity, stating that thirty-six Mexicans were jailed for vagrancy in Fort Worth, Texas. These men had been taken to Fort Worth by an *enganchista* who had had them jailed by compliant law officers until he could provide them with jobs. These unjustly imprisoned Mexicans were freed only through the intervention of Mexican Consul General Alejandro Lubbert (*La Prensa* 1923d).

During most of 1923, San Antonio's Mexican colony was considerably agitated over the maltreatment of Mexican laborers by American labor contractors, public officials, and employers. One phase of the controversy began on February 28, 1923, with a charge printed in *La Prensa* that Mexicans were being "treated as slaves" by the jailers of Grayson County, Texas. This report was followed by a statement that the situation would be investigated by the United States Department of Justice (*La Prensa* 1923a). By March 2, through the efforts of General Lubbert, one of the Mexican laborers' few defenders, these "slaves" were freed. At that time an article in *La Prensa* disclosed that the Mexicans had been suffering maltreatment and privations while being compelled to labor on Grayson County roads (*La Prensa* 1923b).

A number of American companies tried to neutralize charges published in *La Prensa* that they were maltreating Mexican employees. Among the most eager to disclaim any abuse was the Michigan Sugar Company, a producer of beet sugar (*La Prensa* 1923t). The Mexicans claimed that on each of the four days of the journey from San Antonio to Michigan the tortilla-eating workers had been fed sandwiches consisting of "one sardine enclosed within a piece of bread" (*La Prensa* 1923s). The company countered with the accusation that workers were breaking their contracts and published a statement signed by a Mexican worker who testified that the living and working conditions for Mexican laborers were far better in Michigan than elsewhere in the United States.

Although various American companies vigorously denied mistreating *enganches,* San Antonio's Mexicans responded to the published accusations by suggesting several preventive measures. Realizing that many of his countrymen were illiterate, one Mexican admonished all Mexican laborers to read carefully the conditions of any contract or to prevail upon a literate friend to read it (*La Prensa* 1923g). The Mexican Consul General, however, actively intervened to protect the Mexican workers' interests by negotiating directly with American companies on behalf of the *enganches*. The contracts that he signed with American companies guaranteed that the wages, working conditions, and living conditions of Mexicans recruited would be comparable to those of unskilled American laborers (*La Prensa* 1923h). The Mexican Consul General also provided a model contract and recommended that Mexicans seek its adoption by their employers.

Moreover, both American and Mexican officials, reacting to allegations that Mexican immigrants to the United States were suffering from overcontracting and poor conditions of employment, proposed restrictions on the entry of Mexican laborers (*La Prensa* 1923e). Officials of the state of Texas reportedly proposed that "importation on promise of work" was to be stopped (*San Antonio Light* 1923c). Furthermore, officials of the Mexican government apparently agreed that illegal or even unrestricted immigration from Mexico to the United States was undesirable. In 1923, Álvaro Obregón, president of Mexico, declared that "the government of Mexico would take special pains in vigilance to contain the emigration of workers" (*La Prensa* 1923f). Given all the hardships to which Mexicans were exposed in the Southwest, individuals who consented to be transported to distant and unknown industrial cities of the North or the Northeast must have been desperate, highly daring, or both.

Off to the Northeast

In this section we trace the migration of Mexicans to an urban industrial area to complement the above discussion of Mexicans working in agriculture, for the Mexican experience of the 1920s extended well beyond harvesting cotton and sugar beets. As in the previous section, much of the information was gleaned from the pages of *La Prensa*. Our intent is to convey a qualitative appreciation for experiences encountered during migration to northern cities through the description of one particular case (which is further described in Chapter 3).

In 1923, while the American economy was recovering from a recession, the Bethlehem Steel Corporation of Bethlehem, Pennsylvania, once again fired up several blast furnaces that had been shut down. Motivated by the labor requirements of steel mills in full production as well as by a lack of unskilled laborers, the management began to recruit Mexican laborers in San Antonio. "In five shipments arriving between April 6 and May 30, 1923, there were transported from Texas to Bethlehem 912 Mexican men, 29 women, and 7 children" (Taylor 1931:3).

One Bethlehem resident recalls that he learned of Bethlehem Steel Corporation's recruiting in San Antonio when he observed a sign in the railroad station announcing *"Se necesita braceros para la fundicion del estado Pensilvanio"* ("Workers are needed for a foundry in the state of Pennsylvania"). From journalistic accounts one learns that the Bethlehem Steel Corporation was the first American company to recruit laborers while accepting safeguards proposed by the Mexican Consul General (*San Antonio Light* 1923a).

The requirements of this labor contract stipulated a minimum wage of 30¢ an hour, later raised to 34¢, and guaranteed that Mexicans performing the same job as workers of other nationalities would receive the same wage. Mexicans had the option of utilizing company-provided room and board at the rate of $1.10 per day. As an inducement for Mexicans to work in Bethlehem for at least one year, the cost of the railroad transportation including food—$84.00—was deducted from the laborer's wages during the first year but refunded at the end of that time. The agreement further stipulated that if any Mexicans became public charges, the Bethlehem Steel Corporation would transport them to the Mexican consulate in San Antonio (Taylor 1931:4). While the Mexicans resided in Bethlehem, the corporation agreed to be responsible for their medical care and their children's education. Both were to be provided gratis and "without discrimination" (*La Prensa* 1923i). It may be surmised that many Mexicans would have been more reluctant to journey so far to the unknown Northeast had the steel company not made these guarantees to the Mexican Consul General.

But apparently the San Antonio Labor Agency, which had coordinated the recruitment of workers, did not feel that these legal assurances were sufficient to dispel rumors concerning the Mexicans who had by then arrived in Bethlehem. On April 5, 1923, the following public notice appeared in *La Prensa:*

> We wish to announce that we have delivered the 350 Mexican workers who departed Tuesday morning with the M.&K.T. railroad in a special train for the Bethlehem Steel Company, of Bethlehem, Pennsylvania. They have been given adequate provisions consisting of canned fish, peaches, peaches [sic], etc. Also, we telegraphed to all the stations on

the route to give the Mexicans twenty-five gallons of coffee . . . —San
Antonio Labor Agency. (*La Prensa* 1923i.)

Within one week of the first contingent's arrival in Bethlehem,
charges reached San Antonio that the Mexicans had been hired as
strikebreakers. It also was claimed that following knife fights among
themselves seventeen Mexicans had been hospitalized. The Mexican
consul investigated the situation only to discover that there had been
no strike and that only ten Mexicans were in the hospital—all of them
suffering from colds and the grippe, a result of the change in climate[3]
(*San Antonio Light* 1923b; *La Prensa* 1923m). The Bethlehem Steel
Corporation clearly needed new workers; it offered to send
photographs of the Mexican labor camp (houses and barracks
provided by the company) in order to demonstrate that the
accommodations were satisfactory (*La Prensa* 1923k).

What the company omitted from their glowing descriptions of
Mexicans' life in Bethlehem, was that laborers recruited in San
Antonio were assigned to the extremely hot and dirty coke ovens
because few other employees wanted to work there and because of the
stereotype that "Mexicans can take heat." But coming from the North
Central Plateau of Mexico, they were really accustomed to cool
evenings even in summer and several months of uncomfortably cold
weather each winter. Mexican recruits suffered no less than
northerners from the ovens' intense temperatures.

Later the Bethlehem Steel Corporation decided to negotiate a
second labor contract through the Mexican Consul General. The
company stated its intent to hire five hundred additional workers
because of the "industry of the Mexicans and the facility with which
they accustom themselves to their jobs" (*La Prensa* 1923n; *San
Antonio Light* 1923b:10), an evaluation that contradicts stereotypes
about Mexicans. Apparently the negotiations proceeded quickly,
judging by the following classified advertisement, which appeared
but three days later:

> We need about 200 single men to go to the Bethlehem Steel Co.,
> Bethlehem, Pa. Come quickly if you are not working because we
> depart in special trains on Friday. Good houses and good salary.
> We do not charge office expenses. Do not write; come ready if you
> are a good worker.—San Antonio Labor Agency. (*La Prensa* 1923o.)

Advertisements of a similar style and content but decreasing length appeared in each issue of *La Prensa* for several consecutive days.

In compliance with Pennsylvania labor laws, the Bethlehem Steel Corporation was permitted to hire only Mexicans who were common laborers, and the recruiting of foreign "artisans" or "mechanics" was forbidden. Nevertheless, this regulation seems at least partially inconsistent with the Bethlehem Steel Corporation's guarantee that persons with "special knowledge or abilities" would be given the appropriate work with a higher pay scale (*La Prensa* 1923q). The obvious effect of such restrictive regulations was to lower the percentage of *enganches* who had special skills and to ensure that the workers hired would at least in part conform to and perpetuate the stereotype that Mexicans were ignorant and unskilled.

As the spring wore on, *La Prensa's* articles concerning employment with the Bethlehem Steel Corporation presented an increasingly positive picture. For example, the *"pueblo de Mexicanos"* ("town of Mexicans," described in Chapter 3) built by the corporation was described as being equipped with electric fans for the summer and electric heating for the winter, appliances that were available to few Bethlehem natives (*La Prensa* 1923o). Given such advertising, the steel foundries must have had an appeal unequaled by cotton or sugar beet growers.

If *La Prensa* and the *San Antonio Light* present a less than sharp picture of the experiences encountered by Mexicans who boarded trains to Bethlehem, the oral history told by elderly Mexican Americans and their descendants several decades later is yet more ambiguous. The surviving workers tend to reminisce about the box lunches with which "the company" generously provided them, while their children tell about their parents being shipped across the country in boxcars. The truth is elusive, but both accounts may have been accurate.

Conclusions

During the 1920s and other periods, the Mexicans who immigrated to the United States did so to actively seek economic opportunities— and greater opportunities did await them in the United States than in Mexico. However, many Mexicans were destined to leave the United States with less money than they immigrated with because of forces beyond their control. This chapter has provided only a brief qualitative exposure to the obstacles faced by Mexicans who settled permanently, thereby founding today's Chicano barrios.

An anonymous folk balladeer has poignantly captured the feelings of disillusionment that contract laborers and other Mexican immigrants must have felt. Although the lyrics date from the 1920s, much of the message conveyed is a lasting lament of immigrants' acculturation in the United States. The problems and dilemmas raised reverberate throughout this book. The balladeer's *corrido* follows:

El Enganchado
The Contract Laborer (or The "Hooked" One)

I came under contract from Morelia
To earn dollars was my dream
I bought shoes and I bought a hat
And even put on trousers.

For they told me here the dollars
Were scattered about in heaps; That there
were girls and theaters
And that here everything was good fun.

And now I'm overwhelmed—
I am a shoemaker by trade
But here they say I'm a camel
And good only for pick and shovel.

What good is it to know my trade
If there are manufacturers by the score,
And while I make two little shoes
They turn out more than a million.

Many Mexicans don't care to speak
The language their mothers taught them
And go about saying they are Spanish
And denying their country's flag.

Some are darker than *chapote* [tar]
But they pretend to be Saxon;
They go about powdered to the back of the neck
And wear skirts for trousers.

The girls go about almost naked
And call *la tienda* "estor" [store]
They go around with dirt-streaked legs
But with those stockings of chiffon.

Even my old woman has changed on me
She wears a bob-tailed dress of silk,
Goes about painted like a *piñata*
And goes at night to the dancing hall.

My kids speak perfect English
And have no use for our Spanish
They call me "fader" and don't work
And are crazy about the Charleston.

I am tired of all this nonesense
I'm going back to *Michoacan;*
As a parting memory I leave the old woman
To see if someone else wants to burden
himself.

(Taylor 1932:vi-vii.)

Notes

1. A newspaper headline effectively indicated the magnitude of this illegal immigration while also exposing the attitudes of white Texans: "Alien Hordes Seep Across Border: Rio Grande County Too Rough for Adequate Immigration Inspection" (*San Antonio Light* 1923d).

2. Numerous articles appear in *La Prensa* dealing with the treatment of Mexicans in the United States; in contrast, this topic is largely ignored in the *San Antonio Light.* Instead, the *Light* describes the marathon dancers of the day, a train robbery in Ohio, unrest in Russia, indicating a lack of concern on the part of Anglo-Americans for the well-being of Mexican workers in the United States.

3. Bethlehem Steel Corporation was far from alone in denying any use of strikebreakers. The Gulf Coast Employment Service likewise made a similar announcement: "Careful with False Rumors of Agitators: We never send workers where there are strikers" (*La Prensa* 1923q).

References

Gamio, Manuel
    1969a   *The Mexican Immigrant: His Life Story.* New York: Arno Press.

1969b   *Mexican Immigration to the United States.* New York: Arno Press.

La Prensa

1923a   "Será investigado el caso de los mexicanos tratados como esclavos." San Antonio, Texas, February 28, p. 1.

1923b   "Quedan libres los mexicanos tratados como esclavos." San Antonio, Texas, March 2, p. 1.

1923c   "Darse ayuda a los braceros que se hallan en Juarez." San Antonio, Texas, March 11, p. 1.

1923d   "36 braceros libertados en Fort Worth." San Antonio, Texas, March 22, p. 1.

1923e   "Garantías para los braceros mexicanos." San Antonio, Texas, March 23, p. 1.

1923f   "El gobierno de Mexico extremara la vigilancia para contener la emigración de los trabajadores." San Antonio, Texas, March 26, p. 1. (Translation from Spanish by the authors.)

1923g   "No dejaran venir a los trabajadores Mexicanos." San Antonio, Texas, March 31, p. 1.

1923h   "El consulado se halla resuelto a protejer debidamente a los braceros que vayan contratados a diversos lugares." San Antonio, Texas, April 4, p. 1.

1923i   "El consulado asegura a los trabajadores que son contradados en el norte." San Antonio, Texas, April 5, p. 5. (Translation from Spanish by the authors.)

1923j   "Aviso al publico." San Antonio, Texas, April 5, p. 7.

1923k   San Antonio, Texas, April 11, p. 5.

1923m   "Los trabajadores mexicanos despiertan el celo de los obreros de Pensilvania." San Antonio, Texas, April 12, p. 1.

1923n   "Más braceros mexicanos irán a Pensilvania." San Antonio, Texas, April 17, p. 6.

1923o   "Tres mil braceros mexicanos irán a Pensilvania." San Antonio, Texas, April 18, p. 1. (Translation from Spanish by the authors.)

1923p   "Se necesitan trabajadores en Pensilvania." San Antonio, Texas, April 17, p. 7.

1923q   "Ciudado con falsos rumores de agitadores." San Antonio, Texas, April 18, p. 1. (Translation from Spanish by the authors.)

1923r   "Más braceros mexicanos de los que estan sin trabajo en San Antonio van contratados en Pensilvania." San Antonio, Texas, April 18, p. 1.

1923s   "Se quejan varios de los braceros enganchados." San Antonio, Texas, May 26, p. 1. (Translation from Spanish by the authors.)

1923t   "Buena condición de los braceros en Michigan." San Antonio, Texas, June 11, p. 1.

McWilliams, Carey
 1941 "Mexicans to Michigan." *Common Ground* 2 (autumn):5.
 1949 *North from Mexico: The Spanish-Speaking Peoples of the United States.* Philadelphia: J. B. Lippincott.

San Antonio Light
 1923a "Steel Company Recruits 350 Laborers Here." San Antonio, Texas, April 4, p. 4.
 1923b "Will Recruit 500 Mexicans for Laborers." San Antonio, Texas, April 11, p. 10.
 1923c "Would Prevent Trafficking in Mexican Labor." San Antonio, Texas, April 15, p. 6-A.
 1923d "Alien Hordes Seep Across Border: Rio Grande County Too Rough for Adequate Immigration Inspection." San Antonio, Texas, April 26, p. 1.

Tannenbaum, Frank
 1930 *The Mexican Agrarian Revolution.* Washington, D.C.: The Brookings Institution.

Taylor, Paul S.
 1931 *Mexican Labor in the United States: Bethlehem, Pennsylvania.* Berkeley: University of California Press, University of California Publications in Economics. Vol. 7, p. 3.
 1932 *Mexican Labor in the United States: Chicago and the Calumet Region.* Berkeley: University of California Press, University of California Publications in Economics. Vol. 7, no. 2, pp. vi-vii.
 1933 *A Spanish-Mexican Peasant Community: Arandas in Jalisco, Mexico.* Berkeley: University of California Press, Ibero-American no. 4.
 1935 "Songs of the Mexican Migration." In *Puro Mexicano,* edited by J. Frank Dobie, pp. 234-235. Austin, Texas: Texas Folklore Society.

2

Mexican Migration
to the Midwest

Gilbert Cardenas

Introduction

It has been a common, though incorrect assumption that Spanish-speaking peoples reside only in the five southwestern states (California, Texas, New Mexico, Colorado, and Arizona) or along the East Coast (New York, Connecticut, Pennsylvania, and New Jersey). Yet, according to the 1970 census, there are some 1.1 million persons of Spanish origin in the midwestern region of the United States (Illinois, Indiana, Iowa, Kansas, Michigan, Minnesota, Missouri, Nebraska, Ohio, and Wisconsin). Estimates by Chicano and Puerto Rican organizations go as high as 1.5 million. Judging by the published literature, one would hardly know that Chicanos and other Spanish-speaking ethnic populations reside outside the Southwest or East Coast since the literature ignores the Midwest despite the availability of historical documentation on the subject. While the presence of Spanish speaking in the Midwest and Great Lakes states must be understood in a larger framework, it is itself the subject of a complex history that has yet to be written and understood. Since 1919, Spanish-speaking people have worked and settled in the Midwest. Many from the Southwest continue to migrate to the Midwest to work on a temporary and seasonal basis. As early as 1928,

Reprinted with abridgments from *Aztlán: International Journal of Chicano Studies Research* 7 (summer 1976):153-186, with permission of the author and *Aztlán*. Originally published under the title, "'Los Desarraigados': Chicanos in the Midwestern Region of the United States."

the single largest employer of Mexican labor anywhere in the United States was located in the southern shore of Lake Michigan (Taylor 1932). Mexican workers and their families have for decades contributed to the growth and development of key industries in the region such as railroads, steel, agriculture, and cement.

Michigan is the third largest user of migrant agriculture laborers in the United States. In 1967-1968 over 98,213 agricultural migrant workers were reportedly located in the state of Michigan. In the same year, over 214,381 agricultural migrants were located in the Midwest and Great Lakes states (U.S. Congress 1969). In 1969, 23 percent of the hired farm working force in the United States was located in the North Central states (USDA 1970-1976). The majority of the Spanish-speaking ethnics permanently living or working in the Midwest, however, live in urban areas and are not engaged in agricultural occupations. Nevertheless, the farm labor situation has occupied an important place in the history of the Spanish speaking in the Midwest and continues to be a critical area of concern in terms of agricultural activity and settlement patterns (Cardenas 1974b). The more recent growth of the urban Spanish-speaking ethnic population is in part a result of large numbers of Spanish-speaking farm workers who settle out of the migrant stream. While this process occurs in large cities such as Chicago and Detroit, it is particularly significant in numerous small and medium-sized cities such as Saginaw, Michigan; South Bend, Indiana; Racine, Wisconsin; and Davenport, Iowa.

Chicago, Illinois, has one of the largest concentrations of Chicanos in the United States. Chicago also has the highest concentration of Puerto Ricans in any city outside New York. There are large barrios in other midwestern cities such as Detroit, Michigan; East Chicago, Indiana; Kansas City, Missouri; Minneapolis and Saint Paul, Minnesota; Cleveland, Ohio; and Milwaukee, Wisconsin. The employed work force (Spanish language) was heavily concentrated in industrial occupations (33.0 percent in operative category). The urban setting, life experiences, and the urban family in the Midwest have not been adequately researched. Since 1915 the Spanish-speaking population in the Midwest has increased phenomenally. The Mexican population was 69,193 in 1930, more than doubled by 1960, and by 1970 it again increased by nearly three times (see Table 2.1). For example, Faught et al. reported that Chicago doubled or tripled, depending upon the indicator used. There was an

Table 2.1

Mexican Population in the Midwest

State	1970	1960	1950	1940	1930	1920	1910	1900	1850-1890*
Ohio	13,349	9,960	5,959	2,792	3,099	942	85	53	134
Indiana	18,325	14,041	8,677	4,530	7,589	680	47	43	98
Illinois	117,268	63,063	34,538	23,545	20,963	4,032	672	156	240
Michigan	31,067	24,298	16,540	9,474	9,921	1,333	86	56	127
Wisconsin	9,160	6,705	3,272	1,716	1,853	178	39	499	59
Minnesota	4,575	3,436	3,305	2,976	2,448	248	52	162	308
Iowa	4,546	3,374	3,973	3,595	2,760	2,650	620	29	75
Missouri	8,353	8,159	5,862	4,783	3,482	3,411	1,413	24	37
Nebraska	5,552	5,858	6,023	5,333	4,178	2,611	290	27	48
Kansas	13,728	12,972	13,429	13,742	12,900	13,770	8,429	71	126
Total	225,923	151,866	101,578	72,850	69,193	29,855	11,733	1,120	1,252

*1860 and 1870, no data available.

Source: U. S. Bureau of the Census, (1850-1970).

increase of 181 percent (almost tripling) between 1960 and 1970 (22,975 in 1960 to 64,575 in 1970) for the foreign born whose mother tongue (i.e., the language spoken in the person's home when he/she was a child) was Spanish (1975). Migration and immigration patterns and fertility rates indicate that the Spanish-speaking population in the Midwest will continue to grow at a phenomenal pace (see Table 2.1).

This paper presents an overview of Chicanos in the Midwest. No attempt is made to provide a definitive or comprehensive analysis of Chicanos in the Midwest, a task that is needed but beyond the scope of this effort. This brief introduction will be followed by a critique of the literature and an analysis of the origins and significance of migration and settlement. This is followed by a description of immigration and farm labor patterns and then by an analysis of some demographic and social characteristics of the population utilizing 1970 census data.

The term "Midwest" as utilized throughout this report corresponds to a ten-state area—Ohio, Indiana, Illinois, Michigan, Wisconsin, Minnesota, Iowa, Missouri, Nebraska, and Kansas—normally referred to by Chicanos and other Spanish-speaking people as a region in which they identify and in which others, in turn, identify Spanish-speaking people. Like the Southwest (Texas, Arizona, Colorado, New Mexico, and California), the Midwest does not entirely correspond to the regular regional divisions utilized by the United States Bureau of the Census, i.e., Northeast, North Central, South, and West, although a special subject report (*Persons of Spanish Surname*) covering the five southwestern states is published by the United States Bureau of the Census. Thus, when reference is made to the "Midwest," only those ten states mentioned above are included. With the exception of two states—North Dakota and South Dakota—the "Midwest" corresponds to the north central region defined by the Bureau of the Census. The ten-state area defined as "Midwest" is also known in government circles (federal regional councils) as Region V and Region VII.[1]

Review of Literature:
Conceptual Focus

Inadequate recognition and documentation of the history and life experiences in the Midwest has resulted in a dearth of scholarly research, a meagerness of educational curricula, and a lack of public policy. Despite the recent upsurges in attention to minority group problems and ethnic and cultural heritage of minority peoples, Spanish-speaking ethnic groups in the Midwest continue to be neglected and forgotten. There is hardly any mention and virtually no analysis given to their history and life experience in the Midwest in any of the important books, monographs, reports, and articles about the Spanish speaking in the United States. Aside from past tendencies to exclude reference to Spanish-speaking people in the United States and from the more blatant effect of biased and distorted treatment in the literature when it was written, there still remains the tendency to treat Spanish-speaking people as a homogeneous ethnic group. However, Spanish-speaking ethnic groups are not homogeneous but are differentiated in many ways, such as in their historical and cultural conditions of social contact and varying relationships with the dominant society in the United States. In the Midwest, where all Spanish-speaking ethnic groups are substanially represented, these differences are especially significant. . . .

Since the literature available on Spanish-speaking people in the United States has mainly been on Chicanos, we have only to survey treatment in this literature of the Midwest to underscore our point and to clarify its dimensions. The UCLA Mexican American Study, one of the most ambitious studies of Chicanos to date, restricted its focus of Chicanos to the Southwest (Grebler et al. 1970). With the exception of one advance report by Samora and Lamanna (1967), there was virtually no attention given to the Midwest. The United States Commission on Civil Rights since 1970 has undertaken a mass study of the educational status of Mexican Americans (1971). With the exception of one table in the first report, the study and all six reports were based exclusively upon the Chicano experience in the five southwestern states. All of the fifteen books critiqued in John Womack, Jr.'s feature article, "Who Are the Chicanos?" (1972) omitted reference and analysis of the Chicano experience in the Midwest and covered only the situation of Chicanos in the Southwest. Numerous other recent scholarly research and reports have been undertaken and published yet have also omitted the Midwest (Galarza et al. 1970; Johnson and Hernandez-M. 1970; Acuna 1972). The above mentioned research efforts have made an impressive addition to the literature on Chicanos and have influenced the curricula produced and utilized in ethnic studies courses, particularly in Chicano studies.

Moreover, these studies and reports along with others have been taken as authoritative sources, which social scientists, educators, historians, and public officials have relied upon for interpreting the history and status of the Spanish speaking. Public and private agencies have also used these studies as bases for the allocation of funds. The ethnic studies programs focusing on the Spanish speaking that have been started or are in the process of development in colleges and universities throughout the Midwest tend to follow models developed in the Southwest and the East Coast. These programs, however, suffer from the unavailability of resource and reference materials documenting their history in the Midwest.

Despite the omission of Spanish-speaking ethnic groups in the literature and curriculum materials frequently used in ethnic studies and related courses of study, various reports have been recently published and in some cases empirical studies with a Midwest setting, focusing on a specific problem, have been produced (Taylor 1932; Humphrey 1943; Samora and Lamanna 1967; Choldin and Trout 1969; Weeks and Spielberg 1973; Lebeaux and Salas 1973; Lyle and Magadaline Shannon 1973). However, a comprehensive review of this literature and an overall assessment of the situation in the Midwest is lacking (Cardenas 1976a). A systematic attempt to compare and relate the Midwest experience to others requires that one depart from the exclusively regional experience and begin with a national approach. Through this approach it is possible to reconceptualize the history and cultural heritage of Spanish-speaking ethnic groups; it expands the scope of ethnic studies, and establishes a direct method of studying the Midwest. The Midwest experience is not simply an extension of the Southwest experience into the North (nor is it necessarily an extension of the East Coast Puerto Rican experience into the Midwest). A significant proportion of the Chicano population, for example, was born and raised in the Midwest and have never visited the Southwest. Yet, in terms of interregional migration, the study of Chicanos (who left the Southwest) at their destination points rather than their area of origin enhances our understanding of the southwestern experience and the reasons why people left. More often than not, research based in the Southwest only includes "survival" population samples. There are both theoretical (conceptual) and methodological problems pertaining to the study of Chicanos that must be further clarified and modified.

Including the Midwest in the analysis of Spanish-origin ethnic groups not only broadens the scope and focus of a particular group, but also gives the student of ethnic studies a concrete basis in which interethnic relations can be observed. Midwestern cities such as Chicago and Detroit as well as other smaller cities have long histories of ethnic experiences and remain as areas in which ethnic enclaves continue to vibrate. While the history of European ethnic groups (Polish, Italian, Hungarian) in these communities has been the subject of scholarly attention, it is only recently that Spanish-origin ethnics have received serious attention. While the much criticized immigrant analogy approach may not be entirely applicable to the Chicano and Puerto Rican experience in the Southwest, some aspects of the model may be applicable in the Midwest. Similarly, the colonial model advanced by sociologists such as Blauner (1972), Barrera (1976), and Rex (1973) may also be applicable to the Chicano experience. These questions remain theoretical and empirical problems that have heretofore not been raised with respect to the experience of Spanish-origin ethnic groups in the Midwest.

Mexican Immigration to the Midwest

Despite the settlement of Chicanos in the Midwest even before the turn of the century, it was not until the first large-scale recruitment and importation efforts in the 1910s that a Mexican presence became noticeable, particularly in Kansas City and Chicago. The increase in the Mexican population throughout the Midwest was largely due to increased industrial activity and agricultural development. The first significant increase of the Mexican population derived from settled Mexican immigrants in urban-industrial areas and seasonal agricultural workers from Mexico and Texas. The first groups were foreign-born Mexican stock. After World War II, the bulk of the workers and interregional migrants resettling in the Midwest were native-born Chicanos. In other words, prior to World War II, settlement was largely based on immigration from Mexico and step migration of persons of Mexican stock. After World War II, migration and settlement of Mexican persons in the Midwest, while still including Mexican immigrants, became a type of migration that could be characterized as "displaced migration," e.g., being more of a domestic (internal) character. Although we begin treatment with an analysis of immigration, the thesis of displacement as presented above suggests that Chicanos and Mexicanos can be properly considered displaced refugees and that their seasonal and regional mobility (migration) can be compared to that type of migration normally referred to as "depression migration," i.e., a type of migration that occurs during periods of great economic hardship such as that of the 1930s.

Unlike the Southwest, where Chicanos were originally native to the region and predated the appearance of the Anglo-European Americans, in the Midwest the origins of the Mexican population were entirely immigrant. In contrast to the Southwest-bound Mexican immigrant who worked or settled in an area contiguous to Mexico, an area previously ruled by Mexico, populated by Mexicans, and an area retaining cultural, physical, and climatic similarities to the areas of origin, the first waves of Midwest-bound Mexican immigrants were traveling longer distances to areas beyond the Southwest in which none of the above characteristics prevailed. The predominant industrial and other manufacturing-related employment and the urban settlement of Mexican immigrants to the Midwest more closely parallel the European immigrant pattern than the earlier patterns of immigration in the Southwest. The importance of ethnic succession and labor market segmentation of Chicanos in midwestern cities can be more fully understood by drawing from the concrete experiences of European immigrant laborers (aspects of the European immigrant model formulation), e.g., the social relations of production and aspects of the European immigrant model formulation, than normally assumed.

Strong comparisons between Mexican and European immigration can be made with respect to the settlement and employment patterns, particularly in midwestern cities. While the first large-scale movements of Mexicans to the Midwest involved both direct migration from Mexico to the Midwest and step migration (Mexico to Southwest, Southwest to Midwest), the direct migration was the main feature of these movements. Many of the midwest-bound Mexican immigrants eventually made their way there after having passed, worked, or lived in the Southwest. For purposes of this analysis, these migrants would be classified as seasonal workers who did not establish roots in the Southwest before settling in the Midwest. In many respects, this seasonal labor parallels the movement of

European immigrants from the Atlantic coast to the Midwest. (A major distinction, however, relates to the timing of migration particularly with respect to economic development and entrepreneurship.) To this extent, then, such workers would be viewed as direct immigrants. In contrast are those seasonal workers who established roots in the Southwest, their descendants and native Chicanos who eventually left and settled in the Midwest. Thus, in terms of direct migration, the comparison with European immigration is most applicable.

Labor Migration

The distinguishing factor of all major Mexican migratory movements to the United States has been labor migration. The massive shifts and growth of the Chicano population in the United States have corresponded to the movement of Mexican labor to U.S. capital and the settlement of Mexican workers and their families in the centers or fringes of capitalist enterprises. The proletarian status of immigrant workers has been a dominant feature of labor migrants from Mexico since the first organized importation programs in 1917-1922.

One opportunity relatively open to Mexican workers in the United States was geographic labor mobility. For the most part, this mobility, in terms of employment, was lateral rather than vertical. The territorial dispersion of Mexican laborers first within the Southwest and later throughout the entire United States was followed by the settlement of Mexican people in all the states in which they worked. Competition for Mexican labor among employers in the Southwest and later outside the Southwest arose because of the assumed labor demands of their industries, which for the most part was a demand for cheap and unorganized labor (Samora 1971). In the same manner that employment opportunities and recruitment efforts in certain industries were extended to Mexican nationals residing in Mexico, inducing their migration into the United States (legal, illegal, and temporary, etc.), employment opportunities and recruitment efforts were also extended to those settled in the Southwest. The process continued, at the same time, as competition for Mexican labor arose between southwestern and midwestern employers. The first, largest, and most significant mass migration of Mexican people occured along the border, with Texas being the most important state. Later, migration shifted within Texas and was finally directed toward California (State of California 1930).

Gamio (1930) and Taylor (1932) described the process of recruiting and importing Mexican labor by the private sector during World War I and the post–World War I period. During the war, the United States government in conjunction with the private sector initiated a series of administrative maneuvers to import Mexican contract workers.[2] In the Midwest, contract workers were employed in railroad industries, manufacturing plants, stock yards, and in the sugar beet fields. Admittedly less than 300,000 workers were imported through this work program in the period from 1917 to 1922, and while importation was mainly on a temporary basis, thousands of workers never returned to Mexico, while thousands more eventually made their way back to the United States after their contracts expired. The program provided the first major stimulus in the migration of Mexican workers to the Midwest. Midwestern employers who had utilized contract workers actively and illegally advertised and recruited workers from Mexico during and after the operation of the program. Other employers who had not utilized contract workers during the program actively sought Mexican labor after the program was terminated and began recruiting in Mexico and in the Southwest. Throughout the congressional debates and public hearings on Mexican immigration and agricultural labor during the 1920s, midwestern employers and their representatives lobbied for the relaxation of immigration laws, assisted in preventing the enactment of restrictive legislation, and advocated on behalf of the importation of Mexican contract labor.[3]

The importation and employment of Mexican labor in the Midwest increased and expanded into other branches of industry and agriculture during the latter part of the war and extended into the post–World War I period because of the increase in war-related industrial activity, the steel strikes of 1919, the packing house strikes of 1921 in Chicago and the replacement of European immigrant labor with Mexicans as a major supply of "cheap labor" in the agricultural sector. The structure of the Mexican population during the World War I and post–World War I period was largely determined by immigration. Using the Mexican foreign stock population as an indicator, we find a large pattern of growth from 1910 to 1930. During this period the Mexican population grew from 11,733 to 69,193.

While the private employment practices of midwestern capitalists and the World War I government importation program stimulated the first major flow of immigrant workers, the Great Depression, the repatriation activities, and antialien sentiment stimulated a sizable reverse migration flow. Thousands of Mexican nationals were rounded up in places such as Chicago, east Chicago, and Detroit. Virtually "kicked out," Mexicans and their families (many of whom were American citizens) were either returned to Mexico through deportations, voluntary departure removal processes, Mexican-assisted repatriation programs, or were forced to leave the cities on their own initiative for places unknown or to Mexico (Betten and Mohl 1973; Humphrey 1941; Kiser and Silverman 1973; Simon 1974; Spencer 1974). The net change in the Mexican foreign stock population in the Midwest during the decade of the 1930s was less than 4,000.

The importation of Mexican labor power to the Midwest was accelerated during World War II primarily through a combined process of step, drift, and contract labor migration and the internal movement of the resident Chicano population northward. During the war, thousands of braceros were utilized in midwestern agriculture and railroad projects (Rasmussen 1951). Nearly all the states in the eastern North Central region utilized bracero labor at one time or another, yet, for the most part, the midwestern states were not large users of bracero labor. Michigan, Nebraska, Minnesota, and Wisconsin were the largest users. As in the case of the World War I experience, after the termination of contracts, many braceros returned to the Midwest either through legal means or illegally. Overall, the number of "lost" braceros who failed to return to Mexico was not as widespread in the Midwest as it was after World War I. Throughout the bracero program (1943-1947, 1951-1964), employers benefited from the supply of labor provided by a highly developed "underground" smuggling system linking Mexico's surplus labor, southwestern labor pools, and midwestern industries (see Table 2.2).

During the depression and World War II periods, legal immigration was either curtailed through administrative devices or held to a trickle. While Mexican immigration steadily continued during the 1950s, 1960s, and 1970s, it has not been as prominent as it was before the depression (Samora 1971). U.S. involvement in the Korean War and the Vietnam War enabled Mexican immigration to continue

Table 2.2

Mexican Contract Workers Employed in the Midwest

Year	Ohio*	Indiana	Illinois	Michigan	Wisconsin	Subtotal
			S T A T E			
1943-1947	n.d.	436	1,083	7,486	4,817	13,822
1952-1962	94	2,808	1,783	84,800	6,489	95,974
	94	3,244	2,866	92,286	11,306	109,796

Year	Minnesota	Iowa	Missouri	Nebraska	Kansas	Subtotal	Total
			S T A T E				
1943-1947	5,288	4,211	n.d.	4,039	796	14,334	
1952-1962	4,281	858	12,420	16,743	512	34,814	
	9,569	5,069	12,420	20,782	1,308	49,148	158,944

Sources: Rasmussen 1951:226; Hancock 1959:20; U. S. Congress 1958-1962.

* Data not available for Ohio.

  Data not found for 1951 and 1958.

during an otherwise restrictive period. The passage of the Immigration and Nationality Act of 1965 has enabled Mexican immigration to the Midwest to continue at a slightly increased rate compared to the pre-1964 immigration.

Origins

A recurrent interest among observers of Mexican immigration to the Midwest has been on the questions of origins. The data on the origins of Mexican immigration during the 1920s reveal that the central plateau of Mexico accounted for 75 to 88 percent of the immigrants. Estimates on the northeastern region share a range from 9 to 21 percent. Migration from the West Coast and the southern and eastern regions was relatively insignificant. Recent data (Cardenas 1974, 1976) indicate that the central plateau and northwest regions continue to constitute the major sources of immigration, yet the central plateau has declined relative to the northwestern region and the remaining regions have increased as source areas compared to the 1920s (see Table 2.3).

Table 2.3

Regional Origins of Mexican Immigrants to the Midwest

Region	1920s		1970s		
	Taylor[a]	Gamio[b]	Rosales[c]	Cardenas[d]	Portes[e]
Northeast	21.3%	9.0%	18.0%	32.1%	53.9%
Central Plateau	74.8	88.3	80.0	60.7	43.9
West Coast	2.0	.1	1.2	4.8	0
South and East	1.9	.8	0	2.4	2.4
Total	100.0%	100.0%	100.0%	100.0%	100.0%
	(N = 3132)	(N = 3366)	(N = 1017)	(N = 109)	(N = 164)

[a]Taylor (1932)

[b]Gamio (1930:19)

[c]Rosales (1976)

[d]Cardenas (1974a)

[e]Portes (1973)

Undocumented Migration

Undocumented Mexicans (workers without documents) have been apprehended in the Midwest since the 1900s. Taylor (1932) reports specific efforts by the Immigration and Naturalization Service (INS) in the Chicago-Calumet region to apprehend Mexican undocumented workers during the 1920s. During the 1930s, large numbers of Mexicans were located and removed from midwestern agriculture and midwestern industrial centers.

During Operation Wetback in 1954, thousands of Mexican aliens were apprehended in the Chicago campaign (Files of the INS 1954). The more recent efforts by the INS to apprehend the undocumented have been concentrated in the Chicago area. The campaigns, roundups and raids conducted by the INS are greatly resented by Chicanos in the Midwest and elsewhere and the presence of the INS continues to provoke a "reign of terrorism" in Chicano communities in the Midwest. In 1975, Mexicans constituted 62 percent (11,685) of the total number of persons apprehended in the Midwest (18,992). Compared to the proportion of Mexicans apprehended in the United States, 89 percent (766,600), the Midwest Mexican proportion was much lower (U.S. Department of Justice 1975, 1976).

In Chicago, however, where the highest numbers of deportable undocumented Mexicans are located in the Midwest, the Mexican proportion (80 percent) approximates the U.S. proportion.

Undocumented Mexicans apprehended in the Midwest are not the "border runners" of the Southwest. Whereas 76 percent of all persons apprehended in the Midwest had been in the United States for one month or more, the remaining 24 percent were either caught at entry or within thirty days. In contrast, 26.8 percent of the undocumented outside the Midwest had been in the United States for one month or more and 74 percent were apprehended within thirty days. The impact of apprehension is particularly acute in the Midwest. In a recent survey, the majority of Midwest-bound Mexican immigrants surveyed had lived in the Midwest portion of the U.S. for more than three years prior to legal admission (Cardenas 1976). The implications of prior residence are further illustrated by the fact that 50 percent of the sample indicated that their eldest child was born in the United States. The vast majority of aliens apprehended in this region are caught while employed in industry[4] (see Table 2.4).

Recent Migration

Illinois ranks third in receiving Mexican immigrants (U.S. Bureau of the Census 1973a). Cardenas (1976) found that slightly over 10 percent of all Mexican immigrants to the United States in 1973 reported a Midwest state as an intended place of residence. Of the Midwest-bound Mexican immigrants, about 77 percent reported Illinois as their intended state of residence. According to the INS, 62,205 Mexican immigrants admitted in fiscal year 1975 were intending to reside in the Midwest (U.S. Department of Justice 1975). This constituted about 12 percent of all Mexican immigrants admitted in 1975.

The following characteristics were found in the 1973 sample: 80 percent of the Midwest-bound Mexican immigrants had been employed in manual labor occupations; over 50 percent of the sample reported that their main occupation, last occupation, and expected occupation was in the semiskilled urban workers category, the skilled worker, or artisan category; 6 percent reported a white collar, professional, or university professor category occupation; about 57 percent reported that work was the main reason for coming into the United States while 18 percent claimed education and 19 percent

Table 2.4

Deportable Mexican Aliens Located by Length of
Time Illegally in the U. S., 1975

Districts and Sectors	Total	At Entry	Within 72 hrs.	4-30 Days	1-6 Months	7 Months To 1 Year	Over 1 Year
Percent	100.0%	31.0%	26.2%	14.8%	16.1%	4.3%	7.6%
U. S. Total	756,819	234,377	198,194	112,180	121,893	32,455	57,720
District	160,023	537	12,258	26,685	53,615	20,178	46,750
Sector	596,796	233,840	185,936	85,495	68,278	12,277	10,970
Midwest							
Cleveland	1,050	12	16	131	547	126	218
Chicago	10,833	1	412	1,000	3,826	2,050	3,544
Detroit	4,691	871	359	555	1,453	619	834
Kansas City	1,229	-	90	359	391	171	218
Omaha	903	-	32	182	362	160	167
St. Paul	286	-	4	38	105	58	81
Grand Rapids	1,119	176	351	245	215	52	80
TOTAL	20,111	1,060	1,264	2,510	6,899	3,236	5,142
	100.0%	5.3%	6.3%	12.5%	34.3%	16.1%	25.6%

Source: U. S. Department of Justice (1975).

claimed family reunion as main reasons for coming to the United
States; less than 10 percent had earned more than $10,000 during the
previous year, thus pointing to the relatively low earnings of
immigrant workers in the North; the average earnings in 1972 for the
sample studied were about $5,400 (Cardenas 1976b).

One of the salient characteristics of the urban-industrial cities of
the Midwest, particularly Chicago and Detroit, is the ethnic
composition. Since 1957 Mexico has been leading in numbers of
immigrations to Chicago. In 1957 the Mexican alien population
ranked third behind the Polish and German; yet, by 1973 it was
ranked first in size. The INS figures show that 82,303 Mexican aliens
resided in the Midwest in fiscal year 1975. About 74 percent of the
Midwest aliens were reportedly residing in Illinois.

Today, as in the past, Mexican immigration to the Midwest has
been to the city, and the settlement experience of Mexican immigrants
has been largely an urban experience. Yet, while Mexican
immigrants and their children constitute an unusually high proportion of the Mexican population in large urban areas, this segment is proportionally less significant in the many small and
medium-sized cities in the Midwest. In Chicago and Detroit, for
example, the Mexican immigrant population (Mexican foreign
stock) stands out as the single most distinctive segment of the

Mexican population. In contrast to the immigrant population, interstate and agricultural migrants are more evenly dispersed between rural and urban areas and between small and medium-sized and large cities throughout the Midwest. In the small and medium-sized cities, agricultural migrants—particularly from Texas—and other interstate migrants stand out as the single most distinctive segment of the Mexican population (numerically and socially). . . . Moreover, agricultural related migration and resettlement has greatly affected a "Tejano" influence as a dominant factor within Chicano communities throughout these cities. In contrast, the impact of immigration from Mexico has remained a dominant influence in large cities such as Chicago, Illinois; Kansas City, Missouri; Detroit, Michigan; and Gary, Indiana.

Profile of the Population, 1970

Population

It has not been possible in the past to present an acceptable statistical profile of Chicanos in the Midwest because data were not available until reports from the 1970 census of the population were released. With the exception of impressionistic reports, case studies, and research findings based on samples taken in midwestern communities, there has not been any basis to present such a profile prior to the 1970 census of the U.S. population. While the Bureau of the Census used multiple indicators for enumerating the Spanish-speaking population, we shall restrict our analysis to data produced through the identifier, "Spanish origin population." This includes household data obtained from all persons who identified themselves as "Spanish origin." The classification "Spanish origin" includes persons of Mexican origin, Puerto Rican origin, Cuban origin, Central and South American origin, and "other" persons of Spanish origin (cf. Grebler et al. 1970; Hernandez 1973; U.S. Bureau of the Census 1973a, 1973b, 1973c, and 1973d).

In 1970 there were 9,072,602 persons in the United States who reported that they were of Spanish origin (U.S. Bureau of the Census 1973a). The Mexican-origin population (Chicanos) constituted half (50 percent) of the total Spanish-origin population in the United States, 78.6 percent of the Southwest (Texas, Colorado, New Mexico, Arizona, and California), and 35.8 percent in the Midwest. Outside the Southwest and Midwest, the Mexican origin population was proportionately smaller, constituting only 7.3 percent of the total Spanish-origin population, while Puerto Ricans and Cubans constituted over half the Spanish-origin population (56 percent). Over one half (55.2 percent) of the Spanish-origin population was living in the five southwestern states of California, Arizona, New Mexico, Colorado, and Texas; 11.5 percent were in the Midwest; and 33.3 percent were living outside the southwestern and midwestern portions of the United States in 1970. While persons of Mexican origin were distributed throughout the United States in 1970, they were nevertheless numerically concentrated in the Southwest. While 86.9 percent of the Mexican origin population were living in the Southwest, only 8.2 percent were living in the Midwest, and less than 5.0 percent were living in the rest of the nation.

In 1970, the Spanish-origin population in the Midwest was slightly over one million persons. Illinois, with 393,204 persons of Spanish origin, was the top-ranking Midwest state in terms of Spanish-origin population size. Three other states had a Spanish population larger than 100,000—Michigan, Ohio, and Indiana.

It is surprising that persons of Central and South American origin constituted the single largest group: 41.3 percent of the Spanish origin population in the Midwest.[5] Ignoring the validity of the Central and South American count, it appears that in every state in the Midwest, the Mexican-origin population ranged from a high of 57.0 percent of the Spanish-origin population in Nebraska to a low of 20.6 percent in Ohio. The Mexican-, Puerto Rican-, and Cuban-origin populations in the Midwest are heavily concentrated in Illinois. Illinois accounts for 42.9 percent of the total Mexican-population, and 63.4 percent of the total Cuban population in the Midwest in 1970. Persons of Central and South American origins and persons classified as "all other Spanish origin" were more evenly distributed in the Midwest.

Rural-Urban Residence

Over four fifths of the total Spanish-origin population in 1970 were classified as urban, and the remaining as either rural nonfarm or rural farm (U.S. Bureau of the Census 1973a). There were no significant differences by region. Despite the heavy urban concentration of the Spanish population throughout the United States, when comparing regions, the midwestern Spanish-origin population is less urban by only 3.1 percent than the total Spanish-origin population in the United States. In light of the questions raised concerning the classification "Central and South American," it is interesting to note the high proportion of that group reportedly residing in rural portions throughout the Midwest. For example, in Indiana, 30 percent of the Central and South American population were rural. Persons familiar with the Spanish speaking in Indiana would claim that this figure may be entirely incorrect.

Standard Metropolitan Statistical Areas: Chicago and Detroit

The Chicago and Detroit standard metropolitan statistical areas (SMSAs) constituted the two largest concentrations of all persons of Spanish origin in the Midwest counted by the 1970 census. While space does not permit comment on the historical significance of these two urban centers, it is possible to at least characterize the ethnic composition of the population.[6]

According to the 1970 census, the total Spanish-origin population for the Chicago SMSA was 324,215. Persons of Mexican origin comprised 44.3 percent (143,659), persons of Puerto Rican origin comprised 26.6 percent, and other persons of Spanish origin including Cuban, Central and South American, and other Spanish origin comprised 29.6 percent of the total. The city of Chicago ranks fourth in size of the Spanish-speaking population among U.S. cities. The Chicago SMSA reflected a comparable increase of foreign born with Spanish mother tongue of 193 percent—from 27,273 to 80,004— almost a tripling of the 1960 population. Growth in this subgroup of the Spanish-speaking population is occurring mainly in the city, with an increase in Chicago of about 42,000, which is 70.2 percent of the change in the Chicago SMSA. It appears that the traditional concentration of immigrating groups within the city rather than in the urban fringe is clearly being maintained by the geographic settlement of the Spanish-speaking population in Chicago (Faught, Flores, and Cardenas 1975). The city of Chicago has one of the largest concentrations of Chicanos in the United States and the highest concentration of Puerto Ricans in any city outside New York City.

In the Detroit SMSA there were a total of 66,585 persons of Spanish origin counted in the 1970 census of the population. Persons of Mexican origin comprised 40.0 percent of the total Spanish-origin population of Detroit, while the Puerto Rican, Cuban, Central and South American, and other Spanish-origin populations comprised the remaining portion. Other SMSAs having large concentrations of persons of Spanish origin are the Gary–East Chicago–Hammond, Indiana, SMSA; Kansas City SMSA; Milwaukee, Wisconsin, SMSA; Cleveland, Ohio, SMSA; Lansing, Michigan, SMSA; and the Saint Paul–Minneapolis, SMSA.

Nativity and Parentage

About 85 percent of the Spanish-origin population in the United States were native born, while 15 percent were foreign born. The native population is defined as including persons of native parentage (61.5 percent) and persons of mixed or foreign parentage (29.9 percent) (U.S. Bureau of Census 1973b). In community areas of Chicago, where Chicanos are highly concentrated (Westside, Little Village, and South Chicago), the Spanish-language, foreign-stock population was larger than the native stock. In the Chicago Westside, the Mexican foreign stock constituted 66.6 percent of the population, and in South Chicago it constituted 61.6 percent. In these areas the natives of native parentage are outnumbered by the foreign-stock population. The numerical importance of the foreign-stock population is clearly reflected in the social and cultural milieu of the Chicano barrios in Chicago.

Migration

When utilizing the census publications, one finds that interstate migration data on the Spanish speaking is relatively lacking. Moreover, outside the Southwest, migration data is limited to state of birth of the native population, state of residence of the native population, and place of residence. Also, the 1970 published data is only available for the classification "persons of Spanish origin" without further designation (U.S. Bureau of the Census 1973c).

Despite these limitations, the data provides a basis upon which migration (interregional, intraregional, interstate) can be crudely measured. Prior to the availability of the 1970 census data, it was not possible to even provide a crude measure of migration on the Spanish-speaking population in the Midwest.

Interregional Migration

About 97,936 native persons of Spanish origin who were living in the Midwest in 1970 were born in one of the five southwestern states. While this constitutes less than 10 percent of the total Spanish-origin population in the Midwest (1,042,843), it does constitute more than one half (53.9 percent) of all native persons of Spanish origin who had migrated to the Midwest from a different region since birth (N = 181,822). The state of Texas accounted for 79,512 or 81.2 percent, of the southwestern migrants (N = 97,936). The Texas-born migrants were distributed throughout the Midwest but were highly concentrated in the northeast portion of the region, e.g., Ohio, Indiana, Illinois, Michigan, and Wisconsin (87.0 percent, N = 79,512) (see Table 2.5).

In 1970 about 66,141 native persons of Spanish origin who were born in the Midwest were living in the Southwest. Of this group over one half were living in the state of California (54.1 percent) while 30.3 percent were living in Texas (see Table 2.6).

Net Gain Through Migration

Defining migration as the difference between region or state of birth and region or state of residence in 1970 on the basis of the available information, i.e., survival population in 1970, it appears that there was a net gain of 83,330 native persons of Spanish origin in the Midwest. This constitutes approximately 11 percent of the total native Spanish-origin population in the Midwest (N = 789,576). On this criteria the state of Illinois gained 34,490 persons, the highest single gain in the Midwest, while Michigan was relatively close behind with a net gain of 25,506 persons. Iowa, Missouri, Nebraska, and Kansas lost more persons than were gained. In analyzing the composition of the Spanish-origin population in the Midwest, the preceding analysis demonstrates the importance of migration. In determining the composition of the population we shall rely upon data compiled for the North Central region (Midwest and North and South Dakota).[7] By dividing the total Spanish-origin population in the North Central region by residence and birth, we find that a very high proportion of the population (41.6 percent) could be classified as migrant, while only 58.4 percent were born in the region (see Table 2.7).

Table 2.5

Interregional Migration: In-Migration From Southwest to the Midwest
(State of Birth and State of Residence of the Native Spanish Origin Population) 1970

STATE OF RESIDENCE

State of Birth	Ohio No.	%	Indiana No.	%	Illinois No.	%	Michigan No.	%	Wisconsin No.	%	Midwest Subtotal No.	%
Texas	8,527	58.0	6,173	79.5	27,984	86.9	20,563	90.0	5,856	85.3	69,103	86.7
Colorado	122	1.2	466	6.0	1,040	3.2	662	2.9	260	3.8	2,550	3.2
New Mexico	469	4.7	97	1.3	916	2.8	325	1.4	250	3.6	2,057	2.5
Arizona	217	2.2	92	1.2	619	1.9	316	1.4	84	1.2	1,328	1.7
California	704	7.0	936	12.1	1,639	5.1	995	4.4	419	6.1	4,693	5.9
Total	10,039	100.0%	7,764	100.0%	32,198	100.0%	22,861	100.0%	6,869	100.0%	79,731	100.0%

State of Birth	Minnesota No.	%	Iowa No.	%	Missouri No.	%	Nebraska No.	%	Kansas No.	%	Midwest Subtotal No.	%	Midwest Total
Texas	1,692	58.1	1,041	63.0	1,797	47.2	1,797	58.1	4,082	60.6	10,409	57.1	
Colorado	399	13.7	260	15.7	662	17.4	347	11.2	850	12.6	2,518	13.8	
New Mexico	181	6.2	104	6.3	493	13.0	581	18.8	819	12.2	2,178	12.0	
Arizona	129	4.4	82	5.0	194	5.1	58	1.9	171	2.5	634	3.5	
California	510	17.5	166	10.0	660	17.3	310	10.0	840	12.2	2,486	13.6	
Total	2,911	100.0%	1,653	100.0%	3,806	100.0%	3,093	100.0%	6,742	100.0	18,225	100.0%	97,956

Source: U. S. Bureau of the Census (1973).

Table 2.6

Interregional Migration: Out-Migration from Midwest to Southwest
Native Persons of Spanish Origin by State of Residence (Southwest)
and State of Birth (Midwest), 1970

STATE OF BIRTH

Immigration	Ohio No.	%	Indiana No.	%	Illinois No.	%	Michigan No.	%	Wisconsin No.	%	Midwest Subtotal No.	%	Midwest Total
Texas	2,294	32.3	2,070	45.6	4,649	31.5	3,938	44.6	1,220	40.0	14,171	37	
Colorado	276	3.9	98	2.2	585	4.0	211	2.4	285	9.1	1,455	4	
New Mexico	217	3.1	83	1.8	158	1.1	84	1.0	--	--	542	1	
Arizona	707	10.0	100	2.2	612	4.2	273	3.1	319	10.4	2,011	5	
California	3,599	50.7	2,193	48.3	8,740	59.3	4,320	49.0	1,248	40.6	20,100	53	
Total	7,093	100.0	4,544	100.0	14,744	100.0	8,826	100.0	3,072	100.0	38,279	100	

Immigration	Minnesota No.	%	Iowa No.	%	Missouri No.	%	Nebraska No.	%	Kansas No.	%	Midwest Subtotal No.	%	Midwest Total
Texas	888	31.2	443	13.6	1,447	24.7	1,009	16.9	2,064	20.8	5,851	21	
Colorado	292	10.3	224	6.9	410	7.0	1,441	24.2	1,505	15.1	3,872	14	
New Mexico	121	4.3	39	1.2	226	4.5	171	2.9	269	2.7	826	3	
Arizona	217	7.6	98	3.0	494	8.4	385	6.5	371	3.7	1,565	6	
California	1,330	46.7	2,444	75.3	3,240	55.3	2,957	49.6	5,733	57.7	15,704	56	
Total	2,848	100.0	3,248	100.0	5,817	100.0	5,963	100.0	9,942	100.0	27,918	100	66,097

Source: U. S. Bureau of the Census (1973a).

Table 2.7

Mobility Status of Native Spanish-Origin Population in Midwest,
By Region, State of Birth, Region of Residence in 1970,
With Net Gain or Loss Through Interregional Movement, 1970

S T A T E S

Mobility Status of U.S. Native Spanish-Origin Born	Total Midwest	Ohio	Indiana	Illinois	Michigan	Wisc.	Minn.	Iowa	Missouri	Nebraska	Kansas
Total Native Population Born in State	789,576	105,359	97,361	243,231	126,870	50,922	32,746	16,746	51,478	17,962	46,842
Population Born in State	706,246	88,686	83,803	208,741	101,364	45,323	31,762	21,042	55,157	21,268	49,100
Population Born/Living in State	557,096	70,494	69,518	177,297	83,820	37,149	25,485	12,601	37,209	12,219	31,304
Out-migration	149,150	18,192	14,285	31,444	17,544	8,174	6,277	8,441	17,948	9,049	17,796
Within Region	50,681	5,211	6,139	9,835	4,308	3,191	1,853	3,943	8,990	1,779	5,432
Outside Region	98,469	12,981	8,146	21,609	13,236	4,983	4,424	4,498	8,958	7,270	12,364
In-migration	232,480	34,865	27,843	65,934	43,050	13,773	7,261	4,204	14,269	5,743	15,538
Within Region	50,681	4,058	6,905	13,632	6,145	3,897	2,498	1,860	5,602	1,469	4,535
Outside Region	181,799	30,807	20,858	52,302	36,905	9,876	4,763	2,344	8,667	4,274	11,003
Net Gain or Loss Through Migration	83,330	16,673	13,558	34,490	25,506	5,599	984	-4,237	-3,679	-3,306	-2,258
Within		-1,153	846	3,797	1,837	706	645	-2,083	-3,388	-310	-897
Outside		17,826	12,712	30,693	23,669	4,893	339	-2,154	-291	-2,996	-1,361

Note: It is not possible to factor out North and South Dakota from the published data utilized to determine the composition of the population. The S. O. population in these states is small and does not contaminate the analysis. However, since we are not using the same data, this analysis is not precise.

The "migrant population" includes persons who were born in a different region in the U. S.; other native-born in U. S.; born in Puerto Rico and outlying area or foreign-born.

Conclusion

There is a fairly large amount of independent data on demographic, socioeconomic status, and language characteristics that can be utilized in further understanding the Midwest experience and for drawing meaningful comparisons. The longitudinal studies of L. and M. Shannon (1973), the rural to urban migration study of Daniel Price (1971), and the workers in transition study of Choldin and Trout (1969) provide documentation and analysis of data that in many cases remain much more helpful in understanding the Chicano experience in the Midwest than the data provided by the census. While it was not possible to integrate the findings of the independent research into this chapter, their findings greatly augment the data base in which we may increase our understanding of the Chicano experience in the Midwest.

By focusing on the Chicano experience in the Midwest, hopefully the long-standing preoccupation with the Southwest experience will be broken down. Because of the tendency to neglect the Midwest experience, it will be necessary to give this region explicit attention. However, in the long run, the greatest contribution of the midwestern Chicano experience will be toward helping to establish a national Chicano identity. The vitality and persistence of Chicano communities outside the Southwest further suggests the continuity of internationality in the Chicano sociohistorical experience. While a national identity is greatly needed for research and policy purposes, the international identity is one that Chicano activists have long argued.

One of the distinctive features of *la raza* in the Midwest is that all the major Spanish-speaking ethnic groups in the U.S. are substantially represented. In Mexico, the Southwest, and Northeast, or Puerto Rico, only one nationality is dominant, whereas in the Midwest the presence of each group is substantial. In Chicago, for example, the possibilities for coalition and integration are as real as are the possibilities for rivalry and conflict. Indeed, it is still problematic how the diverse groups will work out their differences and commonalities in the barrios as well as how their numbers will translate in the political arenas. Certainly it would not be a mere reproduction of the Southwest experience.

Notes

1. Geographical Areas and Classification:

Midwest	Census North Central Region	Federal Regional Council Areas
Midwest	*East North Central*	*Region V*
Ohio	Ohio	Ohio
Indiana	Indiana	Indiana
Illinois	Illinois	Illinois
Michigan	Michigan	Michigan
Wisconsin	Wisconsin	Wisconsin
Minnesota		Minnesota
Iowa	*West North Central*	
Missouri		*Region VII*
Nebraska	Minnesota	
Kansas	Iowa	Iowa
	Missouri	Missouri
	Kansas	Kansas
	North Dakota	Nebraska
	South Dakota	

2. Ss4, Proviso 9 of the Act of February 5, 1917, 39 Stat. 878.

3. See congressional hearings on agricultural labor and Western Hemisphere immigration in 1921, 1926, 1928, and 1930.

4. In the Southwest region about 90 percent are caught while seeking employment, less than 9 percent in agriculture, and less than 1 percent in industry.

5. Serious questions have been raised with respect to the accuracy of the 1970 census, particularly with respect toward enumerating the Spanish-origin population. The United States Bureau of the Census, despite the allegations that it has undercounted the size of the Spanish-origin population, has acknowledged that it has reason to believe that confusion about the category "Central and South American origin" may have led to an overcount of the Spanish-origin population, particularly in the Midwest and in the South. It seems that the United States Bureau of the Census would have to give very compelling reasons why, everything taken into consideration, the Spanish-origin population in the Midwest was actually overcounted. Note that it is also difficult to make a more accurate determination of the size of each ethnic group because of the confusion about the Central–and South American–origin category. For reasons explained earlier in this paper there

is strong indication that there is an overcount in the category "Central and South American origin" due to the lack of clarity in doing the census for this question. Thus, persons of Mexican origin probably constitute the single largest Spanish-origin ethnic group in the Midwest. It is very doubtful if the proportion of the Central–and South American–origin population is as large as reported by the census publications. This clarification is also applicable to the case for each state in the Midwest.

6. Apart from the 1970 Census Tract Reports PHC (1)-43 and PHC (1)-58 for the Chicago and Detroit SMSAs, the two most recent publications are, respectively: Department of Development and Planning, *Chicago's Spanish-Speaking Population Selected Statistics*, City of Chicago, Illinois, September, 1973, 38 pages; and John R. Weeks and Joseph Spielberg, "The Ethnomethodology of Midwestern Chicano Communities," unpublished paper, presented at 1973 Annual Meeting of the Population Association of America, New Orleans, Louisiana. These materials should be consulted for further up-to-date information about Chicago and Detroit.

7. It is not possible to factor out North and South Dakota from the published data utilized to determine the composition of the population. The Spanish-origin population in these states is small and does not contaminate the analysis. However, since we are not using the same data this analysis is not precise.

References

Acuna, R.
    1972   *Occupied America: The Chicano's Struggle Toward Liberation.*
            San Francisco: Canfield Press.
Barrera, M.
    1976   "Colonial Labor and Theories of Inequality: The Case of Inter-
            national Harvester." *Review of Radical Political Economics*
            (summer).
Betten, Neil, and Mohl, Raymond A.
    1973   "From Discrimination to Repatriation: Mexican Life in Gary,
            Indiana, During the Great Depression." *Pacific Historical Review*
            42:370-388.
Blauner, R.
    1972   *Racial Oppression in America.* New York: Harper & Row.
Cardenas, Gilbert
    1973   *Mexican Immigrant Population Chicago: Social, Economic and
            Language Characteristics.* Notre Dame, Ind.: University of Notre
            Dame, Midwest Council of La Raza.
    1974a   *Socio, Economic and Language Characteristics of Proyecto Ven-
            ceremos Student Population.* Notre Dame, Ind.: University of
            Notre Dame, Centro de Estudios Chicanos e Investigaciones
            Sociales, Inc.

1974b   "The Status of the Agricultural Center for Civil Rights." Notre Dame, Ind.: University of Notre Dame.

1976a   *Bibliography on La Raza in the Midwest and Great Lakes States (1924 to 1976).* Austin: University of Texas, Department of Sociology. Revised.

1976b   "Profile in Midwest Bound Mexican Immigrants, 1972." Austin: University of Texas, Department of Sociology. Mimeo.

Choldin, Harvey M., and Trout, Grafton D.

1969   *Mexican Americans in Transition: Migration and Employment in Michigan Cities.* East Lansing: Michigan State University, Department of Sociology, Rural Manpower Center.

Faught, J. D.; Flores, E.; and Cardenas, G.

1975   *A Profile of the Spanish Language Population in the Little Village and Pilsen Community Areas of Chicago, Illinois and Population Projections, 1970-1980.* Notre Dame, Ind.: University of Notre Dame, Centro de Estudios Chicanos e Investigaciones Sociales, Inc.

Galarza, E.; Samora, J.; and Gallegos, H.

1970   *Mexican Americans in the Southwest.* Santa Barbara, Calif.: McNally & Loftin.

Gamio, Manuel

1930   *Mexican Immigration to the United States.* Chicago: University of Chicago Press.

Grebler, Leo; Moore, Joan W.; and Guzmán, Ralph

1970   *The Mexican American People: The Nation's Second Largest Minority.* New York: Free Press.

Hancock, R. H.

1959   *The Role of the Bracero in the Economic and Cultural Dynamics of Mexico.* Stanford, Calif.: Hispanic American Society.

Hernandez, José

1973   "Public Sources of Data and the Chicano Community." *The Journal of Mexican American Studies* 1, nos. 3 and 4:123-129.

Humphrey, Norman D.

1941   "Mexican Repatriation from Michigan: Public Assistance in Historical Perspective." *Social Service Review* 15:497-513.

1943   "The Migration and Settlement of Detroit Mexicans." *Economic Geography* 19:358-361.

Immigration and Naturalization Service (INS)

1954   Files of the "Chicago Operation." Washington, D.C.

Johnson, H., and Hernandez-M., W. J.

1970   *Educating the Mexican American.* Valley Forge, Pa.: Judson Press.

Kiser, George, and Silverman, David

1973   "Mexican Repatriation during the Great Depression." *The Journal of Mexican-American History* 3:139-164.

Lebeaux, C. N., and Salas, G.
1973   *Latino Life and Social Needs Study of Detroit.*
Price, D. O.
1971   "Rural to Urban Migration of Mexican Americans, Negros and Anglos." *International Migration Review* 5:281-291.
Rasmussen, W. D.
1951   *A History of the Emergency Farm Labor Supply Program.* Washington, D.C.: U.S. Department of Agriculture, Agricultural Monograph no. 13.
Rex, J.
1973   *Race, Colonialism and the City.* London: Routledge & Kegan Paul.
Rosales, A.
1976   "Regional Origins of Mexicano Immigrants to Chicago." Paper presented at the National Association of Chicano Social Scientists.
Samora, Julian
1971   *Los Mojados: The Wetback Story.* Notre Dame, Ind.: University of Notre Dame Press.
Samora, J., and Lamanna, R.
1967   *Mexican Americans in a Midwest Metropolis: A Study of East Chicago.* Los Angeles: University of California/Los Angeles Study Project Advance Report.
Shannon, Lyle and Magadaline
1973   *Minority Migrants in the Urban Community.* Beverly Hills, Calif.: Sage Publications.
Simon, Daniel T.
1974   "Mexican Repatriation in East Chicago, Indiana." *Journal of Ethnic Studies* 11 (summer):11-23.
Spencer, Leitman
1974   "Exile and Union in Indiana Harbor." *Revista Chicano-Requeña* 11:50-57.
State of California
1930   *Mexicans in California. Governor Young Report.* Sacramento, Calif.
Taylor, Paul S.
1932   *Mexican Labor in the U.S.: Chicanos in the Calumet Region.* Berkeley: University of California Publications in Economics.
U.S. Bureau of the Census
1973a   *Subject Reports,* HA201 P. C. (2)-1c: *Persons of Spanish Origin.* Washington, D.C.: U.S. Government Printing Office.
1973b   *Persons of Spanish Ancentry, Supplementary Report,* 1970 Census of Population P. C. (S1)-30. Washington, D.C.: U.S. Government Printing Office.
1973c   *Persons of Spanish Origin. Census of Population: 1970.* Subject reports final report P. C. (2)-10. Washington, D.C.: U.S. Government Printing Office.

1973d   *Persons of Spanish Origin in the United States: March 1972 and 1971.* Current Population Reports, series P-20, no. 250. Washington, D.C.: U.S. Government Printing Office.

U.S. Commission on Civil Rights
1971   *Mexican American Education Study.* Report no. 1, Washington, D.C.

U.S. Congress
1969   *Senate Report of the Committee on Labor and Public Welfare.* Washington, D.C.: U.S. Government Printing Office.

U.S. Department of Agriculture (USDA)
1970-
1976   *Farm Labor.* Washington, D.C.: Statistical Reporting Service.

U.S. Department of Commerce
1960-
1972   Rural Development Service.

U.S. Department of Justice
1975   *Annual Report of the Immigration and Naturalization Service.*

Weeks, John R., and Spielberg, Joseph
1973   "The Ethnomethodology of Midwestern Chicano Communities." Paper presented at the 1973 annual meeting of the Population Association of America, New Orleans.

Womack, John, Jr.
1972   "Who Are the Chicanos?" *New York Review of Books* 19.

3

Cinco Chacuacos: Coke Ovens and a Mexican Village in Pennsylvania

Stanley A. West

Preface

In Bethlehem, Pennsylvania, from 1923 through 1939 several hundred Mexican immigrants as well as laborers of other ethnic groups lived in a steel company's labor camp, an enclave encapsulated by complex industrial machinery.[1] The rudimentary dwellings are overshadowed by gigantic chimneys (*chacuacos*) of the coke ovens that the workers tend during shift hours. For workers, life is spent shuttling between performing the most disagreeable jobs in the steel industry and repose in the adjacent shanties that they inhabit during the remaining hours of day or night. In many respects, this labor camp functions as a total institution that indelibly influences both those Mexican immigrants and their Mexican-American descendants.

Since I lack my own first-hand observations of camp life (these events having occurred before my birth), written historical accounts are few, and local oral history is often contradictory, I offer a vision of and an interpretation of that existence rather than pretending to compile *the* history. I compose this reconstruction by employing

I gratefully acknowledge financial assistance from institutions that supported either field research or composition of this chapter: the Rockefeller Foundation, the Ford Foundation, the Wenner-Gren Foundation for Anthropological Research, and the University of Pennsylvania's Center for Urban Ethnography.

Additional research with Mexicans and Mexican Americans of Bethlehem, Pennsylvania, is described at length elsewhere (West 1976).

To respect the privacy and confidentiality of informants' disclosures, they are referred to anonymously or by fictitious names throughout this chapter.

the concept of paradox in order to convey the richness that life in the camp embodied for its inhabitants. My words bespeak neither the best of all times nor the worst of all times; but rather, both of those conditions as well as intermediate states. If your world view compels you to force a resolution of the paradox, then *you* must do so. I shall not.

Life in the Labor Camp

During interviews with Mexican Americans aged fifty or more years, informants eventually reminisce about their life in the Bethlehem Steel Corporation's labor camp. They indicate that residence in the labor camp strongly influenced them in some significant respect. They usually express intense feelings—ambivalent, positive, or negative—that they continue to hold toward the company camp.

The origin of this camp lies in the acute labor needs of the steel industry that prevailed during and after World War I and the need to provide "temporary" housing for the immigrant laborers hired by the corporation at that time. At least two accounts place the founding of Bethlehem's camp at 1915 or earlier (Daday 1966:8). One informant, who lived there as a child, states that although the Mexicans always shared the camp with families of other national origins— Slavish, Hungarian, Portuguese, Polish, and Spanish—Mexicans numerically predominated following their arrival en masse in 1923 ("Minority Life" 1963:2).[2] However, with the passage of time this predominance diminished as Mexicans found housing elsewhere and members of other ethnic groups became residents.[3] An informant estimates that at any one time the inhabitants numbered about thirty-three families plus a number of bachelors, totaling approximately two hundred to two hundred and fifty persons. Paul Taylor's estimate is 50 per cent less—in early 1929, thirty-four men and seventeen families with fifty-six children, or one hundred and twenty-four Mexicans, resided there (Taylor 1931:12). Thus, although the labor camp corresponded approximately in size to the tiny villages in Mexico from whence had come many of the Mexicans, the camp was by no means ethnically homogeneous. Had it housed thousands of persons, one suspects that former residents might not now so fondly remember the camp's family-like solidarity.

A Mexican American describes life in the camp in a paper written for a sociology class ("Minority Life" 1963). He relates that the housing structures consisted of either six-room frame dwellings or large barracks. To provide housing for small families, some buildings were partitioned into two apartments of three rooms each. Larger families generally rented an entire house, initially at a cost of $8.00 per month. Eventually rent rose to $18.00 per month.

An anecdote recently published by Paul Taylor (1975) sheds some light upon the perceptions and values that influenced Mexicans' decisions about whether or not to remain in the Bethlehem labor camp or to repatriate. In 1931 Taylor studied pottery making in the village of San José Tateposco, Jalisco, Mexico, by observing the craft of Señor (Mr.) and Señora (Mrs.) Ramos, whom he had met in Bethlehem, Pennsylvania (Taylor 1933). One day when Taylor asked Señor Ramos whether he preferred Bethlehem or San José Tateposco, Ramos replied that he liked his village because there was "more liberty" (1975:104). Long antedating women's liberation movements, Señora Ramos replied to the same question that she liked Bethlehem because there was "more liberty" (1975:105). "Then she added in English, 'Turn on the gas,' making with her hand the motion of turning on the cookstove gas. In Bethlehem, she didn't have to scratch around with little twigs and small pieces of wood to make a fire to cook the meals. Nor did she live in an adobe house with one chair and sleep on the ground" (ibid.). By extension, one can infer that Mexican males found life in camp and coke works to be too regimented, but that their wives were "liberated" from some drudgery and appreciated the newly available material comforts.

The Notion of Total Institution

Although this Pennsylvania labor camp fails to display several characteristics of total institutions as conceived by Erving Goffman (1961), the notion of total institution provides an excellent framework for examining the nature of the camp residents' existence. Of the five types of total institutions that Goffman identifies, the labor camp most resembles those "purportedly established the better to pursue some worklike task and justifying themselves only on these instrumental grounds: army barracks, ships, boarding schools, work camps, colonial compounds" (Goffman 1961:5). Much structuring of matter and human activity within the confines of such organizations is based upon "a single rational plan purportedly designed to fulfill the official aims of the institution" (ibid. p. 6). And so it is with the labor camp, which acts as a pool of minimally paid laborers conveniently located within yards of the five coke ovens. One interpretation of the ties that the steel company forged with the Mexican laborers is that provision of company-owned residences was an instrumental strategy designed to protect corporate profit. Although labor camps had long been utilized by American agricultural growers and industrialists, the decision to provide dwellings for Mexicans is entirely consistent with the steel company's policy of attempting to forestall successful unionization of workers by enmeshing employees in various quasi-paternalistic programs. Intriguingly, about 1935 the corporation also constructed a meeting hall at the camp. This structure provided all residents with a site for a kindergarten, dance hall, Mexican cinema, Sunday school, and a meeting place for the Boy Scouts ("Minority Life" 1963:3-4). There, the revered Father Roldan, a Spanish priest who had officiated in Mexico, taught catechism classes, heard confessions, and said Mass for Spanish speakers. Moreover, it was in this hall that twenty Mexicans—both camp dwellers and others—met in order to organize the Mexican Aztec Society in 1937, holding meetings there gratis until the camp closed in 1939.

Although company directives did not closely control Mexicans' minute-to-minute activities when off the job, considerable structuring ensued during their work (jobs that other employees declined). Informants state that until the company signed its first contract with the United Steel Workers in 1942, Mexicans in the coke batteries were compelled to continue working under extremely high temperatures—until they collapsed—rather than being permitted regular rest breaks. After their shifts, the Mexicans departed "black from head to foot." But once at home in the camp, they were relatively free to practice the customs of their homeland, which were most practicable for men who had returned home to natal villages, married their sweethearts, and again journeyed to Pennsylvania as a family unit. Company directives that might pervade work hours were more rare and had far less impact upon family life, unlike other total institutions such as ships or army barracks.

Many total institutions exhibit a stripping process whereby newcomers are separated from the possessions and other symbols of a former existence that might empower them to successfully cling to the past. Entrance into the labor camp caused far less stripping of old ties than the workers had already inflicted upon themselves by emigrating to a hostile United States and by subjecting themselves to a protracted journey far from their homeland. However, the enclosing fence and the gate that guards occupied at the camp's entrance did act as a barrier between camp dwellers and the outer world.

The momentousness of entraining from Texas to distant Pennsylvania is reflected in the lyrics of the folk song "Corrido Pensilvanio" (Taylor 1931:viii-ix):

Corrido Pensilvanio

El 28 de Abril
A las seis de la mañana
Salimos en un enganche
Para el estado de Pensilvania.

Mi chinita me decía,
Yo me voy en esa agencia—
Para lavarle su ropa
Para darle su asistencia.

El enganchista me dijo,
No lleves a tu familia
Para no pasar trabajo
Es en el estado de West Virginia.

Para que sepas que te quiero
Me dejas en Fort Worth
Y cuando ya estés trabajando
Me escribes de donde estés.

Cuando ya estés por allá
Me escribes, no seas ingrato,
En contestación te mando
De recuerdo mi retrato.

Adiós estado de Texas,
Con tu vas tu plantación;
Yo me voy para Pensilvania
Por no piscar algodón.

Adios Fort Worth y Dallas
Por no de mucha importancia
Yo me voy para Pensilvania
Por no andar en la vagancia.

Corrido Pennsylvania[4]

On the 28th of April
At six o'clock in the morning
We set out under contract
For the state of Pennsylvania.

My little sweetheart said to me,
"I'm going into that office—
And say I'll wash your clothes
And take care of you."

The contractor said to me,
"Don't take your family
Or you'll pass up this job
It's in the state of West Virginia."

"So you'll know that I love you,
When you leave me in Fort Worth,
And you have started working,
Write me from where you are.

"When you are there
Write me, don't be forgetful;
In reply I will send you
My picture as a 'forget-me-not.'"

Goodbye, state of Texas,
With you goes your plantation
I'm going to Pennsylvania
But not for picking cotton.

Goodbye, Fort Worth and Dallas,
You're not much to me now,
I'm going to Pennsylvania
To be a vagrant no more.

Al llegar al steel mill worque	When we got to the steel works
Que vemos la locomotora	We saw the locomotive
¡Y salimos corriendo	And we came out running
Ochenta millas por hora!	At eighty miles an hour!
Cuando llegamos allá	When we arrived there
Y del tren nos bajamos,	And got off the train
Preguntan las italianas,	The Italian girls asked us,
¿De donde vienen, Mexicanos?	"Where do you come from, Mexicans?"
Responden los Mexicanos	The Mexicans reply,
Los que ya saben "inglear"	Those who know how "to English,"
Venimos en un enganche	"We came out under contract
Del pueblo de Fort Worth.	From the town of Fort Worth."
Estos versos son compuestos	These verses were composed
Cuando yo venía en camino	When I was on the way;
Soy un muchacho Mexicano	I'm a Mexican boy,
Nombre das por Contestino.	Call me "Contestino."
Y con ésta me despido	And with this I take my leave
Con mi sombrero en las manos	With sombrero in my hands,
Y mis fieles compañeros	And my faithful companions,
Son tres cientos Mexicanos.	Three hundred Mexicans.

As the years passed, various Mexican families moved out of the labor camp in order to reside in the city. In part the gradual exodus was due to the low social and economic status that residence in the camp connoted. Built during World War I, the dwellings had considerably deteriorated during decades of constant use. Industrial pollution further accounted for an especially low environmental quality in the camp's vicinity, and these factors all caused residents to face social stigma and to feel separated from other local Mexicans.

In 1923, when more than 900 Mexicans detrained in Pennsylvania as contract laborers, nearly all arrivals were male and only a dozen or so women and children accompanied them (Taylor 1931). Therefore, the initial composition of the Mexicans who resided in the labor camp potentially appears to be consistent with Goffman's notion that "total institutions are . . . incompatible with . . . the family" (1961:11). However, the majority of these and later arriving Mexicans who remained as long-term residents of the *colonia mexicana* soon transported their wives and children to Pennsylvania. Goffman notwithstanding, the labor camp that began as atomistic bachelor quarters progressively became transformed into a Mexican village, or *pueblo* of sorts, inhabited by dozens of family groups.

Another characteristic of total institutions in Goffman's view is that they tend to work a "disculturation" upon long-term residents (1961:13). In other words, such individuals tend to lose their ability to perform ordinary social roles outside of the total institution. There is no evidence whatsoever that camp dwellers could not function adequately either outside of the labor camp or in their Mexican homeland. All residents did ultimately depart from that setting and many of its first occupants eventually returned to Mexico either during the 1920s or the Great Depression.

To label the labor camp at a total institution is to reify a separateness, isolation, and uniqueness, when this camp also resembled many urban working-class neighborhoods in which other former immigrants resided. In this sense the labor camp was a community situated within an area where the company was the landlord of all individuals and families. However, the labor camp was also clearly set off from surrounding areas.

During the Mexicans' first years as employees in the coke works, the labor camp had an existence separate from the city because while in the camp they felt a security not felt while visiting the more hostile larger community. Paul Taylor (1931:13) suggests that the Mexicans were first viewed by the other workers as "strikebreakers" or laborers whose presence would permit a cut in wages. One local academic has described a photograph of a group of Mexicans detraining in 1923: this photograph shows Mexicans in traditional dress marching between two lines of policemen.[5] An amateur historian, who claims knowledge of local immigrant groups, explains that rather than being present for the protection of onlookers from the newly arrived Mexicans, the policemen actually were deployed in order to protect the Mexicans from the onlookers. Moreover, attitudes of other steelworkers were such that many ethnic groups were accepted because most male members were married and residing with their spouses. Little wonder, then, that when over nine hundred Mexican males arrived in 1923, their advent was hardly welcomed with warmth.

The hostility and misunderstanding of their culture that Mexicans faced in Bethlehem encouraged them to adapt by turning inward to their total institution. For example, by the end of their second week in Pennsylvania, several Mexicans who lived in the labor camp visited nearby Hellertown where they "built a fire into the street and intended occupying a vacant house." Hellertown's Chief of Police responded by sending them home on the trolley, promising to arrest them if the escapade were repeated (*Bethlehem Globe-Times* 1923a). Although Mexican "old timers" usually speak positively about their initial residence in the area, their sons claim that during early years Mexicans who ventured forth from the labor camp did so in groups for their self-protection.

The labor camp also had a unique and fearful image for many non-Mexican residents of Bethlehem. One newpaper article is especially noteworthy when supplemented by details known by one of my informants.

Drunken Mexican Goes on Rampage with Gun

Raul Martinez, a Mexican, residing in the camp at the Coke Works, drank moonshine Thursday night and then ran amuck with a revolver. The intoxicated Mexican fired several shots in the air and later sent a bullet in the direction of members of his family and wounded his eight year old son, Pedro, in the back and then shot himself through the hand. . . . Martinez also suffered from cuts from glass which he broke out of a door. Several persons informed the police that he was drunk and terrorized the community. Maria Martinez said that he chased her and others out of her home at the point of a gun. (*Bethlehem Globe-Times* 1926.)

It is apparent from the date of the article that the protagonist in this drama, whom I call Raul Martinez, was celebrating the Mexican Independence Day of September 16. The day's events were also memorable to an informant, who, forty-four years later, described them as follows:

Raul Martinez liked to drink. One day when he came home drunk, his wife locked him out. When Raul broke in the house, his oldest boy was afraid and ran to hide under the bed. But when Raul saw someone crawl under the bed, he thought that his wife had a man in the house so he got out his pistol and shot at him. And he shot his eight year old son in the rear end.

Because of the stereotype that Mexicans frequently engaged in knife-fighting, because of such alarming news items, or because of the general sensationalism of local reporters, non-Mexicans who did not dwell in the labor camp usually sought to avoid the area unless compelling business required them to brave the camp. In these respects, the labor camp did have a separateness befitting a total institution.

Idealized Views of the Camp

Although the following statements made by informants are presented in rather brief form, this brevity should not be taken as evidence that Mexicans only rarely idealize while reminiscing about camp life. Rather, it is because of the redundancy of informants who praise the camp that little need be written here.

A certain informant credits the Bethlehem Steel Corporation with "providing homes, free light, free coke for heat, some furniture for family use, and land for garden use and the raising of chickens, ducks, pigs, geese, and the like." In fact, to this man as well as to other Mexicans, the camp constituted a "paradise" in contrast with the living conditions that they had experienced prior to migration from Mexico. Some former residents admit that they would never have voluntarily departed from the camp.

Mexican Americans who lived in the labor camp as children frequently recall its physical layout with greater clarity and detail than do persons who resided there only during their adult years. Invariably those who were boys in the camp praise the nearly open countryside that served as a playground well-suited for active youths. This expanse included a creek, where in one location boys and men swam nude, while elsewhere girls and women swam modestly attired in dresses. This creek provided people with an opportunity for some fishing and older boys with a site for sailing the crude boats and rafts that they built ("Minority Life" 1963:4). However, informants agree that those using the swimming hole also faced the possibility of being butted by a heifer that had been specially trained to do so by the farmer who owned the land adjoining the creek. For adventurous youngsters, the farms, fields, and woods behind the camp offered ample opportunity for exploration and adventure.

An anecdote about gardening within the camp illustrates the fairness with which company officials allocated the gardening plots. A former camp resident recollects that each family was assigned a strip of land for its collective use, but from one year to another the size of this parcel grew or contracted in pace with each family's need. He recalls one year when his family was given fifty feet of additional garden. Although he was then a child, he correctly inferred from that event that his mother was pregnant.

Another informant, one who had lived in the labor camp in his youth, praises the general reciprocity that characterized camp life. He recalls that although everyone in the camp was poor, people regularly shared their resources and assisted one another. When one woman had to go into town, a neighbor suckled her hungry infant. The slaughtering of a hog raised in someone's backyard occasioned gifts of meat to other families. Informants also claim that many residents were connected by fictive kinship bonds of *compadrazgo* (coparenthood). The words of one informant express a prevalent sentiment: "There was always someone to lend a helping hand whether it was a Mexican family, a Hungarian family, or any other family." Others stress that "it was just like one big family." Thus, to these Mexican Americans the family-like atmosphere in the labor camp far outweighed any problems of poverty. In analysis one notes that these modes of customary assistance were also effective adaptations to poverty.

The Labor Camp as a Stark Setting

Verbal statements by informants indicate that during the 1920s facilities in the labor camp were of a most rudimentary nature. As late as 1928, residents had to stand in line for water from the camp's single spigot. During ensuing years most families were able to install plumbing, at their own expense; however, at the same time the general condition of the camp's frame buildings was deteriorating. Furthermore, because of its location near the coke works, the residents were confronted by a number of very unpleasant environmental conditions. Whenever the wind blew from one particular direction, it carried gases from the coke battery; whenever the wind blew from the opposite direction, it brought fumes from the tar pits. Thus, people often experienced unpleasant if not noxious odors and women found that their laundry soon become sooted when hung out to dry. A former resident recalls that "I'll never forget that polluted stream that ran through the company's coke plant with its muddy banks and magically colored streams of coke gas floating on its surface. Did you ever take a real mud bath or swallow a mouthful of coke gas?" Not unpredictably, one Bethlehem Steel executive offers health factors as the explanation for the eventual closing of the camp.

Bethlehem Steel Corporation's labor camp and coke oven smoke stack.

A Mexican American who lived in the camp as a child vividly recalls its characteristics.[6] Each house consisted of: "a wooden frame block with six square rooms—one electric cord hanging from each ceiling, one outside toilet, one coke bin and slag stones for a lawn." While making an understatement, he reveals that rats, roaches, and bedbugs were optional. Thanks to Mom and Pop's efforts we were not subjected to these added tortures. Imagine grown people letting their children lose their toes, fingers, ears and nose tips to rats, or to be pestered all night by vermin, or even more to succumb to an overdose of coke gas. It seems my pop was always patching up the exhaust pipes on the coke stove and the coke heater in the parlor. Mom was always scrubbing and spraying and pouring lime in the toilet (ibid.).

In other words, vermin and coke gas provided a hazard from which parents had to protect their children. He continues "the Co. gave us the coke, wood and lime and they also gave us a 'magic' book—it was like money, we could buy anything on it. My folks thought the Co. was so good to us!" (ibid.). But one had to make all purchases in the company store and mandatory deductions were made for one's account on each payday. In this sense the book was not at all magical.

As well as being poignant, this image of frenzied conflict over a supply of scrap wood appears antithetical to the idealized vision of camp life as dynamics in "one big family."

We always knew when winter was approaching for the Co. would park a train on top the slag banks that overshadowed our village and they would dump several carloads of used lumber over the bank's sides. Then the whole village would bustle—fathers, mothers, daughters, and sons—age was no barrier—everyone helping to drag the lumber home to stack in the cellar for the coming winter. It was funny, everyone trying to get the choice pieces—sometimes fights would break out. You would then see whole families pitted against one another and the winners would then take the choice pieces. It was funny. Here and there you would see someone hobbling home and we knew at a glance that they had stepped on a rusty nail—this was common, because we were mostly barefoot or wore a very cheap sneaker. You know, I often wonder now if they knew anything at all about the tetanus vaccine in those days? I know we didn't! (ibid.)

Later each fall the same drama was reenacted, though for a less dangerous commodity:

Then, when the wood was cleaned up, the Co. would dump a couple carloads of coke and the whole village would turn out again. The entire household could be seen converging on the coke pile carrying burlap bags, buckets (25 lb. lard cans), homemade wheelbarrows, wagons, and pop would carry the homemade shovel. He would fill our containers and when we were all loaded up we would start the procession home to the coke bin in the cellar. Pop would pull the homemade wagon with the high sides and iron wheels and I would push at the back—Mom would carry two buckets, one in each hand. Following Mom were my two older sisters, each with a burlap bag of coke strung over their shoulders and bringing up the rear was my little brother carrying the homemade shovel, God forbid what might have happened to our shovel should we have left it unattended even for the briefest moment amongst that pack of vultures! We would repeat these trips back to the coke pile till late at night, sometimes for days at a time until Pop felt there was enough coke in the bins for the winter—then we would sit back and wait for those long, cold, and bitter winters to swoop down on our rickety houses (ibid.).

This Mexican American further recalls introspection about how outsiders might have reacted to camp dwellers who were stocking free coke to fuel stoves during winter:

I could not help but wonder as we walked to the coke pile, I would pause and look up at the people (it seemed like hundreds of them) bent over and filling their containers and then I would look over my shoulder toward the main road and watch the "gringos" drive by in their shiny cars and I used to wonder what they thought of us—what a picture we must have painted for them?

These sentiments connote a sense of "we" versus "they" just as the occupants of a total institution for good reason feel separate from residents of the larger outside world.

The Camp as Self-Contained Total Institution with Subcomponents of Solidarity and Disunity

The most salient characteristic of life at the labor camp that informants recall with nostalgia is their former group solidarity and mutual cooperation. Camp dwellers seem to have preserved more aspects of rural communities than one expects to find with a vast industrial complex. It is possible that Mexican residents, very far away from kinsmen and natal villages, sought to preserve or to recreate former patterns of social relationships with their new neighbors, despite the ethnic diversity of the labor camp. Whatever might have inspired their life-style, Mexicans and other camp dwellers were relatively self-sufficient if one conceives of the camp and the company together as constituting a single system. Labor in the coke works was exchanged for money and residents then took it upon themselves to provide for their other needs.

The petit entrepreneurs of the labor camp did not restrict themselves to gardening and the raising of a few animals or poultry. One man served as a camp barber, working at this trade after finishing his shift at the coke works. During prohibition, another ran a "speakeasy" in his house. One enterprising Mexican youth bought moonshine for $2.00 per gallon, rebottling it into pints and half-pints to sell for a total of either $4.00 or $5.00 per gallon (the expensive liquor contained caramel food coloring while the more economic liquid did not). Another Mexican owned a tortilla mill and sold his product to residents. At least two older women provided the services as folk curers (*curanderas*), dispensing traditional herbal and therapeutic remedies for residents' ills. A Slavic housewife in the camp practiced midwifery, reportedly having delivered between thirty and forty Mexican-American children. Several Mexicans joined together with a few Spanish and Portuguese men, forming a small orchestra in order to provide dance music. Thus, oftentimes disregarding differences in ethnicity, a number of camp dwellers provided their coresidents with specialized services.

Apparently the camp dwellers quite frequently held celebrations. The Virgin of Guadalupe, the patron saint of Mexico, was honored on December 12; Mexican independence on September 16; and the defeat of the French at Puebla on May 5. People generally commemorated their saint's name days rather than their own birthdays. Invariably every other week the Mexicans drank—whiskey and tequila were preferred—and sang far into the night following the bimonthly payday. An Anglo informant who worked with Mexicans in the neighboring coke works recalls that sometimes when on the night shift, he and others would be able to sneak off to a party in the camp—"having a good time" while still remaining on company premises. Based upon these visits he praises the Mexicans' generosity while warmly describing their celebrations. Funerals also were major social events, the accompanying wakes lasting two or three days. Usually the deceased was placed in the front room of his house for "viewing," while traditional Mexican refreshments were served in a back room of the house. Whether for festivities or mourning, such social occasions contributed to the group solidarity that past residents of the camp now fondly recall.

Although many informants continue to emphasize the harmony and well-being of existence in the labor camp, others counter that camp residents also experienced conflicts with one another. For example, Vallarta, a married man whose wife had remained in Mexico, was living in the camp in a consensual union. Because of the scarcity of work during the depression, he was forced to accept "relief" (public assistance) funds in order to support his household. In contrast, his neighbor was a relatively prosperous man who continued in steady employment. So great was the outrage and moral indignation of this neighbor's wife, that she began to taunt Vallarta's "wife," making faces and even throwing dish water at her. Vallarta was forced to solve his problem by promising a severe beating to the neighbor if his wife did not cease her harassment. Furthermore, Vallarta implied that these sanctions resulted more from his consensual union than from his having accepted "relief."

Other informants recount that there was a fight in the labor camp approximately once each week. Some say that one man was killed for having an affair with another man's wife. Indeed, to some Mexicans, the violence that occurred in the labor camp befitted the sensational accounts about Mexicans that had been published in local newspapers.

Although many Mexican Americans idealize their years in the labor camp, others who resided there briefly or not at all tend to be condescending toward former camp dwellers. For example, Mexicans residing in the city who attended dances at the camp's social hall, though indistinguishable in dress from camp dwellers, made themselves noticeable by indictating their attitudes of superiority through their behavior. At least this is the perception that former residents now communicate. Also, Mexicans who resided in the city tend to disparage the structures in the camp as being mere "crude shacks" while at the same time deploring the Bethlehem Steel Corporation's paternalism in providing "free housing, electricity, coke to burn, and garden plots," to name a few of the services. But these Mexican Americans usually neglect to mention that the company always charged at least a small fee for most services and materials that they provided to employees.

Mexican Americans who did not live in the labor camp assert that

Funeral in Bethlehem Steel Corporation's labor camp.

the long-term residents were individuals who in Mexico were of the lowest classes and the least well off. In other words, Mexicans living in the city of Bethlehem hint that their countrymen who lived most contentedly in the labor camp, in Mexico may have lived in rude houses with dirt floors, walls of organ cactus, and thatched roofs. Too, some say that those who remained until forced to move by the closing of the camp had the least drive and initiative. Should such accusations be accepted literally? Or might some Mexicans who did not reside in the camp—for whatever reason—have been envious of their countrymen who were reaping the benefits of life within this total institution? Because the data required for an empirical test of informants' claims are not available, they should be treated only as stereotypes held by one segment of Mexican Americans concerning another subpopulation.

An old Spaniard, who has lived for many years in Bethlehem, eloquently describes the Great Depression as being *"cuando los frijoles estaban tan altos que no podian alcanzar"* ("When the beans were so high that one could not reach them"). From his poetic statement one might construe a very practical reason for remaining in the labor camp: rent was low and one could garden in addition to raising animals. In other words, those who continued to reside in the camp effectively adapted to prevalent economic straits, sacrificing social prestige for the security of being able to produce food and practice functional reciprocity patterns with others experiencing similar conditions. In light of this adherence to traditional Mexican coping mechanisms, non-Mexican informants who refer to the labor camp as the "Mexican village" may be perceptively identifying the key functions that the camp was serving.

Assuming that the hypothesis is correct that Mexican adaptations to the Great Depression were effected via a "return to the village," either through physical repatriation or simulation of village economic and social patterns, 1937 is not merely the time at which the American economy showed first signs of recovery. One can also interpret the formation of the Mexican Aztec Society in that year (over 50 percent of the organizers were then camp residents) as evidence that Mexicans were again willing to chance a mode of adaptation to Bethlehem that did not originate in their traditional Mexican culture. Although members of this voluntary association held their meetings in the camp's assembly hall for nearly three years, the establishment of this organization might have symbolized the replacement of a dying total institution with the establishment and maintenance of a highly respected and much emulated local institution: the ethnic club.

Discussion

One particular city politician, who is critical of the labor camp, converts his Slovak ancestry into political currency by claiming to represent the local immigrant minorities. Given this man's strong ethnic identification, his statement that the demolition of the labor camp ("rows of huts") was "the best thing that ever happened" seems rather callous. Perhaps he condemns the camp because of a conviction that residence in the camp tended to retard assimilation and that assimilation of ethnic minorities should be encouraged. The possibility that the camp might have had a positive function escapes him, as it also seems to have escaped the officials of the Bethlehem Steel Corporation.

On the one hand, many former residents are sensitive about their life in the labor camp though they describe it positively: "We were all poor but everyone was like one big family." On the other hand, nonresidents describe the camp in pejorative terms: "a squalid cluster of rude shacks inhabited by low class Mexicans." Objectively one must say that the camp was an entity both worthy of idealization as well as a reality with very rudimentary housing and exposure to offensive odors. Indeed, the labor camp also served as a transitional buffer for the Mexicans who were least oriented toward acculturation, but in 1939 when the camp closed, its residents were compelled to settle throughout Northampton Heights and other areas in proximity to the steel manufacturing operations. As a result of this dispersal, the pace of assimilation of the Mexicans began to accelerate. The passage of succeeding decades has witnessed considerable acculturation throughout the Mexican-American population.

In keeping with the labor camp's paradoxical character, it was, indeed, an example of the best of times, the worst of times, and an era in Pennsylvania Mexican-American history that fully merits a public record.

Notes

1. I employ the term "Mexican" in order to refer to any individuals of

Mexican birth as contrasted with "Mexican American," which herein denotes any descendant of Mexicans who settled in Bethlehem. I offer my apologies to any resident of Bethlehem who is a descendant of Mexican settlers but who prefers to be known by some label other than Mexican American. Unfortunately, no single term is preferred by the majority of my informants.

The coke works in which most Mexicans labored transforms coal into coke and other gases by raising it to a high temperature within huge ovens.

2. Daday appears to have quoted this paper ("Minority Life" 1963:1) but he neglects to cite any sources. The author of this paper, himself a Mexican American who had lived in the labor camp, supplemented his own recollections by interviewing his kinsmen and other former residents.

3. Although no precise data are available concerning the relative numbers of Mexicans residing in the labor camp as opposed to those living elsewhere, Mexican "old timers" estimate that two thirds of their countrymen resided in the camp during the 1920s but that the proportion declined to approximately one third during the succeeding decade.

4. Reprinted by permission of the University of California Press.

5. This photograph, which I was unable to view, may have recorded an arrival of Mexicans that was also described by a *Globe-Times* reporter (*Bethlehem Globe-Times* 1923b). The four hundred arrivals are included in the nine hundred forty-eight Mexicans recruited by the Bethlehem Steel Corporation.

6. Statements by this individual are parts of a letter, which is placed herein with the author's kind permission.

References

Bethlehem Globe-Times
   1923a   "Mexicans Asked to Move." Bethlehem, Pennsylvania, April 11,
            p. 12.
   1923b   "More Mexicans Arrive." Bethlehem, Pennsylvania, April 26, p. 6.
   1926   "Drunken Mexican Goes on Rampage with Gun." Bethlehem,
            Pennsylvania, September 17, p. 11.
Daday, Rt. Rev. Msgr. Stephen J.
   1966   *Chronicle of the Catholic People in Bethlehem.* Bethlehem, Pa.
            (Pamphlet apparently reprinted from newpaper article.)
Goffman, Erving
   1961   *Asylums.* New York: Doubleday & Co.
Taylor, Paul Schuster
   1931   *Mexican Labor in the United States: Bethlehem, Pennsylvania.*
            University of California Publications in Economics, vol. 7, no. 1.
            Berkeley: University of California Press.

1933   "Making Cantaros at San José Tateposco, Jalisco, Mexico."
        American Anthropologist 35:745-751.
1975   *California Social Scientist: California Water and Agricultural
        Labor,* Vol. 2. Berkeley: Regional Oral History Office, the Ban-
        croft Library, University of California.
Unknown Author
1963   "Minority Life at the Labor Camp." Term paper, Sociology 101,
        Lehigh University. Typewritten (includes a hand-drawn map of
        camp). Cited in Daday, *Chronicle of the Catholic People in
        Bethlehem.* Bethlehem, Pa.
West, Stanley A.
1976   *The Mexican Aztec Society: A Mexican-American Voluntary
        Association in Diachronic Perspective.* New York: Arno Press.

4
Migrants on the Prairie:
Untangling Everyday Life

Brett Williams

It seems strange to find fiestas in the cornfields of the Midwest. Yet in east central Illinois, in the heartland of America, lies a town that embodies many such apparent contradictions. I call it "Prairie Junction" because its history and character have been shaped by the joining of travelers, immigrants, and industrial paraphernalia in what was once a prairie wilderness. Now numbering about 7000 inhabitants, Prairie Junction rose from an isolated pasture when two railroad lines met and crossed there, bringing with them easy access to urban markets and the city's demands for processed foods. Facilities for preserving vegetables were introduced soon thereafter, and a sophisticated industrial technology has supplemented farming in Prairie Junction. Since the late 1800s its economy has been geared toward harvesting, canning, and exporting foods. All other industry in the town is subsidiary to canning, and most residents were drawn there by opportunities to invest or work in the canning operations. Here manual stoop labor is joined with a complex mechanical apparatus to harvest the crops that eventually flow to many major cities. Most farming and canning is done by machine, but to supplement labor needs at harvest time, 2000 migrant farmworkers journey north from Texas. They are Chicanos, ethnically anomalous in the Anglo-Appalachian community;[1] and the primitive hand labor assigned them strikes a stark contrast to the large-scale, highly efficient agricultural scheme that they meet on the prairie. Arriving in April to pick asparagus, migrant workers harvest and can tomatoes in midsummer, and turn to factory labor to process corn, pumpkins, and peas through late fall. During their stay in Illinois, they must live in camps provided by the growers; they then return to Texas until the cycle begins again the following spring.

Migrants' wages are low, opportunities to work erratic at best, and whatever they earn in Prairie Junction must be stretched to last while they winter in Texas.[2] Although many of the forces affecting their lives are remote from Prairie Junction, everyday life in the migrant camps there discloses both the immediate degradations migrants encounter and the creativity with which they meet, manage, and resist them. Daily social interaction also reveals the underlying principles of migrant workers' cultural order.

Responding to rigid environmental constraints and inadequate economic rewards, migrants gather and bind convoys of kin who travel together, steer one another on, share goods and cash, and cooperate in domestic and productive tasks. Because their life circumstances preclude tidy, bounded household groups, for migrants, kinship is something people *do*. I use "convoy" to refer to those who escort an individual through his or her life course, joining concerns of well-being and personal growth, acting together to solve problems, to cushion crises, and to stretch and secure resources.[3] This mutual involvement must be reaffirmed continually in the migrant camps, which, designed to house workers at minimum cost, are squalid and appear degrading to the observer. Upon entering the camps as an outsider, one is overwhelmed by sordidness, and easily misled by appearances of domestic chaos, squandered personal time and energies, and excessive, misguided ritual (cf. Friedland and Nelkin 1971; Coles 1965, 1970). Only when one understands the underlying order to migrants' lives can one appreciate the logic and purpose to everyday activities. I offer here a perspective on everyday life that stems from an appreciation of its testimony to life-long domestic purposes and demonstrates how shared commitments are communicated in the camps. While acting so as to preserve their own and each other's dignity within a demeaning institution, migrants also bind themselves to one another and daily lay a series of "side-bets" assuring mutual involvement.[4]

The Total Institution

The long monotonous buildings in Prairie Junction's migrant camps were constructed during World War II to house German prisoners of war. Today in each camp these barracks are partitioned into living quarters for approximately 500 persons; paper-thin walls and sometimes blankets serve to allot one or two rooms for living space. Each conjugal family has perhaps two beds. Laundry, shower, and toilet facilities are unsanitary and inadequate. Only rarely is hot water available, and the general water supply may be polluted by lead waste from local can manufacturing. Poverty program officials in Prairie Junction suspect a high level of lead poisoning among migrant children, and one outbreak of hepatitis in 1973 was attributed by them to the camp's drinking water. Crowded, unclean living conditions expose migrants to frequent recurring epidemics— most commonly diarrhea, occasionally diphtheria, and one summer an epidemic of tuberculosis. A great pile of hog manure, which is collected for fertilizer, and an overwhelming amount of vegetable processing waste flank one camp's outskirts in the summer, lending an intolerable odor to the environment and augmenting the danger of infectious disease.

The flimsy wooden buildings are vulnerable to hazards of fire and weather: one child was badly burned by flames from a grease fire that spread from the adjoining room to his living quarters. Company officials complain that "they [the Mexicans] can't take the cold," but the camps offer neither heating facilities nor ventilation; and in the cold, wet, and clammy Prairie Junction spring, living there is most uncomfortable. When the hotter weather comes, the absence of trees, awnings, screens, and insufficient windows leaves camp residents exposed to stifling, oppressive heat. The prairie summer is frequently a season of flooding and tornadoes, when the open, unprotected ground is deep in mud and migrants often fear a storm might strike. Then, during pumpkin season in October, the camps are once again too cold.

As well as being exposed to natural calamities, migrants are under continual surveillance by company officials. Camps are policed by a twenty-four-hour guard—"because of people sticking their noses in where they shouldn't" explained one townswoman—who interrogates and inspects suspicious visitors and reports the names of those visited. Until 1973 visitors were not allowed inside the camps at all; now state law grants migrant workers rights as tenants to have guests of their choice.[5] This provision, however, has led to increased surveillance and punitive measures administered to those whose visitors cause trouble. Crew leaders supervise activities within the camp, and the company pays some persons to spy on each other. Visitors can enter only with a specific destination, and having gone to that particularly numbered room, must leave within an hour or so.

Crew leaders have also thwarted all attempts to organize camp-wide meetings; migrants thus know that they must gather in private homes in Prairie Junction if at all. One entire family (including small children and an infant) was evicted and jailed for agreeing to be plaintiffs in a class action suit charging the canneries with using deceptive scales to calculate piece rates. A woman who organized a summer food stamps demonstration was never allowed by the crew leaders to return to the company for work. Another man, pressing for compensation for injuries, saw his entire extended family evicted on charges of "general disorderliness." Migrants can be fired for any reason, and once fired must leave the barracks on the same day; if they do not, the police are summoned to remove them.

But camp residents are subject to visits by certain company-approved outsiders. Two nuns, for example, move to the town every year to survey the camps. According to some migrant women, they seem to function mostly as scouts for the Catholic Church, alert for signs of drug use or surreptitious contraception, and reporting transgressions to the local priest. A public health nurse is frequently present to proselytize for birth control;[6] otherwise, she exhibits (in my judgment) an astonishing unconcern for medical problems and, according to one of the migrants, "thinks we can solve all our problems [by eating] big red apples every day." Migrants are also plagued by hustlers who know when they will have cash. One large jewelry firm, for example, regularly dispatches salespeople to the camps on payday to hawk cheap baubles on an installment plan.

Journalists seeking newsworthy exposés have joined these other visitors in recent years. Although repeatedly warned that the risks they take endanger migrants, some remain oblivious to the consequences of their adventures. One reporter, for example, upon ejection from the camps, returned in a blonde wig and miniskirt disguise. She was instantly detected and forcefully removed, thus creating a scandal that resulted in a rigid tightening of visitation rules and a heightened level of company paranoia, which was unpleasant for all residents. Journalists who are sympathetic to the migrants' plight and even direct advocates such as lawyers and union organizers must be cautious about entering the camps. They must carefully weigh the possibility that they will be unable to provide enough help to mitigate the dangers and punitive measures they might precipitate for migrants.

In the camps, residents are thus trapped,[7] guarded, vulnerable to many natural hazards, and continually exposed to their own bosses and selected outsiders. They are also in one another's constant presence, there being no provision for privacy and no structural regard for what might be their preferred living arrangements or their personal or domestic styles. The camps approximate closely Goffman's characterization of total institutions:

> A total institution may be defined as a place of residence and work where a large number of like-situated individuals, cut off from the wider society for an appreciable period of time, together lead an enclosed, formally administered round of life. (1961 xiii.)

The fourth type of such an institution is the work camp, "purportedly established the better to pursue some worklike task and justifying themselves only to these instrumental grounds" (Goffman 1961:15).

The total institution imposes a consuming definition of the situation and breaks down barriers that ordinarily separate individuals' activity spheres: migrants play, work, eat, and sleep with the same others under continuous supervision. Various degradations emerge in the total institution, including those of paternalistic surveillance, the loss of outside roles, the violation of personal territorial preserves, and rigid constraints on "self-selected expressive behavior" (Goffman 1961:43). In general, the camps deny their inmates control over their own lives. To tolerate institutional life, migrants must present social selves that are appropriate to it,[8] they must identify in some degree with institutional roles. At the same time, those whose lives are nearly overwhelmed by the total institution resist by preserving sacred personal fragments (cf. Goffman 1961). We can best understand the response of migrant workers to institutional degradation by heeding these two aspects of their self-preservation.

Personal Display

Exaggerated personal display can serve in an anonymous environment to compensate for impersonal, degrading life space (cf. Suttles 1968). It seems that migrants cling to their own unique personal styles as a challenge to the inhuman sterility of their camp quarters and as testimony to a vital piece of their lives. While trying to persuade local people that "these camps aren't our homes, we have real houses just like you do," they also stamp their surroundings with significant documents and artifacts from the outside.

Walls are decorated with birth certificates, marriage licenses, and the high school diplomas of various kin. Each family has an impressive set of photographs, featuring "real homes" in Texas, ritual events such as weddings and funerals, and portraits of relatives and friends. Such documents attest both to domestic involvements and to the validity of biographical occurrences that transcend institutional boundaries.

Each two-burner hotplate allotted a conjugal family holds a traditional clay pot for simmering frijoles and every kitchen has a tortilla press.[9] Young men kill and skin animals (usually squirrels or possums) and dry the skins in a designated area. Older women transport figurines of their saints, including their special patrons and, always, the Virgin of Guadalupe—as well as votive candles for them—that they install just above the laundry sinks. Migrant workers travel light, and many have few possessions anyway, yet they choose to carry and display personal artifacts that highlight their own cultural symbols in stark contrast to the definitions imposed by the institution. In these exhibits they seem to be saying of their backdrop: "This is not really us"; these exhibits also act, however, to make the camp their own.

The Domestic Order within the Total Institution

The physical structure of the barracks, having been built for prisoners of war, is geared to lodging single males. The long rows of small single rooms deny conjugal privacy and flexible distribution of space. Beds usually occupy territory shared with kitchen facilities, and there is no other living room; thus, when inside, the migrants' social life is dense and confining. Outside, they suffer full-time public exposure and must consider themselves always on stage (cf. Suttles 1968). Further, those kin actively participating in shared tasks are dispersed randomly throughout the camp, thus located without attention to their cooperative assumption of child care, production and household responsibilities, or their personal preferences. The imposed physical boundaries are unrealistic (and rather insulting)

Figure 4.1

Kinship Diagram of the Sangres' Extended Family

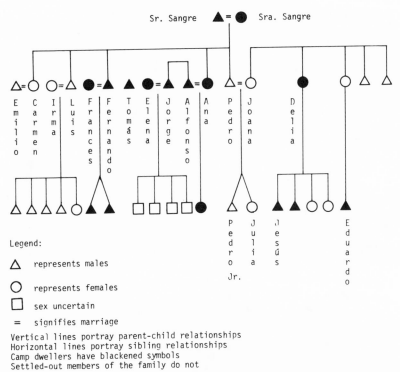

Legend:

△ represents males

○ represents females

☐ sex uncertain

= signifies marriage

Vertical lines portray parent-child relationships
Horizontal lines portray sibling relationships
Camp dwellers have blackened symbols
Settled-out members of the family do not

interpretations of "normal" family barriers, incorrectly stating the primacy of conjugal units by erecting partitions that segregate other kin but do not really allow conjugal privacy. I will discuss migrants' reconstruction of public space in the following section, focusing here on interaction among kin who work out a daily domestic routine that violates the institution's living arrangements.

I will consider first the housing arrangement imposed on a domestic convoy I will call "the Sangres," whose kinship diagram appears in Figure 4.1 and whose residential diagram appears in Figure 4.2. The eldest kin—the grandparents—live alone. Several doors down their son, Fernando, lives with his wife, Frances, and two children;

Figure 4.2

Housing Arrangement Imposed upon
the Sangres' Domestic Convoy

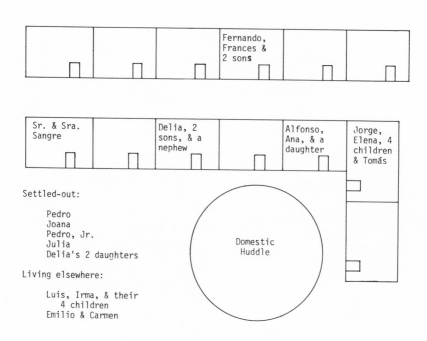

another son, Pedro, has settled in town with his wife, Joana, and teen-
aged children. This daughter-in-law's widowed sister, Delia, lives
with her two sons and a nephew near the elder Sangres. Their son-in-
law's brother, Jorge, is housed with his wife, their four children, and
his best friend, Tomás, who is young, single, and in the camp against
official regulations. Thus, even the Sangres' residential patterns set
forth their resistance to institutional segregation.

But resistance to institutional housing is even more striking in the
Sangres' daily execution of domestic activities. The grandfather
assumes principal child-care responsibilities; when not in the fields,
he brings a chair from inside his quarters, places his infant
granddaughter on his lap, and occupying his family's share of public
(or unassigned) space, quietly tends four or five young children.
Joana's daughter, Julia, joins him almost every evening. His wife

spends much of her time with her twenty-five-year-old daughter, Ana, relying on her for emotional support, cooking, shopping, and transportation. Ana's husband, Alfonso, involves himself mostly with his own brother, Jorge, his sister-in-law, Elena, his brother's friend, Tomás, and Delia's sons and nephew. Delia's daughters live with her sister, Joana, and Delia spends many hours outside of the camp, riding around with Joana to visit people, attending Illinois Migrant Council meetings, or "hanging out" at the local Mexican restaurant. Joana's husband, Pedro, is closer to his other brother, Fernando, and visits that room frequently, even moving in every summer for the corn pack.[10] Pedro Jr. is quite attached to Fernando's wife, Frances, who often cooks for him.

If we assume everyday life to consist of the following routine activities, members of this domestic convoy most frequently pursue them in the following company. While not rigid, these interactional patterns emerged clearly during one summer's observations:

SLEEPING (occurs in all six areas, interchangeably, due to lack of beds):

1. The elder Sr. Sangre, sometimes Sra. Sangre, two or three grandchildren, often Julia
2. Joana, usually Pedro, Delia's two daughters, sometimes Julia, sometimes Delia, sometimes Pedro Jr.
3. Fernando, Frances, sometimes Pedro, sometimes Pedro Jr., usually one child
4. Tomás, Jorge, Elena, one to four children
5. Alfonso and Ana, sometimes Sra. Sangre, sometimes their child
6. Delia's two sons, her nephew, sometimes Delia

EATING (occurs in three of the living spaces, interchangeably, and in the restaurant):

1. Pedro, Pedro Jr., sometimes Julia, sometimes Joana, sometimes Delia, sometimes Fernando and Frances, some of their children, occasionally Tomás
2. Joana, Delia, sometimes Delia's sons and nephew
3. Ana and Alfonso, one to six children, Sr. and Sra. Sangre, sometimes Delia
4. Fernando and Frances, two to six children, sometimes Pedro, sometimes Pedro Jr.

COOKING AND DOMESTIC TASKS:

1. Ana, Sr. Sangre, sometimes Elena, sometimes Julia
2. Frances, sometimes, Pedro Jr.
3. Joana and Delia

EXTENSIVE SHARING OF CONFIDENCES:

1. Pedro Jr., Joana, Frances
2. Julia and Sr. Sangre
3. Pedro and Fernando
4. Joana and Delia
5. Ana, Sra. Sangre, sometimes Elena
6. Delia's sons, her nephew, Alfonso, Tomás, Jorge

SHOPPING AND OTHER INSTRUMENTAL TRAVEL:

1. Varying clusters of young males
2. Joana, Delia, sometimes one to three young males, often Pedro Jr., occasionally Frances
3. Ana, Sra. Sangre, one to three young children, sometimes Alfonso, sometimes Delia
4. Joana, Pedro, Fernando, and Frances

CHILD CARE:

1. Sr. Sangre and Julia
2. Alfonso, Delia's nephew, sometimes Frances, sometimes Tomás, usually Jorge and Elena's older children

These arrangements of course fluctuate with changing circumstances, but the general style illustrates the everyday involvement of kin across conjugal boundaries to perform numerous tasks. Clusters vary with the activity, according to persons, responsibilities, and preferences for particular companions. But the underlying scheme consistently involves sharing the convoy's concerns so that everyone's needs are met and the most productive kin are freed for field labor. Relatives continually redistribute themselves around one another's quarters, mutually allowing privileged access, cooperation, and amenities—such as conjugal privacy (by freeing a room for husband and wife)—that the institution disregards. This ongoing order is not immediately visible in structured living arrangements, but emerges as one witnesses interaction, sociability, child keeping, and domestic acts through time.[11]

Crises frequently puncture the everyday routine, as when Delia's nephew was hospitalized for hepatitis or when Alfonso and Jorge were evicted for alleged drug use. On such occasions, kin rally around those needing aid; in the latter instance the brothers' entire extended family left the camp with them and settled in Joana's backyard while she mobilized her local resources to reinstate them.[12] In addition, relatives intersperse loosely joined, casually pursued daily activities with periodic huddling. The Sangres recognize, and are granted by others, their own portion of public space and huddle there. The huddle offers up testimony to the Sangres' shared lives. In this special space members congregate for consultations, joking, or gossip and frequently check in for news with those stationed there. They request reports on the weather, contrast the Prairie Junction temperature with the forecast in Texas, seek information on the work outlook for the following day, inquire about ill relatives, or seek the whereabouts of well ones. The elder Sr. Sangre most often holds forth there, watching over his youngest grandchildren. After the evening meal all members gather for an hour or so to discuss the day's events and to plan activities. Joana and each of her children almost always stop by during the afternoon and evening. The huddle and cooperative domestic acts unite kin groups, which the institution tends to segregate.

Privacy and Availability

I turn now to a consideration of migrants' management of crowded public space in the camps. Migrant camps are often densely populated; this density, in combination with the lack of private space and consequent full-time public exposure of residents to one another, has led some observers to claim that real social pathology emerges in such settings.[13] My own first reaction to the camps was to long for more privacy. I felt overwhelmed by the perpetual exposure suffered by migrants and expected to find trembling misanthropes hiding in the showers or under beds. I eventually realized that although privacy was scarce for residents, they also value it less than I do. Moreover, residents manage their setting's constraints creatively; they neither yield to chaos nor seek relief through pathological antisocial behaviors. Rather, they cultivate amiable interactional styles, cooperate on parceling out public space for the huddles of each domestic convoy, and ease continuing encounters with a novel provision for privacy.

Preserving one's sanity in what otherwise might be an "insane place" (Rosenhahn 1973) can be largely a matter of perceiving both the necessary and possible relationships among people, objects, time, and space. As Hall (1966), among others, convincingly demonstrates, reactions to crowded conditions are quite variable by culture. While I cannot claim that migrant workers' response to the density of the camps is more a result of their culture than accommodation to the total institution, I feel certain that their style of managing encounters there facilitates self-preservation while remaining consistent with long-term domestic styles.

An uncanny amiability and openness characterize most residents of the migrant camps. They opt for loose, easy personal relations rather than the extreme formality emerging in such setings as the military or the bizarre interactions that can erupt in asylums. Under extremely trying circumstances the most unlikely persons—crowds of adolescent boys, a fourteen-year-old girl who was unmarried and pregnant, her mother, a very ill man—were both friendly and gracious. One day I asked a young woman if she was happy about the arrival of a group of relatives from Texas, and she replied: "I have to be." Another woman said the same of approaching childbirth: "I gotta be excited." Such attitudes may represent the general warmth of Latino culture and perhaps a touch of fatalism, but certainly allows for a humane, realistic approach to crowdedness. Persons continually in one another's presence would find it unpleasant and perhaps futile to react otherwise.

Yet kin who are highly involved in each other's lives must move beyond such surface amiability and make enough of themselves available to one another to reaffirm their domestic ties in daily interaction. Time and space within the institution become metaphors for relationships that transcend the immediate setting, but which must be heeded and even created there as well. The cooperative pursuit of domestic tasks and periodic huddling[14] allow relatives to do this, while giving each individual numerous options in interaction and limiting the intensity of any one person's demands on another. Each finds a variety of relationships among kin concerned with demonstrating their availability.

But to affirm frequently one's availability to those who count on it and look for it is to make privacy rare and personal territories narrow. The constraints imposed by the institution join with the claims of kinship in restricting severely those individual boundaries that Goffman refers to as "territories of the self" (1971:28). Migrants cede these rights of the self to the demands of the institutional setting and to the everyday needs of others; yet, conversely, the diversity of kin responsible to one another allows for mutual provision for privacy in the camp. In front of each building is a stoop, located strategically in between the intensely demanding inside and the less personal outside. While still exposed to surveillance there, persons who remain on the stoop announce their unavailability, and this claim is generally respected. Children rarely assert this right, and I doubt that they would be granted it. But some adults do so frequently and are left alone at these times. Occasionally kin huddle around the stoop, but most often individuals disperse themselves along it, arms folded, eyes almost vacant, silent and contemplative, or resting. They are avoided and ignored.[15] In this instance, time and space become metaphors for the suspension of relationships, attesting again to the construction by migrants of shared perceptions of space according to what actions are felt to be appropriate there (cf. Hall 1966:108). While not valuing or expecting a great deal of privacy in everyday life, persons guarantee some privacy to each other if claims are clear and spatially limited so as to not disrupt the ongoing routine. Through the use of stoops and huddles, migrants interpose an interactional structure between themselves and the potential anonymity and chaos of the institution.

Child Culture in the Camp

Children learn special mediatory skills because they are expected to be ready protectors of adult time and space by caring for each other and by responding to the frequent, pressing demands of the aged, small infants, animals, and visitors. Answerable to many adults for their behavior, and responsible for younger children while at the same time intensely interacting with their peers, children are the caretakers of the area. Suttles (1972) feels that urban neighborhoods are similarly specialized: that people in different age and sex categories have varying investments in the local area. Children, because they are most likely to be confined to the neighborhood, seem to assume greatest responsibility for setting its boundaries and supervising its activities. Certainly migrant children are also likely to spend more time in the camps than adults and to take a greater interest in daily life there. But it is also likely that, as caretakers, children work at lodging themselves in the domestic convoy by purposefully constructing personal connections and serious responsibility for others. Child culture is almost an exaggeration of the careful management of space and sensitivity to kin characterizing the migrant camp, and children's acts thus offer valuable insight into the institutional routine (cf. Denzin and Joffee, in Denzin 1973).

Children readily intercept outsiders to ascertain their business and to direct them where to go. Many times I was met by children who would then escort me to my destination or inform me of my friends' whereabouts: "She's gone shopping," or "their little girl got sick and they had to go to the doctor." The children demanded to know the identities and intents of those who sometimes accompanied me. They frequently asked that I "teach" some sort of spontaneous arts and crafts project or a few words in English. Children wheedled photographs of themselves from adults to give to me. They always knew what would be happening in the camps well in advance of the event, and would invite me to upcoming fiestas or alert me to possible trouble. Thus, children often initiated my contacts and cemented my relations with migrant families: in the camps they learned how to obligate and implicate friends in their personal convoys.

Children roam the camps in great droves and organize themselves into complicated games. They play a good deal of bingo and baseball; they care for numerous adopted dogs; and they spontaneously invent rites as well. I once witnessed, for example, about nine children seriously involved in burying a dead bird; and on several occasions observed clusters of children grooming one another, searching for lice.

While relations with their peers have an everyday prominence, children also interact freely with adults. Children tended by aged relatives reciprocate that care by bringing them food and drinks, braiding their hair, or doing chores under their supervision. Children are responsible as well for the care of babies. One eight-year-old girl, the youngest of six, moves back and forth each day between her mother's and aunt's quarters, watching over her aunt's newborn baby so its mother can work. At a baby shower I attended, the guests were divided equally between women and their young children, who took a keen interest in the activities, the presents, and the plans. When this young woman had her baby, she found that she could count on a perpetual escort of three young children who helped care for the infant, ran errands for her, and generally shared her excitement and concern. As another example, I once showed some children a photograph I had of a small boy. All felt some dismay over the fact that the child was crying and grilled me as to the circumstances in the picture.

To take a near infant's perspective, I will describe the everyday encounters experienced by two children, each only two years old. Ricardo has a puppy that accompanies him everywhere, and these two are often seen rolling in the dirt together, tasting substances like paints, weeds, and mud, and fighting with other children and dogs. Ricardo is so energetic that one could easily imagine his agonizing any single caretaker. Yet he is supervised by his maternal grandmother and grandfather, a great-aunt, two younger aunts and several cousins. Shared responsibility for his well-being means that he is tended at all times without being suffocated. He explores his environment freely and safely; if he grows tired or becomes upset, one of his caretakers hands him over to his grandmother, who bundles him inside for a while. The other child, Isabel, is not quite so active and spends most of her time in her grandfather's care. But when ill, she can expect to receive attention from a variety of relatives. Her teenaged uncles and affines often take her for joy rides, to bars, or out for candy. Neither of these children fares well in the local migrant day-care program,[16] finding even that fairly liberal atmosphere much too stifling. They often refuse to go and pick fights once there. The day-care centers segregate children according to age; thus one program is geared to infants, another to two-year-olds, and so on. Children find it strange to be lumped in dull age sets and continually undermine the formal organization by insisting that a sibling or cousin join their group.

The central location of the migrant children's play area in the camp is telling (Figure 4.3). Here they are watched by concerned adults while at the same time responsive to calls from all sides and alert for visitors from the outside. They are grouped in pivotal territory, and their location emphasizes their roles as mediators and their responsiveness both to peers and to kin of all ages. School

Figure 4.3

General Layout of a Migrant Camp

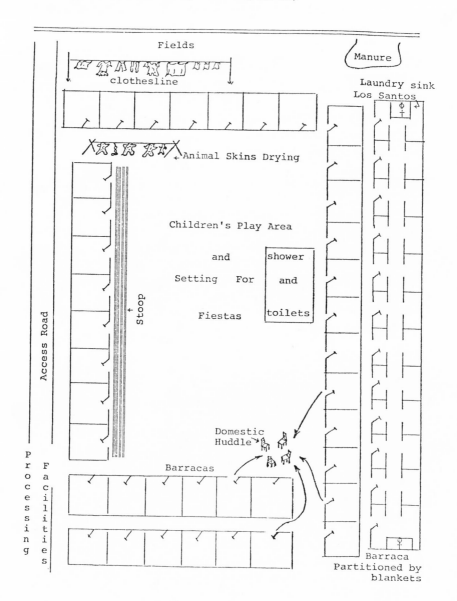

officials complain that migrant children lack individualistic impulses and are too intensely involved with one another's tasks.[17] We can see that they learn that they must be so implicated, that while very young a crowded and exposed life space forces them to begin to learn through interaction the necessary sharing of lives and resources.

Interjecting Ritual

Thus far, I have described the sharing of immediate time and goods, in accordance with long-term domestic commitments, and in an effort to preserve the dignity of the self within the total institution, I have discussed the dilemma camp life presents to migrants: they must abide by its constraints and at the same time organize purpose-ful, dramatically inappropriate[18] resistance to its potential degrada-tions. I have attempted to portray the resolution of this dilemma in an underlying scheme that children learn and adults relearn as relevant to sharing personal and material concerns. And I have claimed that this understanding emerges in daily interaction, whose principles remain consistent with life perspectives and goals.

I turn now to the interruption of routine by periodic ritual, the equivalent in time to the physical resistance migrants express against the institution through the display of personal objects and the re-definition of space. Through ritual, migrants affirm their control over schedules that otherwise run their lives and celebrate their own existence in an environment that denies self-realization. I will conclude this section with a description of a special set of ritual objects that symbolize the whole array of migrants' rebellions to the claims of the total institution.

Migrants work and travel on an agricultural schedule; their yearly rhythms are guided by the season, locally recognized and labeled as the "migrant season." Each year they yield to an annual cycle that calls for stoop labor in the erratic asparagus harvest in April and May, occasional odd jobs from early June to mid July, working the tomato harvest until mid August, intensive fifteen- to twenty-hour days of factory labor through September, and a somewhat slower pumpkin harvest through late fall. In November they return to Texas and attempt to stretch their surplus cash until the following April, when they return to Prairie Junction. Migrants move through periods of frantic activity to times when they have little or no work at all, controlling neither the pace nor the abrupt changes in available work. Yet the agricultural cycle imposes rigid constraints on their lives.

But migrants also resist seasonal controls by imposing their own rituals on each turning point. In Prairie Junction they celebrate lavishly the conclusion of particular harvests with feasts, singing, and dancing. They project their own foods, dress, and music into the monotonous surroundings of the camp and the steady progression of the season. Dances and fiestas appear misplaced with giant processing facilities and long, low barracks as a backdrop. Moreover, the harvest is not its reapers' to commemorate; they share little in its profits, and its conclusion usually ushers in a long slack period for them. Yet inserting ritual at these points seems designed to deny the tyranny of the season, to celebrate the self in opposition to the institution, and to transform economic realities through shared sociability. Through ritual, migrants punctuate the monotonous work routine and interject their own festivities between themselves and the institution.

For example, toward the end of the corn pack, camp residents prepare great quantities of barbecued chicken, corn on the cob, tortillas, and soft drinks. Designated persons, usually influential middle-aged women, remain home from the fields and cook all day. Toward evening everyone gathers around the dirt pits to eat and drink. As night falls, people move over to the open space beneath the water tower and dance to music provided by a teen-aged band. Everyone dances, especially the children, and young girls solicitously invite the hated crew leaders to be their partners. Sometimes the dancing continues until dawn, in defiance of the migrants' work schedule, just as festival expenses mock the approaching period of no pay.

Complementing rites set by the agricultural calendar is a close attention paid religious holidays such as patron saints' days, which are often celebrated with a Spanish Mass. Less formal religious rites include evening music fests such as *Cantando a Dios* ("Singing to God"). One man who researches pop Spanish poetry sometimes rallies his neighbors to listen to religious lyrics that treat topics such as leaving the Mexican homeland and invoking the Virgin of Guadalupe in one's travels. And whenever a friend or relative leaves for a trip, elders insist that everyone kneel and join in long tearful prayers.

Special heed is also given all dates of biographical significance.

Birthdays, baptisms, marriages, and funerals are elaborately noted with great feasts, gift giving, music, and photographs. Here again migrants assert the primacy of their lives against the institution, and also grant the individual the special attention that is generally unavailable, given the needs and demands of other kin.

An interesting example of such biographical ritual is the *quinceañera*, or fifteenth birthday party, given all young girls when they reach that age. On one such occasion a crew of women (the girl's relatives and her godmother) remained home during a peak work period to prepare barbecued chicken, corn, tortillas, and beans, which the extended family had pooled their earnings to buy. The celebrant's mother and sisters bought a large decorated pink birthday cake and cans of soda for the festivities, and some of her male cousins smuggled in beer. At about four o'clock workers began to trickle in from the fields; each one walked directly up to the honoree, kissed her on the cheek and said, *"Te felicito"* ("I congratulate you," or "I wish you well"). She wore a long pink dress; all others remained in their everyday clothes. Everyone ate; then, flanked by two friends in blue jeans who loudly announced the names of donors, the girl opened each gift. Every family in the camp had given something, and when revealed the contents were greeted by loud sustained cheers. Most of the presents consisted of inexpensive jewelry, candy, and handkerchiefs purchased at the downtown dime store, but all were elaborately wrapped. At dark, everyone wandered over to dance, with the feted girl leading off with a crew leader's son, then dancing the second round with her father. Many photographs were taken. Though exhausted, most stayed all night long, to return directly to work.

In similar ways, little children, the aged—and all those whose unimportance is implied in other sectors of society—are periodically reassured that their lives are progressing properly and that their turning points are significant to other people. Even babies receive special birthday parties, and older kin in particular are reassured that their deaths will be commemorated appropriately. Migrant women still wear black for a whole year after the death of a close relative, and funerals are carefully recorded in photographs just as are happier ritual events.

Thus, ceremonies often recur and, through photographs and lore, rituals are frequently relived. Ritual behaviors may appear wasteful and unproductive, and some observers attribute their occurrence to the culture of poverty or to the volatile expressiveness of the tension-ridden poor (see, for example, Friedland and Nelkin 1971). Migrants' rituals are particularly susceptible to such interpretation, because some of their ritual materials suffer from the intrusion of inexpensive Anglo artifacts and from the migrants' own inadequate means to design them as they might wish. We have seen that foods and gifts are sometimes of necessity simply imitations of the wider society's material accoutrements. But, in fact, underlying their unimaginative exteriors and lavish acts is a firm commitment to ritual's larger meaning: the affirmation of the self as something more than that allowed by the total institution and the mutual restaging of people's involvement in each other's lives.

A most interesting ritual counterpoint both to their sterile surroundings and to the farm-labor hierarchy is provided by *los santos*, elaborate ceramic figurines of saints, which migrant women bring with them from Texas. As mentioned above, they install *los santos* above laundry sinks and equip them with candles that they keep lit perpetually. Many different saints and the Virgin Mary are represented, and each extended family generally has its own special patron. Through *los santos*, migrants seem almost to mock the supposed mediatory position of the crew leaders, who company officials claim function to personalize work relations, lending money, easing bureaucratic procedures, settling disputes and the like. Most migrants distrust the crew leaders as exploitative company agents and turn instead to *los santos* when they face such problems. Wolf (1959) explains that the Catholic saints were incorporated easily into native Mexican worship as lower-level members of the Aztec pantheon. The saints are approachable, personal intermediaries, almost like contributing members of domestic convoys; and they form the meaningful mode through which even some modern Chicanos sometimes communicate with the supernatural. Those in the camps interact with *los santos* frequently, making petitions, giving thanks, and demanding their presence when they go north for a season. They approach *los santos* for many types of aid, as when Joana Sangre asked the Virgin of Guadalupe to ensure that her friend pass his bar examinations. When he did so successfully, she took full credit, and insisted over the years that he honor the obligation created by her invocation of supernatural assistance. Thus, *los santos* are both intermediaries with the outside world and powerful extensions of kin connections.

Los santos perform the functions that company executives speciously assign crew leaders, who in turn become the institutional scapegoats for poor living and working conditions and ethnic stooges whose injustices are excused because "they do it to their own kind." By appointing as mediators and foremen migrant workers who have behaved well and curried their favor, owners insure that supervision will be self-righteous and punitive. By paying them on a percentage basis and by granting them license to extract whatever they can get away with from workers' pay, they reward crew leaders for cheating and exploiting workers. Yet owners retain as proof of their own inculpability the excuse that they are not personally involved in the work arena, that they leave details of daily social control to persons who are similar to other workers, and who understand them and look out for their welfare. The entire system is a great farce, and migrants know it to be so. They regard the crew leaders as bullies, cheats, and stooges, and ignore their hypothetical roles as intermediaries. In times of trouble they appeal to *los santos,* thus ignoring company philosophy and insisting on the superiority of their own cultural forms.

This, then, is the daily social order of the migrant camp and its complement in ritual. I have tried to demonstrate that the total institution is not necessarily degrading and certainly not chaotic. The squalor of their surrroundings is overcome by migrant cooperation in self-preserving acts. Joining a powerful respect for narrow private territories with an otherwise easy mingling, camp residents manage a crowded and public everyday life. Elaborate personal display and careful attention to creative uses of space defy institutional indifference to individuals. It seems remarkable that a man involved in menial stoop labor chooses to exhibit the high school diploma of his niece above the family bed, and that a fifteen-year-old who will spend her life in the fields celebrates her birthday with the pomp and attention generally reserved young debutantes. We can see in these episodes that culture-of-poverty-like behaviors are not what they seem; lavish expressive acts are essential in asserting the dignity of individuals and attesting to others' commitment to them. Ritual cannot be dismissed as pedestrian with reference to the objects employed or as wasteful because persons yield work time to prepare for them. Similarly, the apparent unpredictability with which residents emerge from others' living quarters or the corrective work devoted to minor mishaps cannot be understood if they are considered to be random, disorganized diversions of energy. The underlying order of family life is reflected as clearly in such events as in those settings where, for example, an elderly man and his youngest grandchild spend several hours minding one another. Life-long concerns are thus powerfully set forth in everyday encounters, as migrants, resisting the institution, live out their shared understanding of what families are all about.

Notes

1. I term the community "Anglo-Appalachian" because there are very few foreign immigrants and because the majority of the residents are descendants of nineteenth-century migrants from Kentucky, Tennesee, and West Virginia.

2. I discuss these economic, historical, demographic, and social structural constraints more fully in my doctoral dissertation (Williams 1975).

3. My perspective on migrant families differs vastly from those of other observers, for example, Coles (1965, 1970); Grebler, Moore, and Guzmán (1970); Madsen (1964); and Padfield and Martin (1965); and coincides more closely with the view offered by Smith in Helm (1968). Chicanos' attention to extended family concerns has been characterized by the former writers as both unhealthily dependent and maladaptive, in that individuals rarely desert kin to rise into the middle class. But to focus on narrow economic maximization is to underrate the constraints on migrants' lives and to overlook the long-term material and emotional security individuals find in domestic convoys. Nuclear family mobility is precarious, and migrants manage best by sharing erratic, inadequate economic returns and by cooperating so as to most flexibly perform domestic and productive tasks.

4. "Side-bets" is Becker's term (in Neugarten 1968) for those situational adjustments that modify individuals' larger life strategies.

5. I too had a very difficult time gaining access to the camps. I was only able to do so after affiliating myself with an arts and crafts program sponsored by a local church for migrant children.

6. This nurse feels very strongly about birth control for poor women, explaining to me that those without adequate resources to support them should not have children. Her approach is somewhat confusing to migrant women, since it conflicts with Catholic doctrine and is usually not very well presented. Many women refer to the birth control pills that she hands out quite freely as "baby aspirin" and use them for a variety of purposes. On one occasion, it seemed to me that she was being rather punitive to a thirty-nine-year-old mother of five, nine months pregnant and very ill, by refusing her medication and telling her that she could not be admitted to the hospital

until after labor had begun.

7. Migrants are allowed to leave the camps, but are frequently harassed and sometimes denied admittance in the town's restaurants and bars. There are not really very many places for them to go; and thus, they seem trapped in the camps.

8. By "appropriate" I mean demonstrating a formal poetic appropriateness that demands a consistency among dramatic elements. Thus actors, props, setting, and acts are fitting in relationship to each other. Those degraded by the setting present degraded selves, nothing more. By "inappropriate" I mean the presentation of elements incongruous with the institutional scene (cf. Burke 1945).

9. An interesting analogy to migrants' insistence on their distinct culinary tastes occurs when people eat out: many carry jalapeños or little bottles of chili powder with them to enliven restaurant meals.

10. Corn in Prairie Junction is harvested by mechanical pickers, but must be canned soon thereafter. Migrants work in the companies' processing plants at cutting and canning corn, and refer to this work period as the "corn pack."

11. I feel that Grebler, Moore, and Guzmán (1970), who insist on the salience of the nuclear family among modern Chicanos, might have overlooked these domestic patterns in part because they are not easily ascertained through questionnaires or household surveys.

12. It should be noted that housing her kin for even a few days was quite an imposition on Joana Sangre. People were sleeping in her living room, kitchen, and backyard; and the household was very short on food. When I visited, they had nothing to eat other than flour and lard for tortillas.

13. For example, Friedland (1968), Nelkin (1970), and Friedland and Nelkin (1971), writing of black migrants in the Northeast, claim that coerced intensive interaction in combination with low social cohesion leads to high levels of tension and violence. They feel that migrants perceive everyday life as senseless and unpredictable, and react, not with rational, goal-directed behavior, but through simply lowering their expectations and seeking relief. Migrants acquiesce in institutional chaos and find outlets in expressive volatile acts such as drinking, gambling, story telling, and fighting. Perhaps because Friedland and Nelkin studied populations composed largely of single males, the everyday reality they described differed from that found in the camps of Prairie Junction. In any case, my findings are in stark contrast to theirs.

14. Huddling also allows migrants to classify the crowded camp and thus use family categories to make certain predictions about other people's behavior that guide interaction. Some families are labeled "friends of the crew leaders," others "troublemakers," and so on. Classification introduces

an order to interpersonal relations when it is impossible to personally identify those all around. Suttles (1968) demonstrates that inner city residents similarly use categories of sex, ethnicity, age, and territory to organize everyday life.

15. I should note that this designation of the stoop as an arena for privacy was never communicated explicitly to me. But I very frequently observed that persons on the stoop were left alone; and on several occasions noticed that very small children were intercepted when approaching someone there and that conversations in the vicinity took place without any effort to acknowledge the presence of those sitting there.

16. Prairie Junction's day-care program offers a rather enlightened bilingual, bicultural curriculum. Administered by the Texas Migrant Council, day-care services follow the paths of their clients, from Texas to Prairie Junction and back again, seeking to provide continuity of service and personnel. Day-care officials are aware, to some extent, of children's caretaking skills and responsibilities. They noted, for example, that after their program was initiated, older children were more likely to attend school because the centers relieved them of baby-sitting duties. But I do not think that teachers are aware that they might design their curriculum so as to respect and benefit from migrant children's culture, as evidenced in their segregation of children by age. I found, when helping a young seminarian operate a children's recreation center, that children could virtually run the building, direct activities, and provide instruction on their own; children of all ages intermingled, and a sort of natural order seemed to prevail.

17. One teacher complained to visiting Chicano consultants: "Why can't your children take turns like our children do? They always have to butt in and help each other out when we have reading in a circle!" The educators' explanation was identical to mine here. Similarly, Coles (1970) is concerned that when he asked children to draw self-portraits, they always portrayed themselves with their siblings, and never alone. Coles feels that children thus display excessive dependency on others; but I would argue that, on the contrary, their portraits are both an accurate reflection of their lives and a convincing illustration of their healthy involvement with kin.

18. Again, I follow Burke's (1945) discussion of dramatic appropriateness (see note 8).

References

Burke, Kenneth
1945   *A Grammar of Motives.* New York: Prentice-Hall.

Coles, Robert
  1965 *The Migrant Farmer: A Psychiatric Study.* Atlanta, Ga.: Southern Regional Council.
  1970 *Uprooted Children.* New York: Harper & Row.
Denzin, Norman K., ed.
  1973 *Children and Their Caretakers.* New Brunswick, N.J.: Transaction Books.
Friedland, William
  1968 *Field Research in Migrant Labor in New York State.* Ithaca, N.Y.: New York State School of Industrial and Labor Relations, Cornell University. Cornell Migrant Labor Project, second annual report, July.
Friedland, William, and Nelkin, Dorothy
  1971 *Migrant.* New York: Holt, Rinehart & Winston.
Grebler, Leo; Moore, Joan W.; and Guzmán, Ralph C.
  1970 *The Mexican-American People: The Nation's Second Largest Minority.* New York: Free Press.
Goffman, Erving
  1961 *Asylums.* New York: Doubleday & Co.
  1971 *Relations in Public.* New York: Harper & Row.
Hall, Edward T.
  1966 *The Hidden Dimension.* New York: Doubleday & Co.
Helm, June, ed.
  1968 *Spanish-Speaking People in the United States.* Seattle: University of Washington Press. American Ethnological Society Proceedings, annual spring meeting.
Madsen, William
  1964 *The Mexican-Americans of South Texas.* New York: Holt, Rinehart & Winston.
Nelkin, Dorothy
  1970 *On the Season: Aspects of the Migrant Labor System.* Ithaca, N.Y.: New York State School of Industrial and Labor Relations, Cornell University. ILR Paperback no. 8.
Neugarten, Bernice, ed.
  1968 *Middle Age and Aging.* Chicago: University of Chicago Press.
Padfield, Harlan, and Martin, William E.
  1965 *Farmers, Workers, and Machines.* Tucson: University of Arizona Press.
Rosenhahn, D. L.
  1973 "On Being Sane in Insane Places." *Science* 179:150-157.
Smith, M. Estellie
  1968 "The Spanish-Speaking Population of Florida." In *Spanish-*

Speaking People of the United States, edited by June Helm, pp.
120-133. Seattle: University of Washington Press. American Ethnological Society Proceedings, annual spring meeting.

Suttles, Gerald D.
   1968   *The Social Order of the Slum.* Chicago: University of Chicago
            Press.
   1972   *The Social Construction of Communities.* Chicago: University
            of Chicago Press.

Williams, Brett
   1975   "The Trip Takes Us: Chicano Migrants on the Prairie." Ph.D.
            dissertation, University of Illinois.

Wolf, Eric R.
   1959   *Sons of the Shaking Earth.* Chicago: University of Chicago Press.

Part 2
Ethnicity:
Boundary Maintenance, Adaptiveness, and Change

5

La Virgen de Guadalupe and the American Dream: The Melting Pot Bubbles on in Toledo, Ohio

*June Macklin
and Alvina Teniente de Costilla*

Introduction

"Porque voy a dejar mis hijos que pasan por lo que yo pasé?—Why should I let happen to my children what happened to me? That is why I am opposed to what they call bilingual and bicultural education in the schools," says Juan, an American of Mexican descent. But another, Mike, asserts: "One thing I want *my* children to know is Spanish. We have real identity problems here in the United States and need to have culturally relevant education; to know something of our own history, the glory of the Aztecs and Montezuma, something of men like Hidalgo, Iturbide, and Zapata, who were fighting for the freedom of the poor Indians."

These contrasting points of view come from two men who share much in common: both have lived in Toledo, Ohio, for nearly thirty years; both are Catholics; Spanish is the mother tongue of both; both are married to women of Mexican descent; both served in the United States Army; and obviously neither has been able to escape the vocabulary of social scientists when discussing the problems of living

Many, many people gave generously of their time and assistance to make this chapter possible. In particular we would like to thank Morgan J. Barclay, Father Dave Beck, Emilio Costilla, Carlos and Emilio Costilla, Jr., Higinio Corvarrubias, Miguel Corvarrubias, William DeWolfe, Guadalupe Flores, Tom Gillette, Noé Hinajosa, Earl Kalp, Rudy Lira, Linda Martinez, Roberto Martinez, Estela Montoya, Jesse Mosqueda, David Noel, Arturo Presas, Humberto Puente, Stanley Rhonda, and Celso Rodriguez. A special thanks goes to Sue Ann Davis for her cheerful assistance with the manuscript.

they encounter as *toledanos* (a person of Mexican descent living in Toledo).[1] But Juan is fifty-four years old, a father of six, who served during World War II and was a former migrant agricultural worker who settled down in Toledo thirty years ago, while Mike was born and grew up in Toledo. Now thirty, he is a third-generation American who can understand most of the Spanish he hears, but acknowledges that he can speak very little and read even less. His military service came during the Vietnam War. Although his college education included a course in Mexican and Mexican-American culture, his grasp of the details of *la raza*'s history is somewhat tenuous.[2] He recently married a woman of Mexican descent, but his five older brothers all married women who are not.

It is the purpose of this chapter to examine these two opposing but representative models for change found among *toledanos*. The first, which Juan expresses, is explicitly assimilationist while the second, which Mike holds, stresses cultural pluralism, urging that the unique history and culture of Mexican Americans be preserved. We shall look at the beginnings, growth, and implications of both models. Our data suggest that cultural changes (i.e., changes in ideas, beliefs and behavior) and structural changes (i.e., changes in patterns of social interaction among people; e.g., voluntary associations, places of work, intermarriage) are occurring rapidly regardless of the model held by various segments of the *toledano* community. However, social and cultural change is never simple and it is necessary to specify the conditions under which particular changes might be expected to occur. In order to do this, we shall:

1. sketch the ambience of the host community—Toledo, Ohio— into which *toledanos* came and are coming;
2. consider briefly the cultural patterns brought by early *toledanos*; and
3. examine the relations between *toledanos* and their hosts in order to see what kinds of beliefs and behaviors, old and new, have come out of these interactions.

We shall introduce data from the "microcultures"—that is, the hearths, altars, and marketplaces—in which individuals go about handling their daily concerns. It is within these microcultures of individual and family decision making that one can see the processes

An Ohio-born *toledano* expresses his identity with *la raza*. *Miguel Covarrubias.*

of social and cultural change. By looking at how individual and family biographies intersect with economic, political, religious, and social developments, we can consider diversity as well as uniformity in *toledano* behavior (Basham and DeGroot 1977; Pelto and Pelto 1975; Wallace 1952). *Toledanos* are becoming Americans in different ways, many of which were presaged in case materials we began to collect on this community in 1958. We also hope to demonstrate in the last section of the paper that ethnicity—*mejicanidad* or "Mexicanness"—once the major organizer and explainer of behavior in the community under consideration, now often is created, promoted, and shaped by other factors, thus becoming a phenomenon that must itself be explained.

Toledo, Lucas County, Ohio: The Host Community

Twenty years ago, Toledo was among the three finalists in a national competition for the title, "The Typical American Community," no doubt a valid selection. It is typically urban and industrial, as most of America has become, and describable only in superlatives: glass capital of the world; key to the sea; the largest oil-refining center between Chicago and the eastern seaboard; first in Ohio in economic diversification; largest producer of automobile parts, and so on (Toledo 1958). With little to differentiate it in form or culture from other cities between the Alleghenies and the Rockies, with nothing there to evoke exclamation, Toledo is precisely the kind of city of which Gertrude Stein remarked, "There is no there there" (quoted by Passonneau 1963:15).

We suggest that the very lack of "there," of any uniqueness as a city, and the absence of an Anglo-Saxon Protestant history rendered old Fort Industry—as Toledo once was known—a receptive host community to all immigrant groups. Toledo always needed people of diverse skills to man her factories and farms. And they came, hoping to improve their lot in life by their industry. The Irish came to build the Miami and Erie Canal as early as 1832, and formed the nucleus of the large Irish element now found in Toledo; they were followed by others escaping their home island's potato famine (Bartha 1945:1). Many Germans came for both economic and political reasons, fleeing the failed European revolutions of 1848. After 1880, East Europeans began to come, Polish and Hungarian immigrants being the most numerous. By 1890, more than 80 percent of Toledo's 81,434 souls were either foreign born, or of foreign parentage (Bartha 1945:2); their impress is very clear on the 1978 face of Toledo. National parishes stand out and businesses proudly announce un-Anglicized names. Important to our story, however, is that these immigrants were to become neighbors, coreligionists, coworkers, and mediators of their particular inter-pretations of American culture to the *toledanos*. Even more important, they were to marry many of the latter.

This is not to deny that Toledo's white Anglo-Saxon Protestants exercised constraints on later immigrants, as they have done elsewhere from the beginning of American colonization (Hannerz 1974). They apparently disdained all newcomers, regardless of race, religion, or national orgin. The position of nineteenth-century Toledo newspaper editorials may be taken to be representative of the host's attitude. The Germans' personality was considered to be "boisterous," their behavior outrageous and ill bred. However, later editorialists approved when "German men married local women and *learned the English language*" (our emphasis, Barclay 1973).

The Poles—like the Mexicans later—emigrated as peasants with few skills and enjoyed a less attractive image than the Germans. They were considered to be "criminal," "emotional," "hyperactive," and "cruel by disposition" (Barclay 1972). It is clear that the Germans already had aligned themselves with their more restrained Anglo-Saxon hosts, although they were not entirely acculturated. For example, having heard of a fight in a bar that resulted in two dead Poles, a no-longer-boisterous German American remarked, "Mein Gott, dey was woise dan Indians" (Barclay 1972). By the turn of the century, however, the negative Polish image also was beginning to weaken, and by 1920, the press portrayed the "alien" Pole as a "selfmade man who showed concern for his fellow Poles, and *learned English*" (our emphasis, Barclay 1972).

The Anglo-Saxon Protestant host community respected the right of immigrants to maintain their separate religions (Gordon 1978), but not to keep their ethnic identities. Clearly, human nature was not regarded as fixed; foreigners were acceptable as long as they were hard working, industrious, religious people who learned the English language and imitated their hosts.[3]

So it was that when Mexicans began to trickle[4] into this "All American City" in 1900, Toledo was Spanish in nothing more than name; but it also was not peopled by that Anglo-Saxon fundamentalistic Protestant bloc that had greeted them in Texas. Forty percent of Toledo's churchgoers were at least nominal Catholics, while in Lucas County slightly over 60 percent of the members of reporting churches were Catholic (National Council of the Churches of Christ 1957). The vast majority of them still were of foreign stock, and far removed from that controversial borderland between the United States and Mexico; neither hosts nor Mexicans had the bitter history of the Alamo and Texas Rangers to remember. The stereotype these hosts held of Mexicans—when they noticed them at all (Macklin 1976:1)—was patronizing but not particularly negative: they were depicted as "being a miniature of Mexico itself, in their broad-brimmed hats, quaint touches of color in garments and sauntering attitude" (*Blade* 1920).

Three points emerge from these early newspaper accounts, as well as from *toledano* life histories, that bear on our analysis of assimilationist and pluralist models for change among *toledanos*:

1. The host society, as elsewhere in the country (cf. Fitzpatrick 1971), was attempting actively to assimilate all its "foreign groups,"

by conducting "Americanization" programs. What is sometimes ignored in our current pluralistic condemnation of such programs is that at least implicitly, they invited membership in the majority group: one can learn to be a member; he is not judged to be inherently and forever an outsider. And the more open the membership of the majority group, the more likely ethnic minorities are to emulate their values (cf. Brockmann 1971; Ogbu 1974).

2. The Mexicans (like the Germans and Poles before them) were not sitting around passively being stripped of their cultural patterns. They concurred in the assimilationist model proffered, them, being eager to learn English and American customs, even though they reportedly "sauntered" to their evening classes held in a boxcar school (*Blade* 1920).

3. Mexicans, working in railroad terminals, oil companies, and nitrate plants (*Blade* 1920), had begun to occupy several niches in Toledo's opportunity structure, and were beginning to learn urban ways of life.

The cultural pattern for future Mexican-immigrant and Mexican-American behavior was being crystallized (Foster 1960). That is, traditional Mexican patterns were being modified by the contact between these earliest immigrants and their hosts and taking a form with which subsequent emigrants from Texas and Mexico would have to reckon; these emerging patterns were neither "American" nor "Mexican" but a creative adaptation to which both host and immigrant contributed.

Toledano Culture

In order to understand the dynamics of change among the *toledanos*, it is necessary to describe briefly the sources of their culture with particular emphasis on the beliefs and behaviors that potentially were open to modification in the new milieu. In the 1920s, Mexican immigration was stimulated greatly by the passage of the American quota laws that restricted the coming of the Europeans who had previously fed Toledo's labor demands. Mexicans settled first on what was called the old Middle Grounds, an island-like area formed by the Maumee River and one of its tributaries. Here ocean liners from Lake Erie and barges from the canal once met; here the coming of the railroads and the Union Station provided Mexicans with work and homes in "little houses and boxcars." After a half century, this area still is a focal point of their settlement.

Something of past experience—the quality of life in those early boxcar homes—can be inferred from early mission records kept by Reverend José Luá, who served *La Colonia Mexicana de Toledo*. Life was short, and not sweet. The Reverend Luá recorded twenty-seven deaths during the years 1927 through 1930. Of these, nine were children (four less than a year old). The causes of death are mentioned for twenty-three of the twenty-seven and tell a laconic but graphic story: nine died of pneumonia and eight of tuberculosis; "intestinal fever" carried away one baby; a hapless thirty-nine-year-old woman was killed by lightning, and another died of bullet wounds; an appendix operation killed a young man of twenty; yet another, thirty, was murdered. Another man is reported to have committed suicide while intoxicated. The average age of death for the eighteen adults was not quite twenty-nine (*Libro 1°* 1927-1930). Without attempting to extrapolate from these data to the entire group (we are not told how many people Reverend Luá served), the high infant mortality, the high incidence of pulmonary disease, and death by violence bespeak a life of stress, and poor nutrition and medical care—a past difficult to romanticize and not likely to produce a man like Mike or a pluralistic model for change.

All of the marriages performed by Reverend Luá (thirteen from 1927-1930) reflect the importance not only of religion but also of ethnicity and regionalism in the selection of a mate. People came from various communities in northern Indiana and southern Michigan, as well as northwest Ohio to be married by him. All had been born in Mexico, and in nine of the thirteen marriages, both bride and groom had been born in the same village.

Reverend Luá was able to organize the *colonia* officially into a Spanish-language mission without fixed territorial boundaries in 1929. Then, as now, the mission served those Mexicans who had "settled out" of the urban area, and also brought them into the same space to worship with the seasonal migrant agricultural workers and other newly arrived immigrants. Such interaction encouraged renewal and reinforcement of traditional rural Mexican cultural patterns (Macklin 1976:203-204).

Through the first half of the 1940s, "nationals" (i.e., persons born in Mexico; in this case, males) from every part of Mexico were admitted into the United States to assist in the war effort. Eight hundred men were brought into Toledo to maintain the New York Central Railroad alone. They, like their earlier compatriots, regarded the United States as the land of opportunity. Commented one, as he was about to be returned to Mexico in 1945, "There is nothing there [i.e., in Mexico] of the opportunities for study and all sorts of work, that you have here. Here everything is available that you're *willing to work hard for*" (our emphasis, *Blade* 1945).

After World War II, Mexican and Texas-born agricultural workers[5] began to settle out of the migrant stream and it is their model for change that is most evident among *toledanos* of 1978. They, too, thought that hard work would pay off, and were eager for both economic improvement and a good education for their children. While their own migrating lives had made it difficult for most of them to attain much formal schooling (Macklin 1976:227), many were and are enthusiastic about learning. One woman recalls that a sometime school teacher traveled with her father's migrant crew. After the day's back-breaking stoop labor was over, the teacher organized classes and taught his fellow workers to read and write. Our informant reports that he had no problems with truancy. However, the scar of migrant life on most *toledanos* of this era is apparent.[6]

When we began to collect data twenty years ago on this predominantly second-generation, young population, they demonstrated little sense of history. Most of the *tejanos* (Texans) now in Toledo came from three areas of Texas: the valley of the lower Rio Grande, the Piedras Negras–Eagle Pass–Crystal City area, and the barrios of San Antonio. Although most could name the Mexican states from which their parents had come, they themselves had never been in Mexico. No particular regional culture of Mexico predominates in Texas or Toledo because their first-generation parents were bearers of rural Mexican cultures, having come from various Mexican states, and having survived severely disrupted lives (cf. West and Vásquez Chapter 1).

So the culture being lived and transmitted in 1958 had various origins,[7] but its bearers had been subjected to some homogenizing historical experiences. True, they had grown up on farms, in small towns, and urban barrios, but they nonetheless shared the common experience of migrating as children with their families throughout Texas to work in the cotton fields. Later, mechanization of cotton harvesting forced them into the midwestern migrant labor streams.

Migrant camps were both insulating and isolating (cf. Williams Chapter 4; West Chapter 3). One could be in the society of the United States without being of it. Several months following the crops—sugar beets, cherries, tomatoes, and cucumbers—through Kansas, Illinois, Indiana, Michigan, and Ohio, threw families from the diverse Texas communities and regions together. Cultural differences among them were minimized as they all adjusted to the common conditions imposed by migration. Although the richness of a whole society and culture could not be recreated at each stop, some traditional patterns seem to have been intensified, such as family and kin ties. Folk Catholic and folk healing beliefs, rituals, and practices were and are useful in the adaptation to an uncertain and hazardous environment (cf. Macklin Chapter 9; Williams Chapter 4).

Many *toledanos* tend to regard their migrating days fondly like Stanley West's early *beleñeos* (citizens of Mexican descent living in Bethlehem, Pennsylvania) view their past (see Chapter 3). But it was an experience, nostalgia notwithstanding, that they wanted to leave, and one that they do not wish for their children. Errant school children frequently are disciplined by a parent who threatens, "I'll send you out *a piscar pepinos* ('to pick pickles'; considered to be especially arduous work) if you don't study harder." For all of them, the compelling reason to migrate was economic.

Often decisions to settle out of the migrant stream and stay in Toledo were completely situational, but such decisions also reveal much about that life, the migrants' openness to change, and the host community. Recounts a thirty-five-year-old male who has been making Toledo his home for the past fifteen years:

> One day—I must have been about twenty—I was blocking sugar beets with my family, and I kept getting behind the rest. I just couldn't keep up, and it was so hot. My sister was going down her row faster than I was: I couldn't even keep up with my *sister*! I just put down that hoe, and said to my daddy that I was quitting; I remember it was about the middle of the morning. I just hitched a ride into town, ran into a guy I knew from home who told me that they were hiring at the D_____ plant. I said, "Are they hiring Mexicans?" He said that they didn't care. I went to work that day and I have been there ever since. (Macklin 1976:36.)

This case illustrates several of the points underlying *toledano* migration and "settling out." Most came in family units, and this was the unit that was cooperating to improve its economic status. Toward that end, all were willing to work hard even at unskilled, stoop labor. But the work was difficult, unsupportably so in this case, and if that is what being Mexican meant, our hero did not want it. Generalizing from his Texas experiences, he anticipated rejection by the host community, but that did not happen. He was sufficiently miserable and also had sufficient confidence in himself to leave the security of the known, if circumscribed, world managed by his family and protected by the Virgin of Guadalupe. The venture worked: it was the making of an American pragmatist.

Although the "Spanish-American" median family income in 1970 still was somewhat lower than for all families in the Toledo ($8,598 vs. $10,474) and the Toledo Standard Metropolitan Statistical Area ($8,894 vs. $10,932), it was about $1,000 higher than for "Negro" families, a population that is considerably older and lacks the language barrier confronting Spanish Americans. Significantly (Community Planning Council 1973:24-25), "Spanish-American" families have a wide range of yearly incomes, which permits those still living in poverty to look at their more affluent compatriots and optimistically believe that they, too, can realize the American Dream.

Many explicitly measure progress by home ownership, having a good job, and the opportunity to give one's children at least a high school education. From the 1920s on, immigrants of Mexican descent perceived social and economic benefits as accruing from formal education and their aspiration for that education has increased steadily; e.g., in 1958, few women (*toledanas*) worked outside of the home. In 1970, they still had the lowest percent participation in the labor force (Negro women have the highest), but are only slightly below all women in the city of Toledo.[8] Although we do not have a large representative sample for 1978, most *toledanas* with whom we talked are working for those same economic reasons that brought them into the area, not for "self-fulfillment." Several are working specifically to be able to provide a good education for their children in order that "they won't have to suffer what I did."

Most, then and now, were Roman Catholics, at least nominally. In 1958, there were a few Jehovah's Witnesses, and Spanish-speaking Pentecostal congregations came and went, usually comprised of a few interrelated families. These Protestant congregations did not extend the social networks of *toledanos* into the Anglo Protestant community in Toledo. Therefore, such conversions do not indicate social change; they served only to sever ties—social, temporal, and spatial—with other *toledanos*.

In 1958, traditional Mexican beliefs centering around health and illness were widespread. The population was threatened with soul loss from fright (*susto*), the evil eye (*mal de ojo*), vaguely malignant spirits of the air (*los aires*), and personal problems that no Anglo physician could be expected to understand or treat. A curer (*curandera*) whose possessing spirit is the famous Mexican miracle worker, thaumaturge El Niño Fidencio, has been living and practicing in northern Indiana since the 1940s, and serves a large clientele of both *toledanos* and migrants. As we have dealt with her role in detail elsewhere (Chapter 9; Macklin 1967, 1974), we shall simply say here that such is her reputation that many *toledanos* bring relatives from Texas and Mexico to consult her—and, of course, the patients stay on with their Toledo kinfolk during treatment, intensifying traditional family ties and cultural patterns. Therefore, she tends to be a conservative influence, both directly and indirectly. In 1978, her clientele still is enormous, but she says that increasingly, most who come are seasonal migrant workers from Texas, Mexico, and Florida, not *toledanos*.

Toledanos, then and now, hold family and kin obligations to be very important. Most had come into Toledo at the behest of a relative, who also assisted in the search for jobs and housing, smoothing the processes of adjustment; but in 1958, most—even the poorest—found the wherewithal to visit their hometowns and relatives in Texas at least once a year. There were many motivations for more protracted sojourns in Texas: marriage, illness, childbirth, and other life crises were times when they, like Oscar Lewis's (1951) Tepoztecans, wanted to go home.

Several factors have been presented that facilitated change in the social and cultural patterns brought to the Midwest by *toledanos*:

1. The principal reason for coming—economic improvement—is change-seeking behavior.
2. The life of seasonal migrants was uncomfortable, unpredictable, and unsafe.
3. Although shared migrant life experiences tended to reduce regional cultural differences (Mexican or Texan) and pre-

served common denominators (e.g., Catholicism; close family ties; consulting *curanderas*), heterogeneity was still to be found among families and their members. The familial, religious, and economic microcultures were such that some individuals could decide to opt out, and they found themselves in a sufficiently hospitable social environment to make the decision "work."

4. When ethnic migrants are in fact better off financially in their new setting than they were before migration—as are the *toledanos*—they are happier and adjust more rapidly (cf. Price 1971). Carlson (1975) has shown that in 1970 the Spanish-speaking population in ten northwestern Ohio counties enjoyed a median family income of $8,663 as compared with $3,793 for three south Texas counties of the lower Rio Grande valley from which they typically come.

Host and *Toledano* Interactions: The Church and Its Changing Models for Change

As had been true of so many other American ethnic groups, religion was the single most important institution around which *toledano* identity was organized. As we mentioned above, religious differences always have been more acceptable in American society than other kinds of ethnic diversity. Our data corroborate those of Peñalosa and McDonagh (1966), which show that among Mexican Americans, Catholicism rather than Protestantism is found to be most associated with upward mobility. A recent study of *toledano* leadership done by a Toledo-born Mexican American shows that "being affiliated with the Catholic Church" ranks fourth among twenty attributes considered necessary to become an "outstanding" leader in the community (Soto 1974:157).

The Mexican immigrant's Catholicism differed from that of his German, Polish, and Hungarian neighbors (cf. Abramson 1973). His was largely an untutored, family-centered folk Catholicism that venerated the Virgin of Guadalupe, the Dark Virgin, who has been a symbol of Mexican peoplehood since shortly after the Conquest. To Mexicans, Her power is not mediated through Jesus; She is seen as compassionate and caring, an effective actor in Her own right (Northrop 1966; Wolf 1958; Wolf and Hansen 1972).

From the outset, Guadalupe's Spanish-language mission supported and reinforced the ethnic identity of its members. Its masses occasioned repeated interaction of members, strengthening social solidarity and consciousness of kind. Located in the physical center of the community near the earliest settlement of Mexicans, the church building itself encouraged further social and residential concentration. But the relationship between religion and ethnicity is complex and an examination of the church, its officials, and their models for change provides an especially illuminating case of the interaction between the host community and *toledano* culture.

Three models for change can be discerned to have been operating through the church in the past fifty years: the first (1931-1951) urged assimilation with tolerance for selected aspects of Mexican traditions; the second (1952–mid-1960s) was impatiently assimilationist; and the current model is strongly pluralistic. The importance of these models and the priests in charge of them cannot be minimized.

The church began to take notice of her new, growing group of Spanish-speaking communicants about 1930 and the Reverend Luá mentioned above was replaced by an energetic, Ohio-born priest of German descent, Monsignor G. He was fluent in Spanish, having received both master of arts and doctor of literature degrees at the Universidad Javeriana in Bogotá, Colombia. Reverend Luá is not remembered in the *toledano* oral tradition; parishioners credit Monsignor G. with having organized the mission and consider him to be instrumental in the growth of the church-centered community. His model had considerable impact on the direction of social and cultural change, since his firm hand was at the helm of Our Lady of Guadalupe Mission for the crucial "crystallizing," formative years between 1931 and 1951. He sees himself as having "saved" *La Colonia Mexicana* from Protestantism, a judgment corroborated repeatedly by the *toledanos* themselves. Says one longtime *toledana*: "Just before he came, there had been a thriving Mexican Baptist Church with more than a hundred members. Then they just all went back to being Catholics" (Macklin 1976:227). Monsignor G. began to regularize and Romanize the Catholicism of the folk. Baptismal, confirmation, marriage, and death records appear in Latin for the first time. Selectively sympathetic to Latin-American customs, Monsignor G. strengthened the traditional relationship between the church and the parishioner, i.e., that of patron-client. Of his regime, a recent publication reports that:

> He acted as their counselor, helped finance homes, and distributed
> food to the needy. The Guadalupe Center became a place where the
> Mexican community could congregate in masses, fiestas and dramas.
> The dramas became a special event for the community. They were
> written and directed by Monsg. G. (*Creemos* 1975:5.)

Monsignor G. was reassigned to a nearby parish in 1951, but by then
he had helped perpetuate only those traditional Mexican patterns
that he recognized and considered to be appropriate to Toledo.

Occasionally the conflicting views of Catholicism held by Guadalupe's children and by their German-American priest comes through
in the parish records (cf. Betten and Mohl 1973:375-376). Monsignor
G. noted tersely that he could not concede burial in consecrated
ground to one of the "defunct," since he had "died without sacraments, and never, during his life, did he frequent the Church."
However, to one whose "cadaver" had been found in the river, he
did accord an ecclesiastical burial, because that "deceased one was
unbalanced." A stern lesson also was meted out to the parents of a
three-month-old baby boy who had to be interred in unconsecrated
ground because he "died without baptism through [their] negli-
gence" (*Libro 1°* 1945-1951). Father G. presented the *toledanos*
with a dour gringo world where the holy sacraments and church
attendance, even for men, took on a new and awesome importance.
However, the active secular and religious fiesta cycle, the dramas,
and other community activities of which Father G. did approve
tended to ameliorate stress. His fiestas are warmly recalled when
reminiscing turns to the "good old days."

During this period, there also was considerable improvement in
the life chances of Guadalupe's parishioners, although infant mortality remained high (*Libro 1°* 1945-1951). We can infer, also, that
toledanos were using the city's health care institutions since most,
including infants, were dying in hospitals from the early 1950s on.
The adjustments made during these years, when the community was
growing slowly but steadily, informed the direction of changes to
come.

Father S., the priest who replaced Monsignor G. in late 1951,
was strongly assimilationist, and saw himself as culturally distinct
from his parishioners. A converted Presbyterian, he was quite aware
of the differences between himself and them, and discussed these
differences candidly. He consciously set about to change his congregation's behavior. He referred to himself as "very tidy," and felt

that the cleanliness of the "Mexican people" left much to be desired. He was appalled at their tendency to buy things on time, stating unequivocally that *he* would never buy anything unless he had saved the cash to pay for it; he remarked that one of their major problems was that they "do not plan at all." He delicately discussed his predecessor's predeliction for fiestas as a part of church celebrations, and added, "I am doing all that I can to get this element out . . . what goes on there is sin!" (Macklin 1976:205-206).

Before Father S. came, the church had been the center of much secular community activity, but he eliminated that also. The church building was locked except when it was being used officially. He cut the fiesta cycle to two religious celebrations per year—December 12, the day of Our Lady of Guadalupe, and July 26, the day of St. James, *his own* saint's day—because "I just can't take the wildness." He added that he had "two armed policemen at every function, which has reduced the knife pulling." He also was very unhappy with what he saw as an excessive Mexican fondness for drink, and considered that to be the most serious problem in the group. Paradoxically, his stereotyped Anglo attitudes and his eagerness to Americanize his congregation according to his own lights functioned in reverse. In the early 1960s, Anglo organizations began making cooperative, if tentative overtures to the *toledano* community. Their representatives went to its only visible spokesman, the priest. He reportedly told them that "there is no one in the Mexican parish who is capable of representing the group." Thus his ready underestimation of his parishioners prevented one importantt route to structural assimilation, i.e., the interaction of *toledanos* in the voluntary organizations with members of the host community. As we suggested in our earlier study, his judgment of them as backward and inept helped to make them so (Macklin 1976:208).

Although Father S. was able to modify behavior (e.g., in suppressing the old fiesta cycle), the attitudes of the first-generation *toledanos* remained much as they had developed during the first twenty years. Nonetheless—and important to our argument—this model made it difficult for children growing up during his reign to learn appropriate sentiments when symbols of Mexican identity were presented to them.

In the middle 1960s, a major highway came through the largest, densest concentration of *toledanos* centered around the church. Our

Lady of Guadalupe was closed, and the Spanish-language mission was merged with the German national parish of Saints Peter and Paul, only a block and a half away. Black, Red, and Brown power movements were beginning, ethnicity was being rediscovered and recreated, and for the first time the church saw fit to appoint Mexican priests in Toledo. A Michoacan-born priest ministered to the combined congregations, first as an assistant and then as pastor. Soon he was joined by a colleague from Zacatecas who currently is assistant pastor with Father B., a Toledo-born, bilingual Latino-phile pastor of Polish extraction. Of the approximately 600 families in Saints Peter and Paul, 80 percent are now Mexican and, as always, come from other areas in the diocese as well as throughout the city of Toledo. In 1977, the Toledo Catholic diocese (comprising nine-teen counties in northwestern Ohio) estimated that there were 30,000 residents of Hispanic origin in the area and that another 25,000 came as migrant workers each year—a sizable but dispersed, loosely integrated "community." A church spokesman recently commented publicly that "I will be the first to admit that the Catholic Church in the United States has been negligent toward these and the rest of the Spanish speaking," and concluded his interview with the following explicitly—if somewhat limited—pluralistic statement:

> We have to allow for more *diversity* in our parishes, have *interna-tional dinners,* and encourage our neighbors to see the beauty and contribution of all nationalities. About 8 per cent of the Catholic population in the Toledo diocese is Spanish speaking, and unless we are really sensitive to this, we will be hurting a lot of people's faith. (Our emphasis, *Blade* 1977:6.)

Father B., the current priest, is attempting to put more emphasis on Mexican-American culture. He wants to preserve what he con-siders to be the "best" of the Mexican traditional patterns, their "expressiveness, their love of song and celebration, and their emphasis on the importance of the person." He adds that the family seems still to be quite cohesive, and he hopes to preserve that. "The *abuelitos* [affectionate diminutive of 'grandparents'] often are still cared for in the home."

But many *toledanos* have reached a point of no return. They have little in common with their Mexican priests; and they say that they do not know many of the other congregants attending the Spanish Masses, who are "probably migrants" with whom they feel they have little in common as well. Some *toledanos* report that the Mexican priests regard "us as *norteños* or *tejanos* [from northern Mexico or from Texas] who always were very cold in the faith." One *toledano* from Texas shrugged, "They feel that we never did have much knowledge of the Mass and the sacraments, that we were never as devoted as the people from Michoacan or Jalisco or Guanajuato. And, I guess they're right." (Actually, many of the early settlers in both Texas and Ohio came from precisely those Mexican states.) Therefore, the Mexican priests appear to be reinforcing Mexican cultural patterns for only a small minority of the Toledo area's Spanish-speaking population: migrants or those recently arrived from Mexico or Texas. For example, when Father B. suggested that the church's painting of Guadalupe be carried from home to home during Lent in order to spark religious fervor and participation, his *toledano* parishioners gently discouraged him from executing the idea. He remarked, with rueful amusement, that "They didn't think that Guadalupe meant so much to the Mexican people anymore." He thinks that a partial explanation for this may be found in the recent popularity of the *cursillo* (retreat) and charismatic movements within the church itself, both of which are much more Christ-centered than traditional Latin-American religion. But why has an optimistic, powerful, wise, Americanized Jesus become acceptable to a group brought up to venerate a supplicating Guadalupe and a problematic, suffering, and helpless Christ?

We suggest that *toledano* success in the Anglo world (in which Guadalupe has no part)—identification of themselves as Americans, and the ability to enter into non-Mexican marriages as well as non-Mexican friendships and work relationships—has opened that personal, trusted, intimate world of family and kin over which She had presided. As we shall show below, many *toledanos* do feel competent in the public sphere, and do feel themselves to be masters of their own fates. Relations between them and their society have changed; accordingly, so has the arrangement of ideas about the supernatural and their relations to it (Wolf and Hansen 1972:165). The model of a culturally plural society has come too late to be meaningful for many of Guadalupe's children who find themselves unable or unwilling to go "home" again (cf. Benavides Chapter 12).

In summary, although the church's first model—change with tolerance—did tend to perpetuate certain selected aspects of the traditional culture, these did not interfere with *toledano* interaction with neighbors or with their participation in the economic and educational institutions. Nor did any of these behaviors threaten their hosts; rather, they conformed to the notions of the quaintness and charm Anglos thought Mexicans *should* have. The second model, consciously assimilationist, was consistent with that held by many of the *toledanos* themselves; it also served to reduce the frequency of public Mexican behavior (such as religious and secular fiestas, with their rich symbolism), thereby separating the young Ohio-born generation from the evocative power of those symbols. Finally, the explicitly pluralistic model that now is espoused officially by the host community (through federal, state, and local government programs and funding), as well as the church, has come too late for many. A reinterpreted, revitalized Mexicanness has become only one of the several principles of *toledano* identification and social organization.

Host and *Toledano* Interactions:
Settlement Patterns and Intermarriage

From the 1920s on, *toledanos* spilled out from the railroad yards onto both sides of the Maumee River, concentrating in three major older city areas, which they label (not surprisingly) the South Side, the East Side, and the North Side. They have not been very mobile geographically, and while their numbers have increased steadily along certain streets fanning out from those original little houses and boxcars near the tracks, their invasion of German, Irish, Polish, and Hungarian areas has been gradual[9] and their residences dispersed. Even on the South Side (the most concentrated area), they never constituted more than 15 percent of any one census tract and still live among a fine sprinkling of Mahoneys, O'Sheas, Waldcutters, Schwarzkopfs, Stritzels, Blums, and Kachenmeisters. And on the East Side, they coexist with the families Stefanski, Syzmanski, and Szczubiewski as well as Fitzpatrick, McDougall, Mullins, Kleeburger, Schwartz, and Watson.

In 1958, *toledanos* said that while there was some discrimination against them, for the most part they let their neighbors alone and "they let us alone." But they were not letting each other alone quite as much as the *toledanos* claimed. As we have seen, religion, ethnicity, and village of origin at one time appeared to be the determining factors in the selection of a marriage partner. The influence of religion and ethnicity seems to have persisted through 1945, when all of the marriages on which we have data (N = 9, 100 percent of the marriage licenses issued by Lucas County to Spanish-surnamed individuals during six months of 1945) were contracted between Spanish-surnamed spouses. Ten years later, however, the rate of exogamy was astonishingly high. Ten of seventeen marriages were exogamous, which means that ten of twenty-four Mexican-descent individuals (40 percent) decided to marry out of their own ethnic group.

By 1965, our sample reveals[10] that fifteen of nineteen marriages were exogamous, with fifteen of twenty-three Mexican-descent individuals (70 percent) marrying out. Samples from 1974 through 1977 provide more cases, but serve only to emphasize what was suggested by the small number of cases in the earlier years. Here we are dealing with 111 marriages, 65 (60 percent) of which are exogamous; of the 153 individuals of Mexican descent involved, 40 percent married outside their ethnic group. Although our data are neither as adequate nor our hypothesizing as elegant as that of Mittelbach and Moore (1968), it is clear that something highly significant and different from other Mexican-American communities has been going on in Toledo from the 1950s forward. Perhaps more surprising, and indicative of the nature of that milieu is that it is the men who are marrying out at the greater rate, rather than the women as Mittelbach and Moore (1968:53) suggest to be typical for a "subpopulation occupying a low status." Of the 119 Mexican-American males involved in the 147 marriages from 1955 through 1977, 64 (50 percent) married exogamously; of the 81 women, only 26 (about 30 percent) did so.

As always, members of an out-group may hold negative images of a social category, e.g., "Mexican," while at the same time being able to regard those individuals they know as "exceptions." To a woman, the Anglo wives of *toledanos* interviewed in our earlier study insisted that their husbands were hard-working, clean, gentle, and so on, and "just weren't like those other Mexicans."

In one particular, our data confirm earlier studies done elsewhere on Mexican-American intermarriage patterns. Exogamy of both males and females is proportional to the distance of their birth from Mexico.

1. Two thirds of Ohio-born males of Mexican descent marry

out of the ethnic group, while just under 40 percent of the
Ohio-born females marry out.

2. Slightly more than half of the Texas-born males marry out,
   while only 20 percent of the females do.

3. Finally, nearly all Mexican-born males marry in; our sample
   of Mexican-born females includes only one case: she married
   out at age thirty-three, considerably older than the average
   first marriage.

Our data (1955 through 1977) are summarized in Table 5.1.

What are some of the behavioral consequences of such exogamy?
We want to mention only two, both having siginificance for an individual's ethnic identity. First, when the Spanish-surnamed male
marries out, the children do not learn Spanish at all: for good
reason we refer to one's "mother tongue." Even if a Spanish-
speaking husband draws his wife into Spanish-speaking family,
kin, and associated networks, she usually comes to understand and
speak only occasional words of Spanish, but does not master
Spanish as a system that she could transmit to her children. Women
who marry out tend to leave the community, and their children do
not learn Spanish either. Second, the forenames given to children
change: the Deborah Anns, Shirleys, Stanleys, and Wades show up
at once. If, as we argued earlier (Macklin 1976:101), a *toledano(a)*
receives both ethnic and religious identities with his or her given
names, then this source of self-orientation is lost immediately
through intermarriage. Our analysis of all baptismal records from
Our Lady of Guadalupe from 1937 through 1951 (N = 202) shows
that non-Spanish forenames appeared only when there was one non-
Spanish-surnamed parent. However, by the early 1950s, Spanish-
surnamed parents were beginning to Anglicize the Spanish forenames they gave their children (e.g., 10 percent of 115 names in 1952
were Anglicized; by 1962, 20 percent of 139 were Anglicized). By
1965, however, about 30 percent of 62 forenames were non-Spanish
even in families where both parents were Spanish-surnamed (Combined Register 1958-1970). Therefore, it appears that the naming
pattern that tied a child to his religious and ethnic identity is now
on the wane, whether or not intermarriage is present.

Those *toledanos* identified with the Chicano movement, who are
stressing a return to what they regard as traditional Mexican
patterns, see intermarriage as the powerful force for social and

Table 5.1

Mexican-American Marriage Patterns

Nativity	In-Group Marriage	Out-Group Marriage	Total (N)	Per Cent of In-Group Marriage	Per Cent of Out-Group Marriage
Ohio-born					
Males	19	38	57	33	66
Females	35	20	55	64	36
Texas-born					
Males	19	23	42	45	55
Females	20	5	25	80	20
Mexico-born					
Males	17	3	20	85	15
Females	--	1	1	--	100

cultural change that it is. A group of them approached a prominent Texas-born spokesman for the community who is well known for his pride in his Mexican heritage, and asked him to make a public statement condemning intermarriage. They wanted him to assert that it was done only to reject *la raza*, as a way out of one's ethnic group. He refused, he told us, because he does not believe that that is the reason for intermarriage. He also added that six of his sister's children had married Anglos, and that they had married for "love," not for "political" or "social" reasons.

The data we now have seem to suggest several hypotheses, all of which need more exploration.

1. Once people of Mexican descent move into a host community open in the ways we have described Toledo and settle in dispersed patterns (cf. Felter 1941; Lieberson 1961), their rate of exogamy is higher than that of Central and Eastern European white ethnic groups (Mittelbach and Moore 1968).

2. Mexican Americans were not, and are not, relegated to a caste-like position. If males of Mexican descent have as much opportunity to marry women in groups other than their own, then self-identification as Mexican evidently will not deter them from doing so. Insofar as we can infer from surnames, approximately half of the exogamous marriages have been contracted with other ethnic groups, or with whites from Appalachia who are moving into older city areas and becoming *toledano* neighbors. Proximity appears to

be more powerful than ethnicity in mate selection.

3. Traditional patterns for rearing of girls appear to have persisted longer than those for boys, patterns that make it more difficult for girls to participate in American dating patterns (Macklin 1976: 153). Consequently, they may be less available as marriage partners to Anglos, and we hypothesize that the feminine role will be slower to change in other areas also.

4. We suggest that many Mexican Americans are not highly visible physically. Both our intermarriage and qualitative data indicate that once individuals of Mexican descent begin to associate with non-Mexicans, ethnic behaviors—e.g., speaking Spanish, speaking English with an accent, gestures, etc.—diminish. They no longer "look" so Mexican to their Anglo friends. Therefore, at least part of the so-called Mexican visibility is *behaving* in accordance with what others define as Mexican, i.e., a sociocultural category, rather than physical type. Several young single *toledanos* (in their twenties) who have no Mexican friends and participate in few Mexican recreational activities report that their Anglo friends and acquaintances frequently take them to be ethnic something or other—Armenian, Greek, Italian, Lebanese—but not necessarily Mexican.

Viva Mexico! Cultural Persistence, Human Ingenuity, and Emergent Ethnic Behavior

As we have shown, there has been considerable change among *toledanos* in patterns of social interaction (i.e., structural change) as well as in patterns of ideas, beliefs, and behavior (cultural change). In spite of such changes, the community is more visible physically, and the ritual life is richer and more public than it was in 1958. Cultural continuity is to be found among those hearths, altars, and marketplaces, a phenomenon that must be explained.

The visibility is in part demographic: there are now about four times as many *toledanos* as there were twenty years ago, 40 percent of whom were born in Texas or Mexico. The *Testigos de Jehová* ("Jehovah's Witnesses") now have their own building, *Salón del Reino* ("Kingdom Hall") on the South Side, and *Iglesia Sión* ("Church of Zion") with its Mexican-born minister, occupies the same storefront that ephemeral Pentecostal congregations used in the past. And the civil rights movements of the 1960s—including Brown Power—have had an impact. It is not only appropriate to acknowledge one's Mexican heritage, it is incumbent on the successful members of the community to express publicly their ties with the community, the church, Mexico, and *la raza*. Now there are more formal organizations and, although we cannot discuss them here, it is of more than passing interest that insider John Soto's 1974 study of Mexican-American leadership in Toledo corroborated our data of 1958. For example, in 1974 there are still few individuals of the total community involved in formal organizations (304 persons in seventeen organizations, three of which existed on paper only); there is reportedly still much divisiveness and suspicion within and between organizations; jealousy and refusal to accept others as leaders are mentioned as problems both by members of the organizations, and the individuals they view as "leaders." Soto (1974) also shows that, with one exception, all of those designated as being among the top ten leaders were born and grew up outside of Toledo.

Other symbols of *mejicanidad* are more apparent than in 1958. Even though Guadalupe's congregation had to merge with the German national parish, the Dark Virgin is more visible than She was. In early 1978, Her painting was installed front and center above the tabernacle in Saints Peter and Paul where the parishioners— now 80 percent Mexican—voted to place it. Her old temple now houses both the Guadalupe Health Clinic and the Guadalupe Community Center; a mural on its outside wall comprises Her image, hovering protectively behind a noble Indian face. Youth and senior citizen's programs share a building called "Maya." It is important to note that these latter manifestations of *mejicanidad*, along with job training and bilingual language programs, will last only so long as the *toledano* community can show sufficient ethnic solidarity to attract local, state, and federal funding.

However, the most interesting data on persistent ethnicity illustrate how *toledanos* are adapting traditional beliefs and behaviors to meet the constantly changing demands of their lives. These emerging cultural and social patterns can be seen in the manipulation of the godparent system *(padrinazgo)* that has been occurring in Toledo during the past decade. Always a flexible institution (Wolf and Hansen 1972), the Latin-American practice of asking certain individuals to act as godparents *(padrinos* or "sponsors") for the life-cycle rituals is still important in Toledo for baptism, confirmation, and marriage, the first of these establishing the most important set of relationships. The *padrinos* of a child's baptism become coparents *(compadres)* with their godchild's parents, and the terms "cofather" or "comother" *(compadre* or *comadre)* are used reciprocally between the coparents. In this system *(compadrazgo),* the coparents' relationship is more important than that between the godparent and godchild. In 1958 in Toledo, couples selected relatives as *compadres,* which intensified already existing social and kin ties, rather than extending their social network. *Toledanos* usually stated that they would ask a relative for financial and other assistance before they would turn to *compadres,* unless the latter were also "real blood" (consanguineal) relatives. This suggests a situation in which the upward mobility of small family groups was both possible and more important than the upward mobility of the entire local Mexican-American group. For the past ten years, however, the use of the godparent system has been expanded and reinterpreted in two other ritual situations: the *quinceañera* (a coming-of-age ritual and fiesta for fifteen-year-old girls) and weddings.

Twenty years ago, the *quinceañera* was not reported in Toledo although most knew about it vaguely. Nor was the practice customary in the early 1970s, when this ritual for the daughter of a well-to-do family was given television and Sunday-supplement newspaper coverage. "Historically, wealthy families" *(Blade* 1972) in Mexico reportedly practiced such a custom. The family in question actually had gone to Mexico to "research" the ritual in order to do it "correctly." The girl was attended by fourteen couples her own age, the girls wearing identical gowns for which their families had paid. The *quinceañera* (the girl herself) had her own escort, was crowned during the ceremony, and given a birthstone ring by two sets of *padrinos* (or "sponsors" as they more frequently are called nowadays). This particular event cost about two thousand dollars according to the girl's parents, who provided a sit-down dinner for 350 people, dancing to two orchestras, and the "biggest yellow and white birthday cake many had ever seen." This, said her parents, did not prove to be a "burden" to them *(Blade* 1972). They wanted to give their daughter the "best."

Increasingly, however, families who cannot afford a revived ethnic practice so extravagantly executed invite more and more couples of adults to act as *padrinos,* who then cooperate to pay for the dining and dancing hall. There are *padrinos* of the invitations, of the cake, of the orchestra(s), of the crown, and of the ring. Locally, there is much criticism of this extension of the *padrinazgo* system. A Mexican priest protested that "some feel obligated to go to great length and expense—even to the point of going into debt. To give

A girl's important fifteenth birthday can be celebrated in a migrant camp, with all of her kin and friends contributing to the ritual and fiesta, or it can cost her parents $2,000, and include the "biggest yellow and white cake you ever saw." *Herral Long.*

thanks to God, it is not necessary to spend so much money" (*Blade* 1972). Here we have an example of a group wanting to return to Mexican past, yes, but to what they believe to be an elite past, and one that must be researched self-consciously in the country of origin. While the cultural content of the *quinceañera*, as well as the form, appears to qualify as ethnic persistence, the ritual functions much like the Anglo debut: conspicuous consumption announces a family's realization of the American Dream while reaffirming their ties to *la raza* and *La Virgen de Guadalupe*.

Padrinos now serve in much the same way at weddings. Traditionally, there was a set of first *padrinos* to attend the bridal couple as well as three additional couples who provided the token gifts for the marriage ceremony: *arras* (the pieces of silver—dimes in Toledo); the *cojín* ("pillow") on which the rings were carried; and the *lazo* (the knotted cord that symbolically ties the couple). But an analysis of twenty weddings witnessed by informants during 1977 reveals that not one had fewer than ten couples acting as *padrinos;* fifteen to twenty couples was the average, and one actually had forty couples marching in to attend the happy bride and groom. ("Imagine—eighty people!" wailed the Mexican-American photographer charged with the duty of getting them all into one picture.) Many *toledanos* themselves criticise the practice, saying that couples and their parents are simply being absolved of financial responsibility for the wedding. However, some of that hostile concern may be related to the fact that a high status symbol available to everyone (a lavish *quinceañera* or wedding) is no longer a high status symbol at all.

Extension of the *padrinazgo* system to involve many more people from the community in the *quinceañera* and wedding rituals appears to be an adaptation to the local situation: incomes for most are still comparatively low, and inflation is rampant. Reciprocal social ties are established in this manner, even though they are more extensive than intensive. But with such a redefinition of the system, it becomes possible for a large segment of the entire community occasionally to feast and dance together, the expenses being shared—thus effecting wide, if superficial, integration among *toledanos* of every stripe.

Summary and Conclusions

The people of Mexican descent who settled in Toledo, Ohio, and gave shape to today's community, came predominantly from or were channeled through Texas, were mostly from rural or small-town backgrounds, and experienced the homogenizing effect of life in the migrant stream. Once in Toledo as permanent residents, they began to change rapidly both culturally and structurally, dropping some traditional behaviors, modifying and adapting others, while interacting with their hosts and acquiring some new patterns from the latter. The changes seem to have been possible for several reasons. Anglo culture is no more homogeneous and monolithic than is that of Mexican Americans; Toledo was open to the latter in ways that many of the Anglo communities in the Southwest were not, and the host's stereotype of Mexican Americans was rather benign. While there was some residential concentration of Mexicans and Mexican Americans, the group grew slowly and they were never segregated. Finally, the model for change held by the earliest Mexican immigrants was assimilationist. They and their later compatriots had emigrated to change both their economic status and a generally unsatisfactory way of life. They learned English, worked hard, intermarried, and aspired to educational and material success for their children, all of which they could achieve without having to abandon Catholicism, the core of their group identity. The small but steady, continued immigration of both Texas-born and Mexican-born populations (about 30 percent and 7.4 percent respectively in 1970 [Community Planning Council 1973]) does not seem to impede the changes occurring among the Ohio born. On the other hand, after the mid1960s, the pluralist model of change embraced by some urges a return to a Mexican past but offers little agreement on what is "truly" Mexican, substituting "an ideology of relations" for actual, traditional social relations (Stein and Hill 1977:9). Most of these attempts to revitalize *mejicanidad* have come to the *toledano* community from the outside, specifically from the Southwest.

It would appear, then, that we have been looking at a group of people who are perfectly capable of interpreting their own pasts and charting courses toward their own futures, a group comprised of individuals who will arrive at solutions in varied ways, but who need neither academics nor other compatriots, politicized in other times and other places to tell them how to do it. Perhaps better than some anthropologists, they realize that being human and cultured means that you can decide what is real, and you can readily elect to change old definitions of reality if you want to.

Notes

1. We shall use *"toledanos"* to refer to the people of Mexican descent living in the community under consideration, but shall also use "Mexican American." In 1958, when we began to collect data on *toledanos*, the term "Chicano" was used within the group as a descriptive term to identify a person of Mexican descent born in the United States, but carried no political connotation. Neither outsiders nor the mass media knew or used the term. The term "Anglo" to refer to non-Mexicans was not used at that time either; rather, *toledanos* referred to the latter as *"americanos"* or "whites." "Anglo" is now used by some agency people and others familiar with the social scientific literature on Mexican Americans. As in most other Mexican American communities today, "Chicano," incorporated into the concept of *chicanismo*, has strong political overtones and is used by a few *toledanos* to identify themselves; it is strongly rejected by others. *La raza*, although meaning literally "the race" in English, is used—as elsewhere—to refer to a consciousness of and identification with a distinctive ethnic group (Mexican, or sometimes more broadly, Hispanic) sharing both biological and cultural unity.

2. Most North American Anglo citizens share equally garbled notions of Western European, English, and U.S. history.

3. The term "melting pot" seems to have been subverted to mean some thing called "mainstream culture and society," presumably established early and for all time by white Anglo-Saxon Protestants. However, originally the notion was based on the belief "that all could be absorbed and that all could *contribute to an emerging* character" (our emphasis, Handlin 1959). Here emphasis is on the creative, dynamic aspects of the concept, and could be regarded as embracing ethnic diversity.

4. In 1900, only fifty-three Mexicans are reported to have been in the entire state of Ohio. Eighty-five were counted in 1910, and just under a thousand (952) were reported to have been there in 1920. By 1930, however, over 4,000 Mexicans (2,806 males and 1,231 females) were reported to be in the state, 554 of whom lived in Toledo (Bartha 1945:71).

5. In 1958, a 22 percent random sample of the estimated 600 *toledano* households showed that almost 80 percent of the heads of households had come into the area in 1945 or later (Macklin 1958:4).

6. The average for men and women alike in 1958 was less than six years of schooling completed, and while the median year of schooling completed in 1970 still is comparatively low (9.1), the percentage of high school graduates is almost equal to that of the "Negro" population (32.1 percent "Spanish Americans"; 32.2 percent "Negro"; City of Toledo, 49.8 percent [Community Planning Council 1973]). It must be pointed out, however, that these figures are for the post-school-age population and do not reflect the educational attainment of the younger *toledano* population. In 1980,

the census should reveal striking changes within the one generation that has grown up since our earlier study.

7. McWilliams (1949:163) estimates that nearly 10 percent of Mexico's adult population came to the United States during the period 1900-1930, at a time when identification with one's village or region (*"mi tierra"*) superseded national identification. It was, of course, also before the major cultural and social changes that have resulted from modernization, industrialization, and urbanization since 1940.

8. In 1970, all women participating in the labor force for the city of Toledo was 42.4 percent; 40.4 percent for "Spanish American" women; and 51.5 percent for "Negro" women (Community Planning Council 1973:32).

9. In 1940, the Bureau of the Census classified people of Mexican descent under the rubric of "Spanish Mother Tongue," and in 1950 and 1960 as "White," which makes it impossible to determine exactly the rate of growth. Although many more men came during and after World War II (1945) than before, the sex ratio gradually evened out. The judgment, based on city and telephone directories and school and church records, is that the estimated 1960 population of Toledo was about 600 families (ca. 3,000 to 3,500 persons). In 1970, the census again saw fit to count "Spanish American persons," finding 7,352 in Toledo and 12,157 in the Toledo Standard Metropolitan Statistics Area (Community Planning Council 1973:2).

10. The Probate Court of Lucas County issues marriage licenses for both the city of Toledo and the rest of the county. Inasmuch as 18,000 people of Mexican descent now are estimated to reside in Lucas County, these figures provide a better indication of the intermarriage trends than would those from Toledo alone. Our sample includes the following marriage data:

Year	Volume	Period	No. of Licenses Examined	Total the Year
1945	109	February 14–July 13	1,799	5,157
1955	148	April 29–November 8)	2,398	5,345
	149	April 30–December 3)		
1965	188	January 27–July 6	1,199	6,007
1974	238	August 28, 1974–January 9, 1975)	2,398	6,822
1975	239	October 31, 1974–April 19, 1975)		6,299
1975	241	April 8–August 14	1,199	6,299
1976-1977	250	November 8, 1976–April 19, 1977 (latest available to us in July 1977)	1,199	6,452

References

Abramson, Harold
  1973 *Ethnic Diversity in Catholic America.* New York: Wiley-Interscience.

Barclay, Morgan J.
  1972 "Changing Images of the Toledo Polish Community, 1870-1920." *Northwest Ohio Quarterly, A Journal of History and Civilization* 44, no. 3:64-71.
  1973 "Images of Toledo's German Community, 1850-1890." *Northwest Ohio Quarterly, A Journal of History and Civilization* 45, no. 4:133-144.

Bartha, Stephen J.
  1945 "A History of Immigrant Groups in Toledo." Master's thesis, The Ohio State University.

Basham, Richard, and DeGroot, David
  1977 "Current Approaches to the Anthropology of Urban and Complex Societies." *American Anthroplogist* 79:414-440.

Betten, Neil, and Mohl, Raymond A.
  1973 "From Discrimination to Repatriation: Mexican Life in Gary, Indiana, During the Great Depression." *Pacific Historical Review* 42:370-388.

Blade, The
  1920 Toledo, Ohio, April 20.
  1945 "240 Young Mexicans Help Keep Rails Clear in City." Toledo, Ohio, March 1.
  1972 Toledo, Ohio, *Sunday Magazine,* July 30.
  1977 Toledo, Ohio, July 2, p. 6.

Brockmann, C. T.
  1971 "Reciprocity and Market Exchange on the Flathead Reservation." *Northwest Anthropological Research Notes* 5:77-96.

Carlson, Alvar W.
  1975 "The Settling Processes of Mexican Americans in Northwestern Ohio." *The Journal of Mexican American History* 5:24-42.

Combined Register
  1958- Diocese of Toledo, Ohio: Church of Sts. Peter and Paul, Decem-
  1970   ber 14, 1958-June 28, 1970.

Community Planning Council of Northwestern Ohio, Inc.
  1973 *A Profile of the Spanish American Population in the Toledo Metropolitan Area.* Toledo, Ohio.

Creemos en La Raza, A Bilingual Magazine Serving the Hispanic Community of Northwest Ohio
  1975 "The Hispanic Community." Toledo, Ohio.

Felter, Eunice
1941 "The Social Adaptations of the Mexican Churches in the Chicago Area." Master's thesis, University of Chicago.

Fitzpatrick, Joseph P.
1971 *Puerto Rican Americans: The Meaning of Migration to the Mainland.* Englewood Cliffs, N.J.: Prentice-Hall.

Foster, George M.
1960 *Culture and Conquest: America's Spanish Heritage.* Chicago: Quadrangle Books.

Gordon, Milton M.
1978 "Assimilation in America: Theory and Reality." In *Human Nature, Class, and Ethnicity,* edited by Milton M. Gordon, pp. 181-208. New York: Oxford University Press.

Handlin, Oscar, ed.
1959 *Immigration as a Factor in American History.* Englewood Cliffs, N.J.: Prentice-Hall.

Hannerz, Ulf
1974 "Ethnicity and Opportunity in Urban America." In *Urban Ethnicity,* edited by Abner Cohen, pp. 37-76. London: Tavistock Publications.

Lewis, Oscar
1951 "Urbanization without Breakdown: A Case Study." *The Scientific Monthly* 75:31-41.

Libro 1°
1927- *Records, Nuestra Señora de Guadalupe.* Toledo, Ohio: hand-
1930 written in Spanish, no pages. Translation by the authors.
1945- *Records, Nuestra Señora de Guadalupe.* Toledo, Ohio: hand-
1951 written in Spanish, no pages. Translation by the authors.

Lieberson, Stanley
1961 "The Impact of Residential Segregation on Ethnic Assimilation." *Social Forces* 40:52-57.

Macklin, Barbara June
1958 "Preliminary Report: Research on Americans of Mexican Descent." Toledo, Ohio: The National Conference of Christians and Jews, Toledo Board of Community Relations, and the University of Toledo. Mimeographed.
1967 "El Niño Fidencio: Un Estudio del Curanderismo en Nuevo León." In *Anuario Humánitas,* pp. 529-569. Monterrey, N. L., Mexico: Centro de Estudios Humanisticos, Universidad de Nuevo León.
1974 "Belief, Ritual, and Healing: New England Spiritualism and Mexican-American Spiritism Compared." In *Religious Movements in Contemporary America,* edited by Irving I. Zaretsky

and Mark P. Leone, pp. 383-417. Princeton, N.J.: Princeton
University Press.

1976   *Structural Stability and Culture Change in a Mexican-American
Community.* New York: Arno Press.

McWilliams, Carey

1949   *North from Mexico.* Philadelphia: J. B. Lippincott.

Mittelbach, Frank G., and Moore, Joan W.

1968   "Ethnic Endogamy—The Case of Mexican Americans." *American Journal of Sociology* 74 (July):50-62.

National Council of the Churches of Christ in the U.S.A.

1957   *Churches and Church Membership in the United States.* New
York: National Council of the Churches of Christ in the U.S.A.,
Bureau of Research and Survey. Series C, Bulletin no. 10.

Northrop, F.S.C.

1966   *The Meeting of East and West: an Inquiry Concerning World
Understanding.* New York: Collier Books.

Ogbu, J. J.

1974   "Learning in Burgherside: The Ethnography of Education." In
Anthropologists in Cities, edited by G. M. Foster and R. V. Kemper, pp. 93-121. Boston: Little, Brown.

Passonneau, Joseph R.

1963   "Emergence of City Form." In *Urban Life and Form,* edited by
Werner Z. Hirsch, pp. 9-27. New York: Holt, Rinehart and
Winston.

Pelto, Pertti J. and Gretel H.

1975   "Intra-cultural Diversity: Some Theoretical Issues." *American
Ethnologist* 2:1-18.

Peñalosa, Fernando, and McDonagh, Edward C.

1966   "Social Mobility in a Mexican-American Community." *Social
Forces* 44:498-505.

Price, D. O.

1971   "Rural to Urban Migration of Mexican Americans, Negroes and
Anglos." *International Migration Review* 5:281-291.

Soto, John A.

1974   "Mexican American Community Leadership for Education."
Doctoral dissertation, University of Michigan.

Stein, Howard F., and Hill, Robert F.

1977   *The Ethnic Imperative: Examining the New White Ethnic Movement.* University Park: The Pennsylvania State University Press.

Toledo Area Chamber of Commerce

1958   "Factual Report." Toledo, Ohio.

Wallace, Anthony F. C.
  1952   "Individual Differences and Cultural Uniformities." *American Sociological Review* 17:747-750.
Wolf, Eric R.
  1958   "The Virgin of Guadalupe: A Mexican National Symbol." *Journal of American Folklore* 71:34-39.
Wolf, Eric R., and Hansen, Edward C.
  1972   *The Human Condition in Latin America.* New York: Oxford University Press.

6
Home Away from Home: The Jacalan Community in the San Francisco Bay Area

Laura Zarrugh

Although the urbanization literature frequently has shown how migration can contribute to changing identity, less is known about instances in which insularity is maintained. While there are scattered historical references to the phenomenon of European and, more specifically, Italian migrants from the same village resettling together in the United States, few systematic studies, and none involving Mexican examples, have been undertaken of these transplanted or transposed communities and their implications for the adaptation of the people involved.[1] There is little information, then, on how the existence of these village enclaves may affect members' interaction with the host society or their identification with other immigrants of the same nationality. This chapter deals with an example of "community transposition," involving migrants from Jacala,[2] an agricultural village of about 1400 inhabitants in the state of Jalisco, to the San Francisco Bay area, where they have formed what is in many respects an extraterritorial extension of their home village. By examining the properties that make this particular aggregate of migrants a "community," this chapter also demonstrates how this community functions to keep alive the migrants' identity as Jacalans, while retarding their integration into the surrounding society, both Anglo and Latino.

The research on which this chapter is based was conducted in preparation of my doctoral dissertation (Berkeley, 1974). The research was sponsored by the National Institutes of Mental Health (National Institute of General Medical Sciences), Training Grant No. GM-1224. A shorter version of this chapter was presented at the seventy-third annual meeting of the American Anthropological Association held in Mexico City, November 19-24, 1974.

145

In applying the concept of "community" to immigrants, it is sometimes difficult, as Fitzpatrick has observed, to identify the "active reality" that is the community because of geographic dispersion, different stages of assimilation, divergent interests, or a variety of leaders (Fitzpatrick 1966). But because Jacalans, like the aforementioned Italian immigrants of the turn of the century, are bounded populations, having come from the same place of origin, they are not only readily identifiable, but also represent a case in which the immigrant community in many respects approximates the kind of "little community" traditionally described by anthropologists (e.g., Redfield 1955). Despite wide variance in opinion about what constitutes a community, most definitions today include one or more of the following three characteristics: geographic area, primary group interaction, and group solidarity based on common goals and values (Hillary 1955; Fitzpatrick 1966). In this chapter, the position is taken that geographic area, narrowly defined, is not a necessary condition for the existence of "community" due to migrants' ready access to telephones and automobiles, which obviate the need for strict geographic contiguity as a condition for social interaction and communal sentiment. Communal sentiment in this case rests upon a common place of origin rather than upon a shared place of current residence. It is, however, interesting to note that when possible, migrants do make an effort to live near one another. This point will be examined at greater length later. Another point regarding definitions of community that merits comment is self-sufficiency. Because immigrant groups, unlike the classic "little communities" described by Redfield and others, are rarely if ever self-sufficient—one could argue that traditional peasant communities were not self-sufficient either—the nature of the relationship between the immigrant community and surrounding society is also explored.

The case discussed here is of particular significance for several reasons. First, in spite of the fact that Mexico is presently the greatest single source of immigration to the United States (U.S. Bureau of the Census 1972), surprisingly little research has been done on the geographic sources of the migration. Grebler, for example, notes that "much of the data is not only meager but out of date" (Grebler 1966:75); what data do exist suggest that Jacala is situated in an area of traditionally high out-migration. Second, the existing literature has long been burdened by unfounded generalizations that tend to portray all Mexican Americans as victims of a variety of social and psychological problems, although at least one author (Moore 1970) has indicated the need for caution in generalizing about such a large and diverse group. In fact, Jacalans, in contrast to other reported groups of Mexican immigrants, have adjusted relatively easily to life in the United States. Last, and as has already been suggested, Jacalans' insularity raises doubt about the inevitability of second generation assimilation, a question that is also examined in this chapter.

A Note on Methodology

The fieldwork upon which this chapter is based was conducted from January 1972 to September 1973 and involved the use of standard ethnographic techniques: open-ended interviews, participation in a variety of activities, and observations of interactions within the family, within the immigrant community, and between Jacalans and non-Jacalans. Non-Jacalans with whom migrants come in contact (e.g., school couselors, nurses, priests) were also interviewed. The period October-November 1972 was spent in Jacala where I lived with a migrant family. A formal census of the immigrant community was not completed because it proved to be too threatening to the group, which includes many illegal entrants. However, data were gathered on over 200 individuals; particularly detailed information was obtained from members of twenty-five households.

Jacalan Migration as a Way of Life

Fragmented landholdings, inefficient land use, a scarcity of water, and limited employment opportunities in Jacala has resulted in almost uninterrupted migration to the United States since the time of the Mexican Revolution (1910-1921). As in the case of the Italians, whose emigration rates varied by province according to differences in the systems of land tenure (Vecoli 1964:406), landholding arrangements have played a particularly important role in determining the high rate of emigration from Jacala and from the Central Plateau of Mexico in general. In the 1920s, for instance, Gruening ascertained that 96.2 percent of the rural families of Jalisco were landless (Steiner 1970:266). Although no exact figures are available, it is clear that prior to migration, the majority of Jacalan migrants were sharecroppers or landless laborers who barely eked out an existence from land that yielded one yearly crop (corn) rather than the two (corn and wheat) usually cultivated in other areas of the Central Plateau. Immigration to the United States from Jacala over the last fifty years has followed closely the Mexican national trend: Jacalans during the 1920s preferred to migrate to midwestern cities rather than to the Southwest, as they were able to earn substantially more working in midwestern iron and automobile industries than they could hope for in southwestern agriculture. Men, both unmarried and married, went to Illinois, Indiana, Michigan, and Ohio during this period, some of the latter taking their families with them. Although Jacalans, like other Mexican nationals, were coerced by American private and public agencies into returning to Mexico during the Great Depression, some Jacalans managed to remain behind permanently in the Midwest.

The establishment of the bracero (contract labor) program in 1942 induced Jacalans to begin to travel once more to the United States and following the general trend, most village men who took part in the program migrated during the late 1950s and early 1960s. Although contract laborers were sent to several states, the majority of Jacalans went to California during this era, many of them making more than one journey. These later years of the bracero program are often referred to by villagers as a time of "free entry," when it was relatively easy to arrange immigration papers for permanent residence in the United States. Many Jacalans took advantage of this and the wider employment opportunities thereby opened to them in urban areas, since the bracero program involved only agricultural labor. The Jacalan settlement in the San Francisco Bay area, as well as two smaller village enclaves—one near Los Angeles and the other in the Fresno-Bakersfield area of central California—date from the late 1950s.

Village migration to California, both legal and illegal, has continued from that time to the present in a variety of forms and attracting ever-increasing numbers, which has led Jacalans to estimate the number of villagers who are residing in the United States at "half the village." "Going North" has become so institutionalized that it almost constitutes a rite of passage, marking the initiation of adolescent males into adulthood. The trip itself is almost always made in the company of relatives (e.g., siblings or cousins) or friends rather than by oneself, and while some of these migrants settle permanently in California, the majority return to Mexico, marry village women, and resume their temporary migrations. Thus, married men also migrate in order to earn money toward specific goals in the village, such as building a new house, buying land, starting a small business, or paying off a debt. Although these men usually leave their wives and children in Mexico, returning home after spending periods from a few months to two years in California, some men bring their wives or entire families with them, thus greatly increasing their chances for permanent settlement. However, few come with the intention of staying permanently and occasionally families return to Jacala after having lived in California for as long as ten years. Those who have become economically successful in "the North" gain prestige by investing in cattle, land, and elaborate homes in Jacala, a fact that helps explain Jacalans' continuing strong identification with the village, as well as with fellow migrants.

Although economics provides the primary motive for leaving home, with villagers emphasizing that in California they can earn in one hour what it would take them an entire day to earn in the village, Jacalans sometimes leave home for other reasons. Among these are avoiding responsibilities or vengeance, being near relatives—(an especially important motive for elderly women who wish to be near their adult children)—and simple curiosity. Villagers, young and old, speak of their desire to visit the United States just to learn what it is like. On the other hand, few, if any, villagers migrate in order to take advantage of educational opportunities. It is instead their very lack of education that makes urban California a destination preferable to Mexican cities, where stiff competition for jobs requires that applicants have at least a primary school certificate (Balán 1969:18-19). Since few adult Jacalans have completed more than two or three years of school, they have realistically assessed their chances for employment in Mexico and migrate to California with the feeling that there the educated and uneducated alike can find what are by Jacalans' standards well-paying jobs.

The Settlement Pattern of the Jacalan Community in the Bay Area

It is difficult to estimate how many Jacalans (and people from the surrounding ranchos) live in the bay area, since the number constantly fluctuates as individuals go back and forth between the village and California and from place to place within the state in response to employment opportunities and family obligations, but a conservative estimate, based on an analysis of informants' social networks and knowledge of fellow migrants, is about 150 households. Following the classic pattern of other immigrant groups in the United States, the first Jacalan migrants to San Francisco settled in the Mission, an old, low-rent district of the central city, which has a large population of Central and South Americans, in addition to other Mexicans. In succeeding years, some Jacalans found jobs in the suburbs south of San Francisco and moved closer to their work, while a smaller number moved to Oakland and other towns on the east side of the bay. Those who moved south of San Francisco found inexpensive housing in long-established, working class neighborhoods, which, once largely Italian, now contain many Spanish-speaking people, as well as members of other ethnic groups. More recent arrivals from the village frequently move directly into these suburbs, bypassing initial residence in the Mission District. Some Jacalans, however, continue to live in San Francisco.

In spite of the fact that Jacalans are somewhat geographically dispersed in the bay area, the majority live within a ten-mile radius of one another and dispersion is due less to preference than to the exigencies of jobs and finding cheap rental housing where large families or groups of people will be accepted. As many as 90 percent of newly arrived Jacalans stay at least initially with a relative or friend and, because subsequent housing is often secured through the aid of relatives and other fellow villagers, several Jacalan families usually reside on the same street or on several nearby streets. In one case, four related families live in the same apartment building. Of the 10 to 15 percent of Jacalans who have purchased homes in the bay area, almost all have bought them in one small suburban neighborhood, thereby providing the community in recent years with an even more precise geographical referent. In this respect, the Jacalan settlement pattern over time contrasts with that of other immigrant groups in which geographic dispersion often has followed some degree of economic success, as measured by the ability to purchase a home.

Economic Relationships Inside
and Outside the Immigrant Community

Like other immigrant and minority groups, Jacalans occupy a special niche in the economic structure of the area, with the majority employed either as greenhouse workers or garbage collectors. The two next most common occupations are as janitors and kitchen helpers in restaurants; still other Jacalans are employed in a variety of jobs: in small factories, gravel pits, car washes, wrought iron works, and *tortillerías* (tortilla bakeries), and as musicians and singers in the entertainment industry that caters to the large Spanish-speaking population of the bay area. While one common factor among these diverse jobs is that none requires specialized technical skills, a more important one is that none requires more than a rudimentary command of English. With little knowledge of English, Jacalans, by necessity and choice, seek jobs where there are other Spanish speakers and, if possible, other Jacalans. As a result, eighteen of thirty employees in one refuse-collecting company are Jacalans, while in one small nursery, seven of eight employees are from the village.

Villagers usually find jobs in the bay area within several weeks of their arrival, almost always with the aid of relatives or friends who may also be feeding and housing the newcomers without charge. An individual unable to find work within a reasonable period can call upon a large network of kinsmen and fellow villagers in other areas of the state to advise him of job openings; thus, unemployment and underemployment, reportedly widespread among other groups of Mexicans in the United States (Moore 1970), are not serious problems for bay area Jacalans.

Like the men, Jacalan women also rely on friends' and relatives' assistance in finding jobs, and for that reason, most of the women who hold jobs outside the home work together in three types of employment: flower nurseries, laundries, and the San Francisco garment industry. In contrast to many Mexican-American women, virtually no Jacalan women are employed as domestic servants or housekeepers, partially because, as in the village, these jobs are associated with low economic and social status, but also because of language difficulties. However, baby-sitting for fellow villagers and Spanish-speaking neighbors provides an acceptable alternative method of earning money to working outside the home.

A few migrants have attained sufficient economic success in the bay area through diligence and frugality to enable them to become self-employed, a status valued by Jacalans, as it has been by other immigrant groups. Nonetheless small businesses are not common in the larger Mexican-American community. The two main outlets of Jacalan entrepreneural activity are ethnic restaurants and wrought iron works. By providing about a dozen migrants with jobs, these businesses also create economic ties within the group.

Moneylending arrangements form another more important source of economic ties within the Jacalan community, since individuals in need of money almost always prefer to borrow from relatives or fellow migrants, rather than from banks or finance companies. One of the reasons for this is that the consequences of defaulting are not likely to be as serious as when a formal lending institution is involved, since Jacalans are reluctant to resort to legal sanction to force payment of a debt. In spite of the fact that some individuals who lend money find it difficult to collect, others receive repayment often enough when interests of 12 and 18 percent are involved to make moneylending a profitable venture. At least one migrant who has invested in village land is reputed to have amassed his capital for investment in this way. (Of course, the first step in amassing capital for investment in this and other similar cases was the saving of money from earnings in order to lend it at high interest rates.)

Social Interaction Within the Immigrant Community

Notwithstanding these small efforts aimed at financial independence from the surrounding society, Jacalans are economically linked in numerous important ways to the larger community in which they live. However, in forming social relationships, Jacalans tend to restrict informal social interaction to fellow migrants. In fact, their life in the bay area, following village practice, revolves primarily around relatives—most frequently siblings or parents of either husband or wife—only secondarily around fellow Jacalans, and least importantly around Spanish-speaking work mates and neighbors.

As previously noted, new arrivals from the village typically are incorporated into a relative's or friend's household at least until they are ready to move out on their own, thus making for a constantly changing pattern of household arrangements, but one in which siblings, parents, nephews, and nieces are the most common recipients of this form of hospitality. Even when coresidence is not involved, interaction among relatives remains strong. Adult children with parents in the bay area usually visit them once a week, keeping in touch by telephone between visits. Mutual aid between the two generations is also frequent: parents typically baby-sit for grandchildren and, in return, children provide their parents with transportation and assistance with housework. Mutual aid is also well developed between many adult siblings and cousins, as is the pattern of visiting weekly, attending each other's fiestas, and exchanging birthday gifts. As in the village, family ties are also emphasized through the practice of choosing relatives as godparents for one's children; siblings of either spouse, cousins, nieces, and nephews are the most common choices as *compadres.* By custom, parents are supposed to (and actually do) choose the wife's parents as *padrinos de bautismo* (baptismal godparents) for their first-born child and the husband's parents as *padrinos* for the second-born; although either relatives or friends may be chosen for subsequent children, relatives are favored. That this pattern may be related to the Jacalans' migratory way of life is suggested by Madsen's explanation of similar choices made by Mexican Americans in Texas. According to him, relatives are favored over nonrelatives because the latter may move away and become lost, while relatives are more certain to remain in contact and to travel when necessary to fulfill their obligations (Madsen 1964:17).

In addition to kinship, wealth and prestige are also important determinants of social interaction. Migrants may be classified according to whether they look toward the home village or the immigrant community in their striving for economic and social mobility. Village-oriented migrants invest all of their earnings in Mexico, spending only the bare minimum to survive in California, while other migrants strive to improve their economic and social standing directly within the immigrant community. The latter validate their new social status through conspicuous display, which involves purchasing and lavishly furnishing homes in the bay area. Owners of these homes follow a distinct pattern of furnishing that includes the liberal use of massive furniture, gold leaf, porcelain, crystal, velvet, and marble. In one home, the owner's bedroom contained a king-size bed covered with a red velvet bedspread and backed by a matching quilted headboard. The wall behind the bed was done in gold-leaf paper and the sliding closet door was covered with a gold-veined mirror from floor to ceiling. The windows on the opposing wall were hung with heavy red velvet drapery complete with matching cornice and lacy Austrian shade. According to the owner, the draperies and cornice alone cost over two hundred dollars. Dressing "elegantly" and behaving haughtily in their relations with fellow migrants are other ways of validating status. Some, for example, hope to establish their claims to higher status by flaunting the fact that they attend only the fiestas of other individuals who share their pretense of being "high class." Although status differences are a source of divisiveness among Jacalans, the important point is that status striving occurs with reference to other Jacalans and requires their acknowledgment to have any meaning.

On the other hand, interaction among migrants is facilitated by the existence of informal and formal voluntary associations. Similar in function to the coffee houses frequented by Egyptian migrants (Abu-Lughod 1967:397), a centrally located, Jacalan-owned restaurant and several *cantinas* (bars) favored by Jacalans serve as gathering places for migrant men to converse and exchange information. For the women, the three Catholic churches with Jacalan parishoners serve a similar purpose by providing them with the opportunity to visit and catch up on news of fellow villagers after Sunday Mass.

Of the formal organizations, the most important is the Club Jacala, which, although primarily recreational, resembles the benefit societies often organized by migrants in that it also serves as a significant informal channel for mutual aid. First organized as a soccer team in 1969, the club had grown by 1973 to about sixty dues-paying members, in addition to thirty-six players. The majority of the players and virtually all of the club members are from the village, while the few nonvillagers are from the same state of Mexico. A juvenile division of the club was organized in 1971 with the hope that members would provide future players for the adult division, at the same time insuring the club's continued existence among the younger generation.

Monthly dues of five or ten dollars for members and officers respectively are used to pay for the teams' uniforms, insurance, and soccer league fines, but special assessments may be made to help members temporarily unemployed or facing an unusual hardship as, for example, when money was raised for a man whose home burned. Although not undertaken on a formal basis, club members sometimes query one another about jobs and housing for relatives and friends.

Club activities consist of weekly meetings, regularly scheduled dances, and soccer matches. During the soccer season, the club's games become the most important event in the community's social life. Whole families attend, women being as enthusiastic spectators as men; individuals unfamiliar with the fine points of the game at least enjoy the appearance of the teams' *madrinas* ("sponsors") and mariachis, as well as the opportunity to socialize and show off their finery. In addition to these activities, the club also supports civic improvement in Jacala; so far, this has involved financial assistance to the village soccer team, provision of a new church bell and contributions of money toward the construction of a new plaza and jail. In 1972, the club even attempted to organize, albeit unsuccessfully, a charter flight to Mexico for the purpose of playing against the hometown team. As the departure date drew near, the plans had to be abandoned as no one would accept the responsibility for collecting the airfares in advance of the flight. Nevertheless, some members continued to believe that such a flight would be arranged eventually.

Relations Between Jacalan Migrants and the Surrounding Society

Jacalans visit and exchange small favors with their Latino neighbors, but nevertheless remain distrustful and somewhat intolerant of them because of perceived cultural differences. *Tejanos* (Mexican Americans from Texas), for example, are criticized for speaking oddly and having "strange customs," and Central American women frequently receive sharp condemnation from Jacalan women for what they perceive to be their moral laxity, consisting of alleged casual attitudes toward premarital sex, divorce, and adultery, as well as immodesty in dress (e.g., miniskirts and bikinis). Even in Jacalans' relations with other Mexicans, special merit seems to attach to those who are from the Jacalans' home state and especially from the same area as the village.

Of the other ethnic groups with whom Jacalans have contact, the most significant are the Italians, who are frequently their employers and landlords. Jacalans distinguish the Italians from *americanos* (Anglos) because they not only speak Italian among themselves, but they also use it rather than English in their dealings with Jacalans. Because of similarities between Spanish and Italian, Jacalans say that they have fewer difficulties understanding Italian than English. In spite of positive attitudes toward individual Italian neighbors, who may be regarded as friendly and helpful, Jacalans often stereotype and express resentment of Italians in general,

because of the latter's relative economic success and their exploitation of Jacalans. From migrants' comments it is clear that their
resentment stems from the Italians' typically superordinate position
as employers and landlords in their relationships with Jacalans. For
example, the refuse-collecting companies and plant nurseries where
Jacalans typically work are usually owned by Italians.

Because of the language barrier, Jacalans have very limited and
superficial contacts with Anglos and perhaps for that reason are
more apt to regard them with amusement than bitterness, although
much of this humor might also be interpreted as a kind of psychological defense mechanism. Jokes about Americans typically revolve
around the way elderly Anglos try to act young, the way pet owners
treat their dogs like children, and the light way they feel American
couples treat marriage and divorce. Jacalans are forced to rely on
translators—(frequently their own children)—in their dealings with
Anglo school, medical, government, and sales personnel; they find
this procedure not only awkward, but that it also often results in
misunderstandings. Therefore, when possible, they try to find a
Spanish-speaking professional with whom they can deal directly.
One interesting result of this is that by relying on fellow migrants
for their recommendations, many end up patronizing the same
Spanish-speaking doctors, dentists, lawyers, tax consultants, and
stores; thus, in one more way, the reduce their contacts with Anglos.

The Maintenance of Jacalan Identity

Although their national identity as Mexicans is of greater significance to Jacalans in the United States than it was at home, their
identity as Jacalans remains strong. This is perhaps best illustrated
by the fact that Jacalans often refer to fellow villagers in the bay
area as though they constitute a group, using the term *"la colonia"*
("the colony") to designate themselves. Similarly, the phrase "from
Mexico," when used by Jacalans to designate an individual's place
of origin, is often understood to mean "from the village." The
existence of a well-developed community life, a view of themselves
as sojourners, and an intense and continuing interaction with the
village, involving correspondence, remittances, investments, and
annual visits, help support this parochial identity. In the village,
this attachment of migrants to Jacala is accorded recognition once
a year during the fiesta of Jacala's patron saint, when a special pro-

cession is held for "sons of the village living in foreign lands."

As is perhaps inevitable in a complex urban milieu, the migrants' sense and use of identity has become situational. Sensitive to the image of the country bumpkin that their rural origins suggest, migrants sometimes try to conceal these origins from Spanish-speaking outsiders by identifying themselves as having come from Guadalajara. But such efforts are only minimally successful since, as they also realize, they are usually undone by their use of rural dialect or substandard, uneducated Spanish. Such speech negates more extensive attempts at passing and thereby contributes to the inwardness of the migrant group, as does the fact that Jacalans are discriminated against by more-urban Latinos. For example, a priest familiar with several Jacalan families explained their absence from church organizations by the fact that urban Mexicans and Central Americans, who control these groups, would not make Jacalans feel very welcome. That Jacalans are aware of this discrimination was also apparent in the comments of some Jacalan high school students when their school counselor suggested that I show slides of the village at a high school Latin Heritage Club function. Although they were themselves very anxious to see the slides, they opposed showing them before the larger group because they feared that they would be ridiculed for coming from such a backward place. However, discrimination against Jacalans by other Latinos is offset by the group's negative stereotyping of outsiders and their positive evaluation of themselves in relation to the people back home. In comparison to Mexican villagers, migrants see themselves as economically successful, socially sophisticated, and culturally superior. All of these differences are understood in the term *"norteño,"* which is used by villagers and migrants alike to refer to individuals who have lived in the United States; this positive comparison helps to tie migrants to the village.

Because few migrants are able to speak English, the issue of trying to pass as Anglo never arises, and in any case, it is doubtful that Jacalans would see much advantage to that sort of passing, at least at this point, since they do not regard Anglos as a significant reference group. It is for the same reasons that Jacalans often say that they do not understand why other Mexicans and Latin Americans in the United States attempt to conceal their true identities by insisting that they are actually of Spanish or French ancestry. In contrast to Mexican Americans who not infrequently claim at least one Spanish grandparent, Jacalans have no such pretensions; nor do they understand other Mexican Americans who refer to themselves as "Chicanos." In recent years, the word "Chicano," once considered coarse and suitable only for special in-group use, has become transformed into a symbol of ethnic pride. Unaware of the relatively new ideological implications of the word (cf. Cuéllar 1970:149), Jacalans understand it to mean simply a person born in the United States of Mexican parents and consider it and *"pocho,"* another word with the same meaning to them, as uncouth and demeaning.[3] One young Jacalan expressed his feelings about Mexicans who use the term "Chicano" by saying that "instead of trying to advance and be proud of themselves as Mexicans, they are pulling everyone down."

While under certain circumstances behaving as though ashamed of their unsophisticated, uneducated background, Jacalans are, on the other hand, very proud of being Mexican and because of this pride and the belief that they will eventually return to Mexico, no Jacalan has applied for American citizenship, nor are any likely to do so in the foreseeable future. While most cite their anticipated return to Mexico as the principal reason for not seeking naturalization, some add that they see no real advantage of citizenship over permanent residence, feel that it would be traitorous to renounce their natal country, and, in any case, do not think that they could pass the citizenship examination given their language and educational deficiencies. The adolescents are more likely than the adults to remain permanently in the United States, but they, too, express little interest in becoming American citizens. Nevertheless, some Jacalans, both in the bay area and in the village, are citizens by virture of having been born in the United States either during their parents' sojourns of the 1920s or more recent migrations of village women during the last decade. Since these people, most of whom are still children, do not vote or hold government jobs, the principal advantage of their American citizenship is that it permits them easier access to the United States than is possible for Mexican nationals.

Cultural Continuity

With little desire to emulate Anglos in anything other than their economic prosperity, Jacalans have maintained village cultural patterns that serve to express symbolically their identity as Jacalans.

Although many of these cultural patterns are shared with other Mexicans, local differences do exist and are perpetuated after migration. The institution of *compadrazgo* (coparenthood), previously discussed, is one example of a local variation in a widespread cultural pattern. Other examples of local variation occur in the areas of medical and religious beliefs (e.g., the continued veneration of the village patron saint), language, music, and food preferences (e.g., such specialties as *birria*, a dish made with roast kid). More important, through a pattern of restricted interaction, Jacalans in the bay area have been able to maintain a consensus of values and goals strong enough to exact conformity on most issues for fear of criticism or even ostracism from the group. In contrast to lone migrants, for whom migration may be regarded as a pioneering venture, Jacalans' desire to remain a part of the group is stronger than any desire for individual change or mobility within the context of the larger society. To reiterate, economic and status striving occur among Jacalans, but in reference to their own group and frequently in reference to traditional values, such as gaining prestige through ownership of land and cattle in Mexico.

The Second Generation

The discussion would be incomplete without consideration of the second generation (Jacalans born in the United States or brought to California as children), since according to the evidence available on the great European immigrations one would expect the second generation, products of the American public school system, to have lost or abandoned most of the markers of their ethnicity. But the literature on Mexican Americans suggests that this is not an inevitable process and the inappropriateness of the European model to Mexican immigration becomes apparent if one considers the complicating factor of racial discrimination in the case of the Mexicans and the continuing nature of the migration, both of which obscure generational differences. As was mentioned above, the very proximity of Mexico makes the Mexican immigrant's situation quite different from that of his European or Asian counterpart in that there need be less commitment to the demands of the host society when migration is so easily reversible.

It may be premature to try to predict what adjustments ultimately will be made by Jacala's second generation in the bay area, as only a few of these persons have reached adulthood. Nevertheless, there are indications that being a Jacalan retains some salience for them at least through adolescence. Because of continuous migration from the village, there are at any given time substantial numbers of newly arrived teenagers and young adults in the bay area with whom the second generation comes into contact through family connections, the Club Jacala, and jobs. Virtually all male and female adolescents and young unmarrieds belong to cliques made up of first- and second-generation individuals. Within these cliques, peer socialization occurs in both directions, with the new arrivals acquiring some of the sophistication of the second generation, while those of the second generation have the opportunity to strengthen what they have learned from parents about the village, its values and lore (e.g., legends about the existence of buried Indian treasures and accounts of village involvement in the *Cristero* rebellion), and to reaffirm their identity as Jacalans. Moreover, periodic family trips to the village and, in some cases, extended residence there also help reinforce the second generation's sense of themselves as Jacalans. For example, during the period of fieldwork, four of the twenty-five families with whom I was best acquainted, and all with children born in the United States, returned to Jacala to live. One of these families has since come back to California. One result of these practices may turn out to be a continuation of the first generation's practice of village endogamy, according to which migrant men usually marry either women in the village or from the village who are living in the bay area. Too few marriages have yet taken place involving the second generation to say anything with certainty, but during the period of my fieldwork, two young women raised in the bay area from early childhood married men who had recently migrated from Jacala and willingly accepted their husband's traditional authority, despite the fact that neither man spoke English and was thus heavily dependent on his wife.

Other evidence of the importance the second generation attaches to their peer group of fellow Jacalans is the high frequency with which they drop out of school, following a pattern common among other Mexican Americans. As the literature (e.g., Clark 1959; Heller 1966; De Vos 1969) shows, dropping out for many Mexican Americans constitutes a resolution of the potential crisis of being ostracized by the peer group for succeeding in school, and this is, in a sense, also true for Jacalans. But unlike many Mexican-American youths, the kin and friendship networks of young Jacalans help them find what are by Jacalan standards well-paying jobs with little difficulty; thus, the usual consequences of dropping out—unemployment and delinquency—do not occur. When male Jacalans drop out of school it is usually to help their families or to enable themselves to purchase fashionable clothes and automobiles and to entertain friends properly, all of which give an individual high status and prestige within the peer group. Since the status of married women is also highly valued, girls frequently drop out of school in order to marry.

Under these circumstances of high in-group cohesiveness, Jacalans have remained largely immune to the negative self-images and deviant social attitudes that often result in the delinquency that has been reported for other minority groups (cf. De Vos 1969). However, because members of the second generation form friendships with other Mexicans and Latinos more frequently than do their parents, they ultimately may increase their identification with the larger group, perhaps trading the positive adjustments thus far achieved for negative self-concepts. In any case, what is certain is that, although they are more inclined than the first generation to learn English, the second generation is not coming to regard themselves as Anglos.

Barring serious economic setback or a closing of the U.S.-Mexican border to migration, the evidence available for the second generation suggests that the Jacalan community in the bay area is assured a continued existence for at least another generation. What remains to be seen is how long such a community can perpetuate itself, and that only time can answer.

Conclusion

In this chapter it has been argued that the Jacalan experience represents an example of a type of migration here termed "community transposition." The southern Italian pattern of migration and settlement in the United States, mentioned earlier, is another example of the same type. A concomitant of this type of migration is the maintenance of a strong sense of village identity, which, while impeding integration into the surrounding society, provides individual migrants with important psychological and social moorings. Given such moorings, immigration is more accurately described as a process of transplantation than "uprooting" (see

Handlin 1951 for the concept of uprooting).

Although the reasons for "community transposition" are not entirely clear, land tenure, education, and skill level are critical variables. What is clear, however, is that this type of migration has adaptive value. For Jacalans, the existence of a village enclave in the United States permits many individuals who might not be able to make it alone because of a lack of confidence or necessary skills, to migrate and live with relative ease in a foreign and sometimes hostile environment.

Notes

1. Park and Miller, and Vecoli are exceptions. Park and Miller, for example, found that in New York Sicilians settled by village and even by street (Park and Miller 1921), while Vecoli, writing about immigrants from the Mezzogiorno region of Italy, was impressed by "the degree to which the *contadini* succeeded in reconstructing their native towns" in Chicago (Vecoli 1964:408).

2. Jacala is a pseudonym used to protect the privacy of the people involved.

3. Usage seems to have changed over the years. Speaking of the situation some years ago, McWilliams reported that "to the native-born, the immigrant is a *cholo* or *chicano;* to the immigrant, the native-born is a *pocho*" (McWilliams 1968:209).

References

Abu-Lughod, Janet
   1967   "Migrant Adjustment to City Life: The Egyptian Case." In *Peasant Society: A Reader*, edited by Jack M. Potter, May N. Diaz, and George M. Foster, pp. 383-398. Boston: Little, Brown.
Balán, Jorge
   1969   "Migrant-Native Socioeconomic Differences in Latin American Cities: A Structural Analysis." *Latin American Research Review* 4, no. 1:3-29.
Clark, M. Margaret
   1959   *Health in the Mexican American Culture, A Community Study.* Berkeley: University of California Press.
Cuéllar, Alfredo
   1970   "Perspective on Politics." In *The Mexican Americans*, by Joan W. Moore with Alfredo Cuéllar, pp. 137-157. Englewood Cliffs, N.J.: Prentice-Hall.

De Vos, George
    1969   "Minority Group Identity." In *Culture Change, Mental Health, and Poverty,* edited by Joseph C. Finney, pp. 81-97. Lexington: University of Kentucky Press.

Fitzpatrick, Joseph
    1966   "The Importance of 'Community' in the Process of Immigrant Assimilation." *International Migration Review* 1:15-16.

Grebler, Leo
    1966   *Mexican Immigration to the United States: The Record and Its Implications.* Los Angeles: University of California, Mexican American Study Project, Advance Report no. 2.

Handlin, Oscar
    1951   *The Uprooted: The Epic Story of the Great Migrations That Made the American People.* Boston: Little, Brown.

Heller, Celia
    1966   *Mexican American Youth: Forgotten Youth at the Crossroads.* New York: Random House.

Hillary, George Jr.
    1955   "Definitions of Community: Areas of Agreement." *Rural Sociology* 20, no. 2:111-123.

Madsen, William
    1964   *The Mexican Americans of South Texas.* New York: Holt, Rinehart & Winston.

McWilliams, Carey
    1968   *North from Mexico: The Spanish Speaking People of the United States.* New York: Greenwood Press. (Original edition, New York: J. B. Lippincott Co., 1945.)

Moore, Joan W., with Cuéllar, Alfredo
    1970   *The Mexican Americans.* Englewood Cliffs, N.J.: Prentice-Hall.

Park, Robert, and Miller, H.
    1921   *Old World Traits Transplanted.* New York: Harper & Brothers.

Redfield, Robert
    1955   *The Little Community.* Chicago: University of Chicago Press.

Steiner, Stan
    1970   *La Raza: The Mexican Americans.* New York: Harper & Row, Harper Colophon Books.

U.S. Bureau of the Census
    1972   *Statistical Abstract of the United States.* Washington, D.C.: U.S. Government Printing Office.

Vecoli, Rudolph
    1964   "Condadini in Chicago: A Critique of *The Uprooted.*" *Journal of American History* 51:404-417.

Death joins the bogus partners in Teatro Desangaño del Pueblo's *Silent Partners*. The author, center, plays Death. *Peter T. Marshall.*

7

Folklore in Chicano Theater and Chicano Theater as Folklore

Nicolás Kanellos

Historical Background of the *Teatro* Movement

The eleven years that have passed since Luis Valdez gathered together a group of striking farmworkers in Delano, California, to create a farmworkers' theater in support of the historic grape boycott and strike, have seen the emergence of numerous Chicano theaters in the Southwest and Midwest, and of Puerto Rican theaters in the East. The exact number of Chicano and Puerto Rican theater groups is not known, but certainly must exceed one hundred.[1] These groups have developed from and serve such diverse communities as tomato pickers in New Jersey, factory workers in New York, Chicago, and Los Angeles, assembly line workers in Detroit, steelworkers in Northwest Indiana, cannery workers in San José, and farmworkers throughout the Southwest, Midwest, and Northwest. Many of the *teatros* ["theaters"] are short-lived and are barely aware of the existence of the majority of their counterparts. Some do not hold regular rehearsals and performances, but meet together occasionally when an important community or Chicano movement issue needs to be dramatized. Only a few groups have achieved stability and managed to operate for as long as five or six years.

Most of the *teatros* share similarities in theme and purpose, but their styles and levels of sophistication vary. They range from the

Reprinted with abridgments from the *Journal of the Folklore Institute* 15, no. 1 (1978): 57-82, with the permission of the author and the Folklore Institute.

unpolished and homespun groups like Teatro de la Sierra of rural New Mexico, to the agitprop,[2] Marxist-Leninist esthetic of Los Angeles' Teatro Movimiento Primavera, to the highly artistic, university-related Teatro de la Esperanza of Santa Barbara. Regardless of their level of sophistication, all of these groups incorporate folkloric material, some consciously and others quite naturally and without any artistic, anthropological, or ideological criteria for doing so. In fact, the majority of Chicano theaters in the Southwest and Midwest, and to some extent the Puerto Rican theaters in the East, are folk theaters: they unselfconsciously reflect the life, mores, and customs of the grass-roots communities from which they have sprung and perform mainly for these communities. These theaters not only represent the world view of their *pueblo* ["people"], but often carry on traditional forms of acting, singing, and performing. Many times they exhibit the vestiges of various types of folk drama practiced historically by Chicanos and Puerto Ricans (Kanellos n.d.). . . .

The first and only Chicano theater to become a professional company is the Teatro Campesino, which also operates a commune and cultural center in San Juan Bautista, California. It left the exclusive service of the farmworkers' struggle in 1967 to address broader issues and further develop *teatro* as a Chicano cultural and artistic form.[3] Despite its professionalism, its national and international tours, and its winning of Broadway's highest awards, the Teatro Campesino is still nourished by the folk culture that it represents, although its use of the folklore is now very astute, scientific, and purposeful. That is, as the Teatro Campesino has become more artistically sophisticated, it has very carefully selected and elaborated Mexican folk motifs to (1) enlighten its audiences as to the basic elements of Chicano culture, (2) please these audiences by providing material that is not only familiar but cherished, and (3) purposefully create a type of theater that is consistent with Mexican-American tradition. For example, the Teatro Campesino has fully explored the Mexican attitude towards death and its symbolic representation in Mexican folklore and popular culture. Consequently, it created the character, Death, who is everpresent and fatefully manipulates the action in such works as *La Gran Carpa de la Familia Rasquachi* [*The Tent Theater of the Rasquachi Family*]. Heavily inspired by folk customs revolving around the *Dia de los muertos* [*All Soul's Day*], as well as by the works of the Mexican engraver and illustrator of *corrido* ["folk song"] broadsides, José Guadalupe Posada. Campesino has created this dramatic figure, Death. Campesino also attired its musical ensemble, La Banda Calavera ("The Skull Band"), in death masks and skeleton costumes, and has illustrated its publications and posters with copies of Posada's work. Also, El Teatro Campesino's experiments with the *corrido* as a dramatic form are a result of this artistic elaboration of folklore. In these and other experiments with Mexican and Mexican-American folk arts and culture, Teatro Campesino has influenced the other Latino theaters in the United States as well as in Mexico. In the eleven years of its existence, El Teatro Campesino has risen from the leadership of a limited and rather unknown group of folk theaters to become one of the leaders of experimental theater arts in the Western world. Today one can truly join the name of its director and mentor, Luis Valdez,[4] with those of Peter Brook, Jerzy Grotowski, Richard Schechter, Enrique Buenaventura, and Augusto Boal.

The early Teatro Campesino functioned in two manners: (1) it promoted solidarity among striking farmworkers and attempted to proselytize strikebreakers; and (2) it served as a propaganda organism for the grape boycott among nonfarmworkers. The majority of its actors at that time were farmworkers who created their material through improvisations based on their personal and group experiences. Their main audience was constituted by farmworkers like themselves. Thus their *actos* ["acts"] like *La Quinta Temporada* [*The Fifth Season*][5] demonstrated the seasonal nature of their work and the need for unionization. The desired effects of the grape boycott were projected in their *Las Dos Caras del Patronicito* [*The Boss's Two Faces*]. From the beginning Teatro Campesino incorporated the singing of traditional songs into their performances and began changing the words to reflect the reality of the strike. "Se Va el Caimán" ["There Goes the Crocodile"] became their "El Picket Sign" (cf. Valdez 1971:99-103), whose infectious tune and lyrics have been sung by thousands of striking farmworkers and sympathizers. New songs like "Viva Huelga en General" ["Long Live the General Strike"] were soon composed to document the progress of the strike and boycott. Later some songs and *corridos* would become the bases for their dramatic material.[6]

The Teatro Campesino's most important contribution to the fast-spreading *teatro* movement, however, was the *acto*. The *acto*, which is highly indebted to agitprop threatre and to *comedia dell'arte* (cf. Valdez 1971:6), was introduced by Luis Valdez to the farmworkers, who subsequently made it their own. The *acto* is basically a short, flexible, dramatic sketch that communicates directly through the language and culture of the Chicanos in order to present a clear and concise social or political message. Humor, often slapstick, is of the essence as the opposition is satirized. According to Luis Valdez, *actos* are supposed to accomplish the following: "Inspire the audience to social action. Illuminate specific points about social problems. Satirize the opposition. Show or hint at solution. Express what people are feeling."[7] The *acto* is usually improvised by the *teatro* collectively and then reworked into final form. It thus arises from the members' common experiences and reflects in an uncontrived fashion their participation in the culture and folklore of their communities.

Because of the *actos'* flexibility and its introduction as a grass-roots Chicano theatrical form, it soon became the dramatic vehicle for the varied experiences of Mexican Americans not only in the fields of the Southwest, but also in factories and steel mills, on college campuses, and even on the welfare rolls, as shall be seen later in this chapter. Also aiding in the fast growth of the *teatro* movement was the Teatro Campesino's leadership in founding in 1971 the Teatro Nacional de Aztlán (TENAZ),[8] the national organization of *teatros,* and the publication of its book of *actos.* But it must be emphasized that much of *teatro* is learned and transmitted orally and visually without the use of scripts or notes. Very few of the community groups ever use scripts, preferring to collectively improvise their material and then memorize the parts. It is an effective means, quite suited to *teatro*'s spontaneity and its objective of remaining up-to-date and tailoring performances to specific audiences. But of course this procedure also makes for an ephemeral and easily lost body of dramatic work. It is easy to see that for the most of these groups, creating a lasting dramatic statement is far from their minds. Nor are most of the groups mindful of the need to circulate their works so that other *teatros* may adopt them. Much of the material developed by Campesino and other theaters has been imitated or adapted in oral form only. I remember how, as a member of the Teatro Chicano de Austin, I learned my first role in *Los Vendidos* [*The Sell-Outs*], an *acto* "borrowed" from Campesino. We called it the "Tex-Mex Curio Shop." I learned my role only by copying its enactment by the director, Juan Chavira, without the benefit of a script or notes, or of ever having seen the Teatro Campesino. It was not uncommon in those days—and this is still true for many *teatros*—for one member of our group to teach us an *acto* from memory that he had seen performed by another *teatro*. And this was how other *teatros* adapted some of our own original material. In fact, I was surprised to find material that our group had created in Texas being performed by other *teatros* as far away as Seattle. . . .

The oral nature of *teatro* transmission is also apparent in the way community groups, not *teatros*, adopt an *acto* to perform on their own. For example, the Teatro Chicano de Austin had developed various *actos* to support the national boycott of lettuce for the United Farmworkers Organizing Committee (UFWOC). The local UFWOC workers, after seeing the *actos* performed at a rally, learned the material and began performing the skits on picket lines in front of supermarkets. This also occurs, of course, with the *corridos* that *teatros* compose and sing. In fact, many *teatros* provide sheets of lyrics to assist audiences in singing along.

A Short Survey of Latino Folk Theaters

While many *teatros* began by performing Teatro Campesino material, the groups that were most closely tied to their own communities soon developed their own material by adapting Campesino's style and the *acto* to their own sociopolitical reality, a reality that was more often than not an urban one. Such was the case with groups like El Teatro Chicano de Austin, Gary's Teatro Desengaño del Pueblo, Chicago's Teatro Trucha, Denver's Su Teatro and Teatro la Causa de los Pobres, Los Angeles' Teatro Urbano, Tierra Amarilla's Teatro de la Sierra, and Camden's Teatro Alma Latina.

El Teatro Chicano de Austin was founded and directed by Juan Chavira in 1969 after he had worked with a farmworker theater in the Rio Grande Valley of Texas. The group combined University of Texas students and high school students from East Austin. While continuing to perform works relevant to the farmworker struggle and life in South Texas, the group gradually developed material that was more oriented to East Austin. Much of the new material propagandized the need for bilingual education and the teaching of Chicano history and culture in the schools. This was accomplished through the short, satirical schoolroom scenes of *Escuela* [*School*], *High School,* and *Brainwash.* Discrimination in local hospital emergency services was attacked in *Hospital,* while *Juan Pistolas* satirized police treatment of Chicanos. The group also supported local Mexican-American candidates for election to the city council and became heavily involved in voter registration drives. The burlesque of the politician and his campaign practices in one *acto,* and the demonstration of the need for Chicano poll watchers in another became so well known that during election time the group was called to perform not only throughout East Austin, but in neighboring towns and cities whose Chicano citizens were beginning to organize for political representation. Like many other *teatros,* El Teatro Chicano was ready to improvise *actos* on issues that emerged overnight, such as the police killing of an unarmed teenager in East Austin, racist incidents at a local Catholic church, a local furniture workers' strike, a rally against the practices of the Department of Housing and Urban Development program (in San Antonio), and various protest marches. While the group's main sphere of activity was Austin, it was often called to perform in neighboring towns and as far away as San Antonio, Dallas, and Houston. Once the group made the long trip to perform in Eagle Pass and on another occasion traveled to Washington, D.C., where it had been invited to perform at the American Folklife Festival held by the Smithsonian Institute. Today the members that were formerly high school students have inherited the group and converted it into a theater that mainly serves the needs of Chicano students at the University of Texas at Austin.

El Teatro Desengaño del Pueblo was founded in Gary in 1972 by this author and a combination of Indiana University Northwest students and nonstudents from the surrounding community. Over the past four years, Desengaño has lost most of its student membership and is presently made up of community people ranging in age from five to forty. But even when the group was dominated by students, they were nontraditional students who were often full-time steelworkers besides being registered students at the urban, nonresidential campus. From the outset the group created material not on student life but on life in Gary and East Chicago as seen by the Mexican, Chicano, and Puerto Rican residents. Desengaño dramatized community issues like Chicano and Puerto Rican unity in *Frijol y Habichuela* [*Beans*], discrimination in employment in *The Employment Office,* the need for bilingual-bicultural education in *Escuela* and *Brainwash,* drugs in *Juan Bobo,* local politics in *La Política [Politics]* and *El Alcalde [The Mayor],* dehumanizing work in the steel mills in *Burundanga.* Other material was designed to provide a sense of history, culture, and identity through *teatro: Papá México, El Grito de Lares [Puerto Rican Independence], Identity* and *Baile [Dance].* Like El Teatro Chicano de Austin, Desengaño performs extensively throughout the community at rallies, holiday celebrations, schools, churches, and parks. But the group has also traveled throughout the Midwest performing for the little Mexican colonies in Ohio and Wisconsin, and at universities in Indiana, Illinois, Wisconsin, and Michigan. A long, protracted struggle in which the group has been involved is the battle for the establishment of bilingual-bicultural education in northwest Indiana. Over the past four years the group has performed for teachers, P.T.A.'s, conferences, and rallies in an effort to sensitize the populace and the public institutions to the educational needs of Latinos. Desengaño has also been a faithful member of TENAZ and attended festivals as far away as Mexico City, Los Angeles, San Antonio, and Seattle.[9]

Founded in 1973, Compañía Trucha of Chicago's Eighteenth Street barrio, began as a very earthy and raucous satirical group that was associated with the Casa Aztlán Community Center. Hard-hitting but humorous satire, through a style that is as unsophisti-cated as it is relevant and direct to the people of the barrio, is Trucha's stock in trade. The ills of urban life, monotonous and dangerous factory work, and dramatizations of actual events fill their *actos.* In one of their pieces a local Mexican entrepreneur's exploitation of illegal Mexican labor, and of community radio and television, is satirized in such a direct and outrageously funny manner that the barrio audience's instant recognition and delight fulfills the highest expectations of direct and concrete relevance of this type of theater. In another *acto, El león y los crickets [The Lion and the Crickets],* the people's struggle as a minority within the United States is allegorized through a timeless folktale. Their current *acto, El Hospital de San Lucas [St. Luke's Hospital]* is the result of their work with a community organization that is making demands on St. Luke's Presbyterian Hospital to serve the needs of the barrio in which it is located. Compañía Trucha is one of the local theaters that has weathered the storm of leftist organizations and protest theaters that have tried to transform such grass-roots theaters into more sophisticated "cultural arms" of the international class struggle. While at one point swayed to produce more ideological drama, Trucha has returned to its original role in the community and its authentic style.

Two theaters in Denver, Su Teatro and Teatro la Causa de los Pobres, work extensively within their own communities. Su Teatro, while originating as a student group that applied Aztec and Mayan mythology to contemporary issues, has gradually redirected its efforts towards the dramatization of community issues. Its latest work, *El corrido de Auraria* [*The Ballad of Auraria*], relives the tragedy of the destruction of some of its own members' former neighborhood, Auraria, to make way for the building of a college. Ironically, one street of the barrio was preserved in the middle of the new campus to serve as faculty offices and a "living monument to historic Denver." La Causa de los Pobres, on the other hand, is made up of welfare mothers and their children. It began as an expression of Denver's Chicano Welfare Rights Organization and continues to dramatize the injustices of the welfare system that the poor mothers—there are no men in the group—continue to experience in their daily lives. The group's natural concern of course is with its children and their development. La Causa de los Pobres' material, therefore, criticizes not only the welfare system but the schools and the police as well. Drawn from life are their outlandish and biting parodies of such people as the superintendent of schools, Chief of Police Dill (Sour Pickle), and school board member, Mrs. Bradford (Mrs. Bratfart).

More rurally oriented than the others are New Mexico's Teatro de la Sierra and South Jersey's Teatro Alma Latina. Sierra is made up mostly of high school students along with a few other people ranging in age from five to thirty. Once again in a *rascuachi*[10] ("down to earth and unsophisticated") but direct manner, this group addresses issues relevant to Mexican Americans in New Mexico's Tierra Amarilla region. Its current *acto, Narangutang* [*The Orangutan* or *The Monster*], is an exposure of a corrupt, *caudillo-* ["boss"] type sheriff, and of the lack of community services like paved streets. El Teatro Alma Latina, on the other hand, serves Puerto Rican agricultural workers in South Jersey. Their *El Emigrao* [*The Emigrant*] demonstrates why Puerto Ricans leave their island to work in the tomato fields of Jersey and shows their exploitation by agribusiness. Their other *actos* dramatize poor working conditions, unemployment, and abuses by the State Employment Service. Their most imaginative and comical satire is expressed in their exposure of the *espiritistas* ("spiritualists" or "mediums") that take advantage of the Puerto Rican laborers, especially around payday.

Each of these groups, as well as the more experienced and professionalized theaters, has in one way or another used various types of folklore in communicating their sociopolitical messages. By far the most popular and effective folkloric media adapted by *teatros* are the *corrido* and the *cuento* ["folk tale"]. In addition, *teatros* emulate popular language patterns, diction and dialects, and enrich their theatrical language with popular phrases, sayings, and proverbs. *Teatros* also make use of folkloric artifacts like masks, costumes, and musical instruments.

The Corrido

From the beginning, Chicano theaters have combined singing with their dramatic presentations to warm up the audience in preparation for the *actos,* to create variety, or to reinforce the themes presented in the *actos* themselves. The usual reason given for the incorporation of *corridos* was that the barrio audience liked them and, if copies of the songs were handed out to the audience, people would sing along. The *corridos,* especially the border ballads and the ones that deal with historical themes, also coincided in spirit and impact with a great deal of *teatro* material. A few *teatros,* moreover, were fortunate enough to have as members *corridistas* ("composers of *corridos"*). They in turn had in *teatro* a great means of distributing their compositions, which at times gained for them a minor following and the opportunity to have their songs recorded. The most famous of the *teatro* composers are Agustín Lira and Daniel Valdez[11] of Teatro Campesino, Ramón Moroyoqui Sánchez (Chunky),[12] formerly of Teatro Mestizo, and Rumel Fuentes, formerly of Teatro Chicano de Austin.

The *corrido* in Chicano theater became so important that in 1971 TENAZ sponsored a workshop on the *corrido* and the ways of incorporating it into *teatro* performances. In truth, many *teatros* had already been experimenting with the incorporation of the *corrido* into the *actos* themselves. Some, like Seattle's Teatro del Piojo, had presented tableaus of the Mexican Revolution through the dramatization and singing of the most famous *corridos* from the revolution. Others, like the *teatro* of the Colegio Jacinto Treviño in Texas, created abstract mimic routines to *corridos* like *"Valentín de la Sierra."* The Teatro Chicano de Austin indicted the power of Texas ranchers and their use of the Texas Rangers to subdue Mexican Americans who once owned the ranchers' lands. The *teatro* turned the tables on the ranchers and the rangers by bringing to life the hero of the *"Corrido de Jacinto Treviño,"* who was treated as an historical personage. The *acto* would begin with the singing of the "Corrido de Jacinto Treviño," followed by a monologue in which a rancher gloated over his lands, power, and wealth. The rancher would then train two, dumb, doglike Texas Rangers to attack Chicanos and blacks. When the rangers attacked picketing farm-workers, from backstage would be heard the following verse of the *corrido*:

> Entrenle, rinches cobardes.
> El pleito no es con un niño,
> Qué bien conocen su padre.
> Yo soy Jacinto Treviño.
>
> Come on in, you cowardly rangers.
> You're not dealing with a child,
> Come and meet your father,
> I am Jacinto Treviño.

As this verse is sung, Jacinto Treviño himself comes on stage with guns-a-blazing and, after being confronted by the rangers who grab him by the lapels (as in the *corrido*), he shoots them dead. The *corrido* is once again sung, this time with the audience joining in.

It was the Teatro Campesino, however, that pioneered the *corrido* as a dramatic form and demonstrated its artistic and cultural possibilities in one of its finest works, *La Gran Carpa de la Familia Rasquachi* [*The Theatre Tent of the Rasquachi Family*] (cf. Kourilsky 1973:44-46). The *Gran Carpa* is a very fast-paced collage of scenes that follow three generations of an archetypal Chicano family. A series of *corridos* provide the narration to the action and create the rhythm and mood to which the actors execute their mime and dance. The *Gran Carpa* has been performed throughout the nation and abroad, and has been strongly influential in populariz-ing the *corrido* dramatic technique. Another work by El Teatro

Campesino, *El Corrido,* has also had great impact, mainly due to its nationwide television broadcast.

The *Gran Carpa* is not, however, the best example of the *corrido* as a dramatic form; it is too extensive and diffuse. El Teatro de la Gente's *Corrido de Juan Endrogado* [*The Ballad of Juan Endrogado*], written by Director Adrián Vargas, is the finest illustration of the *corrido's* formalistic qualities. It is a light, dramatic piece whose performance consists of constant mime and dance movement to the beat of the *corridos* and other songs which provide the narration. The actors wear exaggerated makeup, as the *corrido* is designed to depart from realism; for the *corrido* is lyrical, satirical, lightly philosophical, and somewhat reminiscent of ballet. As the *corrido* concentrates on themes already familiar to the barrio, it can help to coalesce the public's opinion on the matters at hand, but it is in no way comparable to the directness of the agitprop *acto.* The *corrido* wins over the audience with the use of familiar songs, esthetically attractive costumes and acting style, and the creation of easily recognizable scenes and situations. As in the *acto,* there is no scenery, and props are minimal.

El Corrido de Juan Endrogado accomplishes these objectives delightfully, and still manages to deal with the important theme of Mexican-American addiction to the ever-elusive American Dream. *Juan Endrogado* takes as its musical theme the well-known and very popular "Corrido de Juan Charrasqueado," a ballad that recounts the life and death of a hard-drinking, hard-loving gambler. Vargas changed the lyrics to tell the story of Juan Endrogado ("John Drugged"), a poor man who becomes addicted to the pursuit of the American Dream with its enticing material symbols and sexual fantasies: high-paying jobs, beautiful cars, fast women. Juan, after failing to attain these, achieves his dreams only in the stupor of drugs. But along with the addict's highs come the waking nightmares of withdrawal, theft to finance the habit, hunger, and ultimately, death.

Throughout the piece, which is interspersed with only sparse dialogue, the thematic music returns with the narrative line. *Juan Endrogado* opens with the singing of these lines, which can be compared to the original "Corrido de Juan Charrasqueado":

Juan Endrogado

Voy a cantarles un corrido de mi pueblo,
lo que has pasado muchas veces por acá,

la triste historia de un hermano endrogado
que por poquito con las drogas se mataba.

I'm going to sing you a *corrido* of my people,
about something that happens often out here,
the story of a dope-addicted brother,
who little by little was killing himself with drugs.

Juan Charrasqueado

Voy a cantarles un corrido muy mentado,
lo que ha pasado en la hacienda de la Flor,
la triste historia de un ranchero enamorado
que fue borracho, parrandero y jugador.

I'm going to sing a *corrido* that's quite famous,
about what happened at the Hacienda de la Flor,
the sad tale of an enamoured rancher
who was a drinker, a good-time Charlie and a gambler.

As the play progresses the new *corrido* becomes less and less like its model, and other types of songs are introduced to correspond in theme and mood with the action. At times the music is very somber and elegiac; other times it is fast and happy and the actors must keep pace by almost doing a two-step or a polka. Included in the repertoire of songs used and transformed in the play are these very popular numbers: "Cuánto Sufro en esta Vida" ["How I Suffer in this Life"] (ranchera), "El Muchacho Alegre" ["The Happy Boy"] (*corrido*), "Creí" ["I Believed"] (*bolero*), "Put on Your Red Dress" (rock and roll), and the melody to a Chevrolet television and radio commercial.

All of the lyrics, tunes, and actions are perfectly synchronized. At times, a song's original lyrics are not transformed per se but used to create stage irony. This is so with "A Medias de la Noche" ["At Midnight"]. It is sung to a scene where Juan is seized with hunger pains and the song's original lyrics take on a new, ironic meaning. It is no longer a loved one that is embracing Juan, as in the song, but Hunger herself:

A medias de la noche te soñaba.
Te soñaba abrazándote conmigo.
Te soñaba abrazándote conmigo,
pero ¡ay qué angustia
me ha dejado esta mujer!

> Around midnight I was dreaming of you.
> I dreamed that you were embracing me.
> I dreamed that you were embracing me,
> but oh what anguish
> this woman has caused me!

Thus, the *corrido* is a dramatic piece that brings the audience and actors close together. The barrio audiences have lived with these songs and love them. Both the actors and the audience, through the performance, are joined in a type of poetic union that arises spontaneously from the shared values and experiences. The *corrido* as a dramatic form is an innovation in Chicano theater, but hardly a departure from tradition. . . .

Folktales, Legends, and Personal Experience Narratives

Teatros throughout the country use several types of folk narrative techniques and structures in their works because their audiences are familiar with traditional types of oral communication. In Mexican folk culture, the *cuento* ("tale") has often been used to illustrate a moral or practical lesson. It is quite natural that Chicano theatres appropriate the *cuento* as a means of furthering the didactic purposes of the *acto*.

At a rally in Austin, César Chávez illustrated the need for unity among Chicanos by telling the tale of "Las Avispas" [*The Wasps*]. The Teatro Chicano de Austin, immediately impressed by the lesson and the form that it took, soon thereafter transformed the tale into a dramatic piece. This tale, which deals with the skill of an expert whip handler who tyrannizes all the animals of the forest except the wasps (does not mean White Anglo-Saxon Protestant here) who are organized, was also adopted by Mexico's Teatro Mascarones quite independently of César Chávez and Chicano theater. Los Mascarones used the tale to demonstrate the need for unity and organization to campesinos in Southern Mexico. Under similar circumstances, the Compañía Trucha heard Reies Tijerina use the tale of "El León y los Crickets." As mentioned above, Trucha gave the lion the identity of the dominant society in the United States, and the poor, powerless, little crickets became the Chicanos.

Many of the *teatros* have dramatized legends or helped to further elaborate them. The best known and most dramatized legend is that of La Llorona, "the Crying Lady." Legendary figures like Emiliano Zapata, Pancho Villa, and now Che Guevara continue to appear or be invoked in *actos* from coast to coast. Beyond the legend, religious figures taken directly from the miracle plays and *pastorelas* ["shepherds' plays"] have also made their way into *teatro*. San Antonio's Teatro de Artes Chicanos used to perform an allegory of a Poor Man, God, Death, and the Devil (complete with the devil's mask and costume from the *pastorela*). The Teatro Campesino and a few other groups annually produce the Virgin of Guadalupe miracle play for their local parishes on the Mexican patron saint's feast day.

Teatros have not only recreated and adapted certain folktales and legends, but also appropriated various folk figures like Pantaleón, Juan Pistolas, el Pelado, and Juan Bobo and placed them in new, urban surroundings. The *teatros* have also helped to solidify the characters of various other popular stereotypes like the Pachuco, the Vendido, the Coyote, and the Militante that have appeared in contemporary times. El Teatro Chicano de Austin characterized Pantaleón Manso as an unsuspecting, gullible Chicano who falls prey to the scheme of the ghetto used car, electrical appliance, and real estate salesmen. El Teatro Campesino based its *Carpa Cantinflesca* [*The Cantinflesque Theatre Tent*] and its *La Gran Carpa de la Familia Rasquachi* on the poverty-stricken, luckless character known in Mexico as *el pelado* ("the naked one") and made famous by the world-renowned comedian, Cantinflas. The Teatro Desengaño made use of Puerto Rico's most famous picaresque figure, Juan Bobo, in an *acto* designed to show teenagers that taking drugs is dumb.

Certain popular stereotypes have been forming in the course of the development of Chicano culture in the United States and they have steadily made their way into Chicano theater scenes. First and foremost of these popular figures is the Pachuco or zoot suiter, the teenage rebel who developed his own subculture in the forties and fifties. Almost every *teatro* has at one time or another paraded this swaggering, marijuana-smoking, *caló*-speaking hipster on its stage. Another character that was ubiquitous in early Chicano theater was the Vendido or Sell-Out, sometimes referred to as Tio Taco. He was the Mexican American who was bought by the system to deal with his own kind or to serve as token minority representation. The Coyote, of long tradition in the *corridos* that deal with Mexican labor in the United States, is the despicable labor contractor who exploits his own brothers on both sides of the border with his illegal gambit. The Militante is of course a parody of young Chicano militants who are seen as being very loud and menacing but assimilated to the dominant culture and thus rendered ineffective. Many of these character types are represented in Teatro Campesino's *Los Vendidos*, as robots for sale to the governor of California who is in need of someone to get him the Mexican-American vote. Also included in this *acto* is the Frito Bandito, Frito-Lay's corn chip bandit who has served as a gross stereotype of Mexicans in the mass media.

Chicano and Puerto Rican theaters have also taken the personal experience narrative as a basis for some of their work. New York's Teatro Calle 4 conducted a series of interviews with Puerto Ricans on the Lower East Side in preparing their *¿Qué Encontraste en Nueva York?* [*What Did You Find in New York?*] The result is a work that follows the misfortunes of a newly arrived *jíbaro* [Puerto Rican peasant], a country bumpkin who gets a rude awakening as an introduction to life in the New York ghettoes. He is duped, robbed, beaten, and finally becomes disillusioned. He resembles the protagonists of many a joke or tale about the transition from the Caribbean "paradise" to the urban jungle.

El Teatro de la Gente's *El Cuento de la Migra* [*The Tale of the Immigration Service*] is the story of an illegal immigrant from Mexico and his misfortunes at the hands of the border patrol, the labor contractor, the factory owner, and the Immigration and Naturalization Service. The *acto* begins with the following *corrido* stanza as historical background:

> Año de mil ocho cientos
> cuarenta y ocho corría
> firmaron dos gobernantes
> y a mi pueblo dividián.

> In the year eighteen hundred
> and forty-eight
> two rulers signed a contract
> and divided my people.

This is followed by a monologue effected in the style and speech patterns of an old-timer relating his personal experiences:

y desde ese entonces ha existido esa frontera por allí por el sur. Sí, pero una frontera muy caprichosa, no reconocida por el pueblo mexicano trabajado. Y si a mí me dicen que soy espalda mojada porque crucé un río asina de ancho, bien se sabrá el super-espalda mojada quien cruzó ese marezote. Sí, señor, porque a estas tierras yo he venido. También de estas tierras yo he nacido. Por eso les vengo a contar este cuento, el cuento de la migra. Sí, señor, esa víbora, ese animal que en estos días les está dando en la madre a nuestra madre. El cuento comienza en mil novecientos setenta cuando de repente. ¡Ahí viene la migra![13]

This example of the personal experience style as well as the other examples of narrative techniques used by *teatros* illustrate popular theater's attempts to communicate in the vernacular and to employ performance techniques that are familiar to Latino communities throughout the United States.

Language and Language Usage

The context in which a *teatro* uses English or Spanish is an extremely complex matter and depends on many variables, including the Spanish-English language dominance of the community and the dialects in use, the Spanish-English language dominance of the theater members, the social context of the *acto*, and the type of character that is speaking. Generally speaking, *teatros* use the language of their audiences, unless typing a character through dialect and other speech patterns. Various degrees of dominance of Spanish and English are represented in the communities and can depend on such factors as the length of time the individual community members have resided in the United States, their age and amount of schooling, or simply their language preference. The Puerto Rican *teatros* in New York and New Jersey use Spanish almost exclusively. Most of the Chicano theaters perform bilingually and have devised various strategies to deal with community language diversity. As always, *teatro* performances are flexible and subject to improvisation on the spot. Thus accommodations in language as well as content are often made during performances.

However complex the problem of bilingualism may be, *teatros* exhibit a gusto for oral expression that manifests itself not only in a richness of popular sayings, phrases, and proverbs, but also experimentation with different dialects and bilingual word play. The heterogeneous makeup of Latino communities is often reflected in *teatro* dialogues. The *caló* of Chicano youth and particularly of the Pachuco, the sing-song accent of immigrants from rural Mexico, the English-Spanish switching of many Southwesterners in particular, the lisping of the Spaniards, the rapid fire dialect of the Puerto Ricans, the hip language of the New York Puerto Ricans all can be found in the *actos*. El Teatro Desengaño del Pueblo depicts in linguistic form the conflict that has existed between Mexicans and Puerto Ricans in northwest Indiana in their *Frijol y Habichuela*. What is a bean to a Mexican (*frijol*) is not a bean to a Puerto Rican (*habichuela*). The *acto* goes from this initial lexical difference to differences in accent, culture, and race as the two characters, both of whom are identical beans, fight over their authenticity. After calling each other a series of names that have double meanings within the context of the *acto*, the beans unite and decide that their differences are not great enough to divide them.

Teatros explore all of the possibilities that bilingualism offers for creating humor, irony, and dramatic conflict. A standard bilingual ploy is the translating of the characters' names from Spanish to English. Such names as Juan Paniaguas, María Dolores de la Barriga, and Casimiro Flores are names that approach the ordinary in Spanish. But in English they become John Bread and Water, Mary Stomach Pains, and I Almost See Flowers. An unsympathetic character or a sell-out may be named Ben Dejo (*pendejo* means stupid or naive) or Ben Dido (*vendido* or sell-out). As far as dialogue is concerned, one can imagine the many misunderstandings between Anglos and Latinos that are depicted on stage because of misunderstanding each other's language.

Professionalism and Sophistication

Since the founding of the national Chicano theater organization (TENAZ) in 1971, a continuous effort has been made towards professionalizing *teatros*. The primary focus of the organization and its leadership, a coordinating council of regional representatives, has been on assisting theaters in developing acting and staging techniques and in creating more esthetically and politically sophisticated material. . . . Nevertheless, there is also a large number of groups that have looked upon these efforts at professionalization suspiciously and have considered them to be too fancy and too removed from their everyday reality and their issue-oriented theaters. The members of these groups have formed *teatros* not because they consider themselves actors, performers, or artists, but because *teatro* is a means of serving their communities in their struggle for civil rights and human dignity. . . . TENAZ, on the other hand, sees only a naive lack of discipline, commitment, and organization in those groups that fail to perform up to the level of their artistic potential. While there has always been an apparent respect in *teatros* for the *rascuachi,* TENAZ has had to impose standards of discipline that somewhat remove the organization from the groups that are probably closest to being folk theaters. El Teatro de Artes Chicanos de San Antonio, for example, was turned away from the TENAZ festival in Mexico City in 1965 because it had failed to register in advance. This has occured quite often because many groups, through their lack of business planning or organization and because they are not professionals, do not spend time corresponding by mail, filling out questionnaires, establishing checking accounts, or even maintaining a permanent address. In many cases, their own performances are arranged strictly by word of mouth. If they decide to attend a festival or workshop, they often do so at the last minute possible and often with the idea that they are going basically to perform and to see what the other *teatros* are up to. In many cases improving their art or having a study session on radical politics is the furthest thing from their minds.

In spite of all of these efforts at professionalization, the only *teatro* that has succeeded in becoming a full-time, professional theater is the Teatro Campesino. . . . For Campesino, professionalism was a goal fostered and realized through the efforts of the university-trained playwright and director, Luis Valdez. It represented the only avenue to a full exploration of the esthetic and cultural possibilities of the Mexican-American theatrical form that Campesino had helped to invent. . . . While it is assumed that the ultimate goal of some groups is to serve as the cultural and propagandistic arm of a proletarian revolution, their theaters relate more directly to advanced political study groups than to the working classes in the barrios. In that they do not have this intimate relationship with the barrio and its culture, they find themselves often performing for audiences that are made up of people like themselves, politically sophisticated students or graduates involved in radical political movements of the Left. Their purpose is therefore defeated if they fail to reach the real working class that is supposed to effect their desired revolution. These groups have merely become more specialized in the type of community that they serve. Where once they related to the entire barrio, they now serve one segment of the

El Teatro Desengaño del Pueblo's *Inflation. José Gonzalez.*

Teatro Campesino's *El Fin del Mundo* (*The End of the World*). *Nicolás Kanellos.*

El Teatro la Causa de los Pobres, Denver. *José Gonzalez.*

El Teatro de la Gente's *El Cuento de la Migra* (*The Tale of the Immigration Service*). *Nicolás Kanellos.*

El Teatro de la Sierra's *Narangutang. Nicolás Kanellos.*

barrio, a segment that is probably in transition and in the process of leaving, the young Chicano leftists.

As Chicano and Puerto Rican theaters become more known and accepted, the demand for their performances and their presence within the academic community increases. Because of the solid, popular base that *teatros* have created over the last eleven years, today more and more Chicano and Puerto Rican playwrights are appearing on the contemporary scene, more Chicano and Puerto Rican drama classes are being taught at universities and high schools, and more plays by Latinos are being produced in legitimate theater houses on Broadway, off-Broadway, and at universities. The appearance of the playwright in *teatro* is an indication of professionalization in many cases. There is a conversion from collective creation to the specialization of services that is taking place in the most professionalized groups. Luis Valdez was a playwright even before founding the Teatro Campesino, but Campesino did not produce any of his plays before taking that great step to leave the service of the farmworkers' union. Adrián Vargas, after his initial involvement in *teatro*, returned to the university to receive advanced training in playwriting. Groups officially supported by universities, such as El Teatro de la Esperanza, El Teatro Aztlán of California State College at Northridge, the Bilingual Repertory Theater Company at Texas A&I University, and Teatro Libre of Indiana University at Bloomington, have customarily produced plays written by a single member of their group, a well-known Chicano author, or a professor at their school. Finally, the playwright without the theater group is also becoming a reality, as a more middle class and academic audience for Latino theater develops. Of course, the works of these writers, which are destined to be performed for a heterogeneous, theater-going public, and by professional actors unknown to the author, have less and less folkloric content. Perhaps as the Latino middle class grows, the need for the type of grass-roots theater that has been examined here will diminish and instead Latino life will increasingly be reflected in the mass media, on Broadway, and on television. But for now, *teatro* is alive and well in the United States.

Notes

1. For a partial list of Chicano theaters and their addresses, see *TENAZ Directory* (1974).

2. According to R. G. Davis (1975:166), agitprop "is agitational propaganda. Agitprop theatre is made up of skits performed by people who, like their audience, are directly engaged in the content of the skit. For example, Teatro Campesino, when performing in Delano, California, in 1965-1967, presented agitational propaganda for the members of the National Farm Workers Association (NFWA). Their songs and *actos* "were designed to inform the workers of union negotiations, grievances, and programs. The performers were engaged in organizing work, and their *actos* were extensions of that work."

3. For a detailed history of the Teatro Campesino, see Kourilsky (1973).

4. Sylvia Drake (1970:56) compares Luis Valdez to Jean-Louis Barrault and François Rabelais. R. G. Davis (1975) compares at length the work of Luis Valdez with that of the five other radical theatre directors: Joe Chaiken, Richard Schecter, Julian Beck, Peter Schumann, and himself.

5. Most people are unaware that the lyrics to "El Picket Sign" and "Viva Huelga en General" were composed by Luis Valdez (n.d.) and are included in a mimeographed songbook, ca. 1967-1971. They also have circulated anonymously hundreds of song sheets and songbooks distributed free, or sold by *teatros* throughout the country.

6. Prior to founding El Teatro Campesino, Luis Valdez worked with the San Francisco Mime Troupe, where he learned some of the agitprop techniques that he would later apply in *teatro*. He also performed in the Troupe's *comedia* style performance of Lope de Rueda's sixteenth-century *paso* (the Spanish version of the *comedia*), *Las aceitunas* (*The Olives*) (cf. Huerta [1973:15]).

7. TENAZ was founded at the first conference of Chicano theater directors held in Fresno, California, in 1971 and sponsored by El Teatro Campesino.

8. During the last two years El Teatro Desengaño del Pueblo has become increasingly more professionalized and sophisticated. Its current production, in fact, is a play, *Silent Partners*, written entirely by its director rather than by the group as a whole.

9. The term *rascuache* is defined by Santamaría (1974) as an adjective meaning (*"miserable," "ruin," "pobre"*); that is, it is usually a miserable, run-down, or poor place. The term used by *teatros*, however, is often applied to the poor people of the barrios, or their poor, earthy, or unsophisticated lifestyle. Many *teatros* have preferred to spell the word *"rasquachi"* either in deference to its Aztec derivation or because of the influence of English orthography. Its termination in *"i"* instead of *"e,"* in my text and in *teatro* usage, is related to the word's common pronunciation.

10. An album of Valdez's songs, *Mestizo* (CAM Records Sp-3622), was recorded in 1974 and sold at *teatro* performances.

11. A few *corridos* by Chunky were published anonymously (Teatro Mestizo 1974). The lyrics to his "La Guitarra Compesina" and "El Corrido Rasquachi" have also been published (Chunky 1974:4-5).

12. The words and music to a few of Rumel Fuentes' *corridos* have been published (1973:3-40). His "Soy Chicano" and "Corrido de César Chávez" were recorded by Arhoolie (45-529B) in 1975. In 1970, the Teatro Chicano de Austin recorded his "Yo Soy Tu Hermano" ("I Am Your Brother") and "Mexico-Americano" to be sold at *teatro* performances. The five hundred copies were all sold, and this album was never distributed. However, Arhoolie recorded "Mexico-Americano" on its album, *Music of La Raza*, vol. 1 (3002).

13. "And from that time on the border just south of us has existed. Sure, but it's a very capricious border, not recognized by Mexican workers. And if somebody has the nerve to call me a wetback just because I crossed a little river just so wide, he better find out who's the super wetback who crossed that great ocean to get here. Yes, sir, because I came to this land. But I was also born in this land. That's why I've come to tell you this story, the story

about the *migra* (The Immigration and Naturalization Service). Yes, sir, that snake, that animal that's putting it to our mother (literally "Mexico," figuratively "fucking our mothers"). The story begins in 1970 when all of a sudden: Watch out, here comes the *migra!*"

References

Alvarez, George R.
1967   "Caló: The 'Other Spanish'." *ETC. A Review of General Semantics* 34 (March):7-13.

Chunky
1974   *Revista Chicano-Requeña* 2 (summer):4-5.

Davis, R. G.
1975   *The San Francisco Mime Troup: The First Ten Years.* Palo Alto, Calif.: Rampart Press.

Drake, Sylvia
1970   *"El Teatro Campesino:* Keeping the Revolution on Stage." *Performing Arts* 8:56.

Fuentes, Rumel
1973   *El Grito* 6 (spring):3-40.

Huerta, Jorge
1973   "Concerning Teatro Chicano." *Latin American Theater Review* 6:15.

Kanellos, Nicolás
1976   "Séptimo Festival de los Teatros." *Latin American Theatre Review* 10 (fall).
n.d.   "Elementas Hispánicos en el teatro chicano." *Actas del XVII del Congreso del Instituto Internacional de Literature Iberoamericana.* Madrid: Instituto de Cultura Hispánica, forthcoming.

Kourilsky, François
1973   "Approaching Quetzalcoatl. The Evolution of El Teatro Campesino." *Performance* 7:37-46.

Loo, Guillermo
1976   "Editorial." *El Boletín Cultural de TENAZ* 1:1-2.

Santamaría, Francisco J.
1974   *Diccionario de Mejicanismos.* Mexico City: Editorial Porrúa.

Teatro Chicano de Austin
1974   "Las Avispas." *Revista Chicano-Requena* 2 (summer):8-10.

Teatro Mestizo
1974   *Cantos Rebeledes de América.* San Diego, Calif.: Toletcás en Aztlán.

TENAZ Directory
1974   *Chicano Theatre Three.* Pp. 50-54.

Valdez, Luis, and *El Teatro Campesino*
1971   *Actos.* Fresno, Calif.: Cucaracha Press.
n.d.   *Cancionero de la Raza.* Fresno, Calif.: Teatro Campesino. Mimeo.

8

Flesh Pots, Faith, or Finances?
Fertility Rates Among
Mexican Americans

María-Luisa Urdaneta

Introduction

Mexican Americans have the highest birthrate of any ethnic group in the United States (Moore 1970:84-85). This rate is about 50 percent higher than that of the overall U.S. population (U.S. Commission on Civil Rights 1968:11; Uhlenberg 1973:34-35).

This exceptionally high fertility has been attributed to cultural factors such as Catholicism[1] (Johnson 1975; Leñero-Otero 1968); *machismo*[2] (Stycos 1968; Madsen 1964:49); and a socialization process that leads Chicanas to regard childbearing and childrearing as their main function in life (Clark 1959:119; Madsen 1964:48-53; and Murillo 1971:104). Of particular concern to this paper is the fact that family planning clinics' staff accept this cultural explanation and are organized and administered accordingly. However, when the data are examined closely, it becomes apparent that the group is not homogeneous. Census and survey data show that it is only Mexican-American women of low income and low educational levels who have the larger families, while professional Mexican-American women exhibit almost exactly the same average number of children as do similarly educated whites in the United States (Bradshaw and Bean 1972:10). Because only a small percentage of all Mexican Americans have completed four years of high school,[3] the low fertility of the better educated has little influence upon this ethnic group's birthrate (Uhlenberg 1973:35).

I collected and compared data on fertility regulation practices of two distinct groups of Mexican-American women: the medically indigent (poor) and the business and professional Chicanas (non-poor). My data suggest that neither the cultural patterns of Mexican Americans nor the structure of Anglo society alone is sufficient to explain the high fertility rate of lower-class Mexican-American women. Rather, one must analyze the macrosystem that is comprised of both Anglo and Mexican-American microsystems. This chapter will (1) argue that the cultural explanations advanced in the literature inadequately account for my observations; (2) offer a more complex model for explaining fertility regulation behavior; and (3) suggest a broader applicability of my analysis.

Field Methodology

Preliminary data for this study were gathered during a period of eighteen months (April 1972–November 1973) when I was working as a registered nurse and researcher with the Model Cities Family Planning Clinic in Alcala[4] (pseudonym), a Texas city of 400,000 people. Additional visits to the clinic were conducted intermittently in May through August of 1974, 1975, and 1976. The Model Cities Family Planning Clinic is a recently instituted clinic (1971) for the medically indigent—those people officially recognized by the government as unable to afford medical services. Most of its clients (81 percent) are Mexican-American women; 16 percent are black women, and 3 percent are Anglo women and others. By virtue of a previous arrangement with the clinic director, there was an opportunity to interview most (72 percent) of the Chicanas. In addition to the clinic-eligibility interview required for acceptance as a client, many Chicana clients voluntarily permitted several sessions of intensive interviewing in their own homes.

This particular clinic was chosen for study because it serves a higher proportion of Chicanas and has a much lower drop-out rate (18 percent) than the other two service providers. The other providers are: Planned Parenthood, with a drop-out rate of 45 percent; and the Family Planning Outpatient Clinic of Alcala's city-county hospital, with a drop-out rate of 50 percent.

In June 1974, the writer was chosen by the Mexican-American Business and Professional Women of Alcala (MABPWA) to be a member of the subcommittee on health care. The MABPWA membership, upon learning of my activities with the family planning clinic in the barrio voted to hold several "rap sessions" for their members on topics dealing with sexuality, birth control, and sensitivity training and encounters. This arrangement resulted in many private, intensive interviews of these members. Out of these "rap sessions" an additional committee was formed entitled "Chicana Counseling." This committee provided significant data and new informants for the research.

In my role of participant observer, I accompanied clients throughout Alcala's city-county health care system and related agencies (e.g., clinic and hospital admitting offices, social service, surgery, obstetrical department, labor and delivery, public welfare, legal aid, food stamp program headquarters, child-care centers, clergy consultation services on problem pregnancy, abortion clinics, and private M.D. abortion services).

Findings

This section will explore a number of variables that have been advanced as *the* explanation for high birthrates. Each will be examined in turn and their weaknesses revealed.

Catholicism

Eighty-nine percent of Model Cities Family Planning Clinic Chicanas are nominally Catholic. Yet of those intensively interviewed (125) not one voiced objections to birth control on religious grounds. Instead, clients (92 percent of whom are using one of the birth control methods that requires a physician's prescription) justify the use of effective contraceptives as physician-prescribed behavior in which one engages to prevent aggravation of illness. Thus the typical clinic client acts as if the pill and the intrauterine device (I.U.D.) are medicine prescribed by a physician and have little if any relation to the church's doctrinal stand on birth control. Others believe the Catholic Church to be changing, shifting from its secular role (where edicts are institutional and binding) to one primarily comforting and traditional. These findings support those of Kay (1974), Alvírez (1973), and O'Grady (1973), in which Catholic Mexican Americans seem unfettered by Catholic legalistic dicta on the use of birth control. This is illustrated by the following case study.

Maria Alicia Guerrero is a 25-year-old housewife, and an obese (5'2", 202 lbs.) Mexican national. One of her brothers is an ordained

Catholic priest. Maria Alicia is the mother of two girls. When she first came to the clinic she was seven months pregnant with her third child. She and her husband are here without legal papers, and reside at the home of Mr. Guerrero's divorced sister.

The Guerreros were planning to have this baby delivered—like the previous two—by a *partera* ("midwife"), but due to Maria Alicia's umbilical hernia which has grown progressively larger with each pregnancy (along with her obesity), they decided to risk seeking medical services. They were advised by their doctor in Mexico (prior to their emigration to Texas) to have the hernia repaired. Also, on the advice of their doctor, they would like to avoid having more children for a while.

After the usual clinic admission conference, Maria Alicia enrolled for prenatal services and the clinic secretary helped her to make the necessary arrangements with the city-county hospital for weekly payments on the future bill for her obstetrical delivery and hernia repair. Mrs. Guerrero delivered a son at the city-county hospital in March 1974, and soon thereafter a hernia repair operation was performed. On her four weeks postdelivery medical checkup visit at the Family Planning Clinic, she began an oral contraceptive regimen. The last field note entry on Maria Alicia is dated August 1976. She is still a successful oral contraceptor.

The Guerreros are not unique in viewing the use of effective contraceptives as a medical rather than religious concern. As generalized health care becomes a matter of knowledge and control, more and more Mexican Americans move in this direction. One aspect of the religious dimension that needs to be explored is the effect of the ideological split that has existed since colonial times among Latin-American Catholic clergy. As Tannenbaum (1960:60-61) has noted, traditionally in Latin America the lower clergy—being mostly *mestizos* (mixed descent) and the poorer members of the Catholic hierarchy—have disobeyed their bishops and identified themselves with the specific clientele with whom they have greatest contact— the poor. Catholic Church dignitaries, being mainly European, have aligned themselves, traditionally, with the papacy in Rome. In my experience, it appears that parish priests who are Chicanos rather than European or South American are less prone to oppose openly their parishioners' use of effective contraceptives.

Both of the Chicano priests in parishes within the model cities area are quiet supporters of this clinic's efforts. In 1974 there were seven referrals for family planning services from priests in these parishes and in 1975 there were nine (according to the records of the Family Planning Clinic from 1974 and 1975). Also, for the past three years the clinic's RN's have received at least two invitations per year from the above-mentioned Catholic parishes to speak about fertility regulation to several young couples engaged to be married.

Machismo

Less than one percent of clinic Chicanas reported that their husbands or sexual partners oppose the use of birth control. This striking finding can be explained if one adequately understands what is meant by *machismo*. This concept forms part of a configuration of male dominance that investigators have ascribed to the Mexican-American male. The most strongly emphasized aspect of this configuration has been the masculine need to demonstrate virility through the siring of many children. However, *machismo* is more than sexual prowess; it also includes elements of courage, honor, respect for others, as well as adequate provision for one's family. Thus, there are some inherent contradictions in the idea (Alvírez and Bean 1976:277-278).

Siring as many offspring as possible often would conflict with the fulfillment of the other components of *machismo*, e.g., providing fully for one's family. Furthermore, individual components of the concept may be valued differently by different males, e.g., one individual may order "sexual virility" higher than "providing for family." If so, he may discourage his wife from using fertility regulating methods. Or, he may believe that having many children now will provide social insurance in his old age. This again could cause him to discourage his wife from using family planning services. If he ranks virility higher than family honor, he may encourage his wife to use Family Planning Clinic services to avoid the expense of raising and educating several children because he would rather use that money in courting and making sexual conquests.

Instead of male opposition to his partner's use of birth control, data from the target population of this study suggest that a large proportion of these women's mates appear to view contraception as a woman's problem and a woman's choice; e.g., if she does not want to conceive, she is the one that selects and obtains the means to prevent pregnancy. (Due to time and financial limitations affecting this research it was not feasible to interview Mexican-American males.)

Social Roles of Chicanas

My data indicate that indigent Chicanas do not perceive themselves exclusively as wives and mothers. Whether by choice or necessity, over 20 percent of Model Cities Program–area Chicanas suggest that more would seek employment if their work options were not severely limited by their low educational achievement, their minimal job skills, unavailability of child-care services, inadequacy of public transportation, and lack of money to pay for the medical history and physical examination—a usual prerequisite for employment. The jobs available to these Chicanas are undesirable because of low wages, temporary or seasonal employment, split shifts (cafeteria and restaurant food servers and waitresses), minimal employment benefits (e.g., lack of hospitalization insurance), and poor working conditions such as excessive heat (laundries), or contact with hazardous materials (fiberglass-boat factory). The following case study illustrates some of the problems that limit the employability of Chicanas who desire jobs.

Maria Gomez first made contact with the clinic when she was three months pregnant and desired an abortion. Six weeks earlier when her husband had gone to live with another woman, Maria had no financial resources other than welfare. She was offered an evening-shift job at a chain store close to her home, and it was possible for her to accept employment only because her *comadre* ["comother"] and Maria's oldest daughter (13 years old) were available to baby-sit with her younger children. However, before she could qualify for the job, Maria had to submit to a medical history and physical examination. At that time (December 1973) pregnant women were not hired because the store manager did not want to train an employee contemplating only temporary employment.

The Model Cities Program Family Planning Clinic nurse was able to get Maria a staff (charity) card at the city-county hospital; and the private gynecologist, Dr. Jones (whose services were paid by Medicaid), was able to post Mrs. Gomez's procedure on the following day's hospital surgical schedule. This in itself was quite a feat because at that time (late 1973) the local medical association—pressured by a local university feminist group and the recent federal ruling legalizing abortion—had reluctantly agreed to allow physicians who wished to do so to perform abortions, but only three local gynecologists (out of a total of fifty-six) are willing to perform therapeutic abortions in Alcala. Prior to December 1973, poor women desiring an abortion had little choice but to travel eighty miles to another city. This entailed arranging for transportation, obtaining child-care services, and being away from home for ten or more hours.

Mrs. Gomez tolerated the termination of pregnancy procedure quite well. A week later she started work in her new job. The last field note entry on Mrs. Gomez is dated July 1975. She has left the chain store and is now employed as a teacher's aide—making 17¢ more per hour—at a nearby grammar school.

There is further evidence that Chicanas who are poor do not necessarily desire large families. My research findings reveal that by the time clinic clients have borne three children, 96 percent of them have used some contraceptive, although for many the use was sporadic and haphazard. But this sporadic use my be less the result of disinterest in fertility control than due to the unavailability of effective contraception. Some of the factors that inhibit availability and effective use of contraceptives are:

1. None of the effective contraceptives (birth control pills and I.U.D.'s) are available over the counter. They must be dispensed by a physician and only after the client has undergone a medical history and physical examination.

2. Some women who desire to use effective contraceptives cannot tolerate them physically. For example, the pill may be contra-indicated in women with a medical history of breast or uterine cancer, liver disease, and blood clotting disturbances. Women with history of diabetes, high blood pressure, or migraine headaches can use the pill but only under close medical supervision. Also, physicians will not fit women with intrauterine devices if they have histories of pelvic inflammatory disease or caesarean sections, or have not given vaginal birth.

3. Obtaining effective contraceptive devices through (charity) clinics requires clients to interact with bureaucrats whom they fear. For example, a Chicana who has a venereal disease knows that the family planning physican or nurse is required to report the case to authorities in the health department. She further knows that the health department in turn will advise (and at times coerce) her to make the costly sacrifice of work time in order to recover or to

undergo further diagnostic studies. Further, approximately 14 percent of Chicana clients at this clinic are believed to be undocumented aliens. The illegal immigrant fears any transaction that she imagines might bring her to the attention of immigration officials for subsequent deportation.

4. Unschooled and/or minimally schooled clients often are embarrassed at their inability to read and write; hence, they try to avoid situations where they must fill out required forms, thereby requiring the help of some patronizing bureaucrat who will remind them of their inferior status and inadequacies.

5. Health care personnel seldom translate cryptic medical nomenclature into easily understandable concepts because most cannot speak Spanish and lack familiarity with the barrio's ethnomedical taxonomy. Notable areas of difficulty in communicating are:

Standard Questions in Clinic Intake Form	*Barrio's Ethnomedical Taxonomy*
A. Do you suffer from constipation?	A. *Batallas para obrar el cuerpo?*
B. Menstruation	B. *Regla*
C. Urinate	C. *Hacer las aguas*
D. Pelvic Exam	D. *Examen de la parte*
E. To become pregnant	E. *Quedar gorda*
F. To deliver or give birth	F. *Aliviarse*
G. Sexual intercourse	G. *Panochar*
H. Vagina	H. *Verija*
I. Penis	I. *El miembro, la picha, or la verga*
J. Intrauterine device or I.U.D.	J. *el aparatito*

Attempts to apply those translations commonly used in family planning programs in Latin America have failed because they are too technical to be of use in this setting where local dialect and idioms are the main means of communication.

6. Forms may require information that clients lack (e.g., their husband's yearly incomes). Also, many have no telephone number to place on the proper line and are unaware that "none" is an acceptable response. A Chicana may also be unaware of the address of the relative in whose home she is temporarily staying. Each of these situations may be most embarrassing to a client.

7. Lack of transportation is one of the most prevalent problems faced by clinic clients. Forty-three percent of Model Cities Program-area families lack automobiles (Model Cities of [Alcala] 2nd Action Year 1972-1973:4-20). Autos owned by Model Cities Program–area families are not always in good running order, and are customarily monopolized by males.

8. Hours of clinic sessions was a problem until 1973, when they were staggered to facilitate access to its services.

9. Correct use of effective contraceptives and coping with their frequent, minor, but annoying, side effects requires early instruction, reassurance, and encouragement; these supportive services have often been lacking in health care services to the poor.

The following case study illustrates several of these problems: e.g., the indigent are more prone to have problems other than access to fertility regulation methods; a client's responsibility to family supersedes medical demands; and the use of effective contraceptives is a complex matter involving synchronization of various related aspects (such as accessibility of services, the client's organic tolerance of contraceptive method, and her life circumstances). It also documents that clients are discouraged, by delay and cumbersome requirements, to become users of the effective contraceptives; confidentiality is crucial when counseling clients; and that there are Chicanas who, because of lack of knowledge about how to obtain contraceptive services and/or fear of the birth control pill, make no concentrated effort to seek help until desperation leads them to think of sterilization as the only way out.

Elva Madrones was married to a heavy drinker who spent both of their salaries in drinking sprees; after seven months of marriage and before their son was born, Elva left him and went to live in a rented room in east Alcala. Her baby was three months old when Elva began to work twelve hour shifts—from 11:00 p.m. to 11:00 a.m.—at a nursing home. While on this schedule, she earned $115 every two weeks until she came down with pneumonia and was forced to go back to her parent's home. When she was ready to return to work, there were no openings available at the nursing home. Elva found a job managing an old, two-story rooming house in the barrio section of Alcala. She earned $20 per week and lived rent-free in a large first-floor front room.

At the suggestion of one of her girl friends, she went to the family planning clinic requesting an I.U.D. She was instructed to return to the clinic on the second day of her next menstrual period when it would be possible to have one inserted. Although Elva would have permitted a physician to fit her with an I.U.D. during her original visit, she did not keep her later clinic appointment because of her work, transportation problems, and babysitting needs.

The second time she was seen at the clinic she was eight months pregnant with her second child who was fathered during a short-lived affair with one of the tenants of the rooming house. Although she was planning to have this baby delivered by a local midwife—who charges only $35 per delivery—she came accompanied by and at the insistence of one of her neighbors who had become quite concerned at Elva's appearance, physical weakness, and lack of appetite. At the clinic Elva was found to be markedly anemic and was tentatively diagnosed as suffering from infectious hepatitis. To treat her anemia, two large injections of iron were administered to Elva and the clinic dietitian in charge of the Women, Infants, and Children Nutrition Program (WIC) was summoned. It was agreed that her neighbor, the dietitian, and the outreach worker would try to manage Elva's treatment at home.

Elva's dwelling place was uncomfortably warm. The room was cluttered, in spite of the fact that it was sparsely furnished, with two unmade beds with thin, soiled mattresses, a small brown plastic radio, a black-and-white TV and a small portable electric fan whose frame had been bent by repeated falls from the window sill. A strong smell of urine permeated the room. Elva tried to use the washe-teria—located two miles away—to wash her son's diapers every other day. In the interim, she stored soiled diapers in an open, plastic laundry basket that she kept in a corner of the room. Eduardo's toys, cracker crumbs, and a large, half empty box of sugared puffed rice were strewn on the floor. Two pillow cases stuffed with laundered clothes were on one of the beds; one of the pillow cases contained the only set of bed linens.

Elva shared the only kitchen with fourteen other tenants (mostly single young adults). For weeks the absentee landlord had been notified that the gas stove needed repairing. In spite of the fairly clean and orderly kitchen, the cockroaches thrived, boldly marching everywhere in full view.

With food stamps from the WIC program plus some additional funds the dietitian and the clinic outreach worker purchased a week's supply of groceries for Elva's special diet and for Eduardo. Two days later, from the laboratory exams done on Elva it was learned that she did not have hepatitis. Her marked anemia (six grams of hemoglobin instead of the normal twelve to thirteen) had been most likely due to poor eating habits.

Her daily diet had consisted of sporadic handfuls of dry cereal and cookies chased down with powdered fruit or soft drinks. Elva's idea of a large square meal was the hot bowl of canned soup that mother and son had enjoyed as their evening meal every other day. By the time her second son, Miguel, was born (in the hospital), through dietary and vitamin therapy Elva's hemoglobin had been raised three grams—a nice accomplishment and insurance, since at childbirth a woman loses approximately a gram of hemoglobin.

Ten months after the birth of Miguel, the outreach worker and the researcher casually dropped by for a visit with Elva at around four in the afternoon. The windows and door in her room had new screens; the broken door latch had been repaired, a sturdy shelf about five feet from the floor had been built and the TV securely anchored on it. A larger exhaust window fan had been installed. In a newly acquired crib slept her younger son. The beds were made and the floor was swept. Elva, pregnant again, answered from the community shower down the hall; she and her son Eduardo had showered and were getting dressed to go out.

Shortly after, a man (who appeared to be in his fifties) named Fernando Guerrero came in. Elva introduced the outreach worker as one of the persons who had helped her at the clinic. Fernando and Elva exchanged a knowing glance and then he suggested that perhaps the outreach worker could help them. Specifically the Guerreros (they had married) wanted to know whom the nurse would recommend to do a sterilizing procedure (bilateral tubal ligation) on Elva, how much it would cost, and how soon after a baby is born the operation could be performed safely.

The outreach worker suggested the possibility of having the sterilization performed following the baby's delivery at no cost to the Guerreros and asked Elva to drop by the clinic so that she could fill out the required paperwork. The following day at the clinic the nurse suggested that Elva should manage the delivery of this pregnancy in the same way as her previous one except that this time she should request a tubal ligation. This meant that: (1) on the birth certificate the child would be registered under Elva's maiden name; (2) only Elva's signature—since she is divorced—would be required on the surgical sterilization permit; and (3) the bill would be paid partly by the city and partly by the Department of Health, Education and Welfare (HEW).

Under present (1974) income guidelines Mr. Guerrero's salary is overscale; this disqualifies the entire family from receiving staff medical services. By not reporting their marriage to the welfare worker until after the infant was delivered and Elva's tubal ligation was performed, the Guerrero's avoided a $1,500 to $2,000 health care debt.

The last field note entry on Elva is dated July 1976. Three months after their daughter was born and the tubal ligation was performed, the Guerreros had moved to the outskirts of Alcala into a second-hand mobile home. Their home has all the modern conveniences, but Elva's proudest possessions are the trailer's portable washing machine and the fence that Fernando has built around the yard in front of the trailer. During this visit Elva commented:

> Fernando is a good man. I am lucky to have him. He only drinks an occasional beer. He loves me and loves my kids. The kids are not lacking in a thing. We like it out here where the kids don't have to watch scandals and "dope heads" and where at all times I know where they are at. Besides, out here Lupe (Elva's ex-husband) cannot pester us as often (he does not have a car) as he used to at the rooming house where he would come in drunk at any time of the day or night wanting to take Eduardo with him for the weekend.

The desire for many children that is usually ascribed to Mexican-American women is less evident in Alcala Chicanas with more formal education than in the clinic population discussed above. Chicanas with higher academic degrees have lower fertility ratios. The following statistics are based on interviews with fifty-seven active[5] Mexican-American Business and Professional Women of Alcala (MABPWA). Of 20 MABPWA members who have had a high school education or less, only one (5 percent) had no children.

Of thirty-three Chicanas with B.A. degrees, twenty-one (64 percent) had no children. Of twenty Chicanas with M.A. degrees, fourteen (70 percent) had no children. Of four MABPWA members with Ph.D. degrees all had no children. A MABPWA member offered the following explanation to account for fertility differences between these two groups: "A Chicana with a college education can get a better paying job . . . [thus] educated Chicanas more readily can afford and negotiate to obtain the pill than can their indigent sisters."

In summary, although Chicanas do have a high fertility rate, this is not due to ideological components such as their religion, their mates' opposition, or to their disinterest in the use of effective contraceptives. It appears that fertility regulation among medically indigent Chicana clients is influenced overwhelmingly by variables within the structure and operation of the health care delivery system rather than by ethnicity or individual motivation.

Conclusions

Earlier in the study it was noted that this particular clinic has the lowest drop-out rate of all three family planning service providers to the medically indigent in Alcala. I have identified several characteristics of this family planning clinic as being responsible for its success. The same characteristics may well be essential to the success of other family planning services for medically indigent Chicanas in other locations. These factors are:

1. Accessibility of clinic. The clinic should be located within walking distance (one to two miles) of the highest concentration of the low income population expected to be clients.
2. A clinic coordinator aware of socioeconomic, educational, and cultural differences between clinic staff (physicians and RN's) and clientele, who is bright and resourceful, knows the health care system, and knows what the system can and cannot do.
3. Convenience of clinic hours.
4. Preference given to indigenous job applicants.
5. Personal rather than impersonal manner with clients.
6. Bidirectional communication between staff and clients.
7. Privacy and confidentiality during counseling and examinations.

8. Relaxed, informal atmosphere.
9. Multipurpose in-services offered.
10. Community health volunteers recruited for their known rapport with clients.
11. Family planning services provided free of charge.
12. Message of concern about client's total health.
13. Education as well as contraception.

This research has shown, in the case of one clinic, that reasons for the high Mexican-American fertility do not stem out of the microsystem of the Mexican-American population and their cultural beliefs. Rather the problem stems from the disjuncture of Anglo implementation of family planning services and Mexican-American perceptions of those services. Rather than examining microlevels or single sectors of the macrosystem separately, I have defined a macrosystemic interface model. If the situation analyzed is typical, it is a complex interplay of a number of components— Mexican-American clients, Anglo health care personnel, economic and political factors; transportation and other spatiotemporal factors in the urban milieu; language barriers, etc.—that causes success or failure. It is macro- and microsystems interacting compatibly and with minimal conflict that has made this particular clinic successful; and it is conflicts between the systems that can lead to failure.

It would be worthwhile for the staff or planner of other family planning clinics to consider examining the setting and personnel in their locales, with an eye to adapting and/or implementing the guidelines that have been provided here. Attention to sociocultural dynamics will improve the quality of health care services provided to all minorities, not only Mexican Americans. Most important, such review will generate a more genuine dialogue between those who wish to provide a service in its most effective and (in the broad sense) "economic" fashion to those whose needs should and must be met despite external factors that inhibit and minimize the full potential of this and other clinics.

Notes

1. Leñero-Otero (1968:24) states that the teachings of the Roman Catholic Church have an important role in either rejection or ignorance of

contraception in Mexico—a predominantly Roman Catholic country. The Chicano population continuously absorbs a steady stream of Mexican migrants. Furthermore, approximately 95 percent of the Mexican American population is nominally Roman Catholic (Moore 1970:84-85).

2. The masculine need to demonstrate virility through the siring of many children—a supposed aspect of the Latin American man's *machismo*— has frequently been cited as a cultural deterrent to fertility regulation even though the scholar who suggested this hypothesis subsequently rejected it (Stycos 1968:vii-viii).

3. As a group, disproportionate numbers of Chicanos live well below national standards in income, education, housing, and health (Grebler, Moore, and Guzmán 1970:13-33). In the 1970 census of the United States, 17 percent of households headed by persons of Spanish origin reported annual income of less than $4,200 as compared to 10 percent of all other households. Fifty-two percent of the Spanish-surnamed group from the ages of twenty-five to twenty-nine have not completed high school as compared to 29 percent for Anglos.

4. All persons and places mentioned will be provided fictitious names to protect those who aided so graciously and willingly in this research endeavor.

5. In 1973 MABPWA of Alcala had a membership roster of 252 members; of these only 57 were active members (had paid their yearly dues).

References

Alvírez, David
   1973   "The Effects of Formal Church Affiliation and Religiosity on the Fertility Patterns of Mexican American Catholics." *Demography* 10:19-36.
Alvírez, David, and Bean, Frank D.
   1976   "The Mexican American Family." In *Ethnic Families in America: Patterns and Variations*, edited by Charles H. Mindel and Robert W. Habenstein, pp. 271-292. New York: Elsivier.
Bradshaw, Benjamin S., and Bean, Frank D.
   1972   "Some Aspects of the Fertility of Mexican Americans." In *Demographic and Social Aspects of Population Growth*, edited by C. F. Westhoff and R. Parks, Jr., pp. 139-164. Washington, D.C.: U.S. Government Printing Office.
Clark, Margaret
   1959   *Health in the Mexican American Culture.* Berkeley: University of California Press.
Grebler, Leo; Moore, Joan W.; and Guzmán, Ralph C.
   1970   *The Mexican American People: The Nation's Second Largest Minority.* New York: Free Press.

Johnson, Carmen Acosta-
  1975   "Fertility Differentials Among Mexican Americans of the Five
          Southwestern States." Ph.D. Dissertation, University of Texas
          Health Science Center School of Public Health, Houston.
Kay, Margarita
  1974   "The Ethnosemantics of Mexican American Fertility." Paper
          presented at the Seventy-third Annual Meeting of the American
          Anthropological Association, Mexico City. November.
Leñero-Otero, Luis
  1968   *Investigación de la Familia en México.* Instituto Mexicano de
          Estudios Sociales, Mexico.
Madsen, William
  1964   *The Mexican Americans of South Texas.* New York: Holt, Rine-
          hart & Winston.
Model Cities of [Alcala]
  1972   *Model Cities of [Alcala] 2nd Planning Year 1972-1973.* [Alcala]:
          Model Cities Printing Office.
Moore, Joan W.
  1970   *Mexican Americans.* Englewood Cliffs, N.J.: Prentice-Hall.
Murillo, Nathan
  1971   "The Mexican American Family." In *Chicanos: Social and Psy-
          chological Perspectives,* edited by N. W. Wagner and M. J.
          Huags, pp. 97-108. Saint Louis: C. V. Mosby.
O'Grady, Ingrid P.
  1973   "Childbearing Behavior and Attitudes of Mexican American
          Women in Tucson, Arizona." Paper presented at the annual
          meeting of the American Association of Applied Anthropology,
          Tucson, Arizona.
Stycos, J. Mayone
  1968   *Human Fertility in Latin America.* Ithaca, N.Y.: Cornell Uni-
          versity Press.
Tannenbaum, Frank
  1960   *Ten Keys to Latin America.* New York: Vintage Books.
Uhlenberg, Peter
  1973   "Fertility Patterns Within the Mexican American Population."
          Social Biology 20:30-39.
U.S. Commission on Civil Rights
  1968   *The Mexican American.* Washington, D.C.: U.S. Government
          Printing Office.

9
Curanderismo and *Espiritismo*: Complementary Approaches to Traditional Mental Health Services

June Macklin

Introduction

It is a hot Sunday afternoon in a small Indiana town, and people of all ages are waiting both inside and outside the well-built *templo* ("temple") for the healing session to begin. They talk of the great Mexican miracle worker and healer, El Niño Fidencio. Myths about his prowess are recounted; some eagerly repeat stories of how his spirit comes to assist Mrs. A., the *curandera* (traditional curer) for whom they are waiting. These accounts reaffirm the faithful in their beliefs and create confidence among newcomers and skeptics. The motives for visiting El Niño are varied. Many who come are migrants, and want to thank him for having given them safe conduct on trips from Florida, Texas, or Mexico; many come to express gratitude for a miracle he performed for them, while yet others carry with them carefully typed and framed testimonials describing how he "alleviated" their problems. Grateful patients frequently leave votive offerings—small-scale silver or tin figures of an entire human body, a leg, or an arm—on the altar in the *templo* to commemorate the healing Fidencio effected for them, much as the ancient Greeks and Romans did (Foster 1960).

It is the purpose of this chapter to (1) describe one of these

Slightly revised for this volume by the author from a paper of the same name to appear in *Modern Medicine and Medical Anthropology in the U.S.-Mexico border Population,* edited by Boris Velimirovic (Washington, D.C.: Pan American Health Organization, Scientific Publication no. 359, 1978), pp. 155-163. Reprinted with permission of the editor and the Pan American Health Organization.

traditional folk healers; (2) examine her immense popularity in the midst of a secular "scientific" society like the United States; and (3) suggest that with modernization and urbanization, traditional *curanderos(as)* may evolve into literate Spiritist and Spiritualist mediums who offer their followers a "culturally constituted world view" that provides a "blueprint" for reflection, decision, and action (Hallowell 1963:258). These healers are eclectic and pragmatic and therefore are able to construct flexible belief systems adaptable to the changing environment of their clients. What differentiates both the *curandero* and the medium from the practitioner of Western medicine, however, is that while the former seldom hesitate to recommend that a patient consult a physician, that same physician is likely to consider a patient who seeks medical care from "irregulars" as one "so far deficient in education that he cannot . . . understand and apply" the "opinion and advice" of "the man educated in scientific medicine" (Shelley et al. 1971:15).

Further evidence of the medical profession's attitude toward folk healing is revealed by a cursory examination of the subject heading of the *Index Medicus*. No entries appear for categories that anthropologists deem appropriate: folk healer, faith healer, shaman, marginal practitioner, medium, witch doctor, medicine man, or quasipractitioner. What pertinent material is listed can be found under the rubric "Social Problems," subheading "Quackery."

Mexican and Mexican-American Healing Cults

Healing cults that center around the traditional *curandero* and those that involve Spiritist and Spiritualist mediums represent two ends of a continuum of cultic belief: the healer may receive the spirit of folk-Catholic saints such as El Niño Fidencio, Don Pedrito Jaramillo, and "Santa" Teresa; study the works of Allan Kardec, the nineteenth-century French "architect" of spiritism; and yearn for the day when their followers will be developed enough—spiritually, intellectually, and educationally—to comprehend the profound "scientific" truths of Joaquin Trincado, the Argentine who adapted Kardec's teaching during the early part of the twentieth century.[1] Mexican Spirtualistic cults also fit along this continuum remarkably well (Lagarriga Attias 1975; Kelly 1961; 1965). Highly syncretic and variable, they are all compatible with folk Catholicism and Mexican traditional medicine. They also represent the religious pluralism that developed in Latin America during the second half of the nineteenth century. Although the Catholic Church had earlier gained at least nominal control over all access to the supernatural, it was unable to maintain its "monopoly on salvation" (Willems 1975:361-362).

An understanding of the ways in which *curanderismo* and spiritism help individuals adjust to the world in which they live might best be gleaned by a presentation of the background and approaches of two different practitioners. The first, Mrs. A., the folk-Catholic *curandera* mentioned above, practices half of the year in Indiana, and the other half in Mexico. She works with only one spirit, that of the famous *curandero* and folk saint of Nuevo León, Mexico, El Niño Fidencio (1898-1938); once possessed by his spirit, she is able to diagnose and treat health and other problems characteristic of traditional and rural Mexico. The second, a healing medium who organized a Spiritist group among Mexican Americans living in San Antonio, Texas, studied the works of Trincado, whose twelve books provide a complete cosmology for his followers. The concept of reincarnation is central to the beliefs and practices of this group and provides the individual member with social and emotional support, as well as explanations for events in his or her life.

The *Curandera* and El Niño Fidencio

The spirit of El Niño Fidencio assists a number of *curanderos* from Florida to California, and from Illinois and Indiana to Guatemala, including Mrs. A., whose beliefs and practices vary only in detail from those of other traditional *curanderos* (cf. Hopgood 1976; C. Madsen 1966; W. Madsen 1964; Olson 1972; Rubel 1966; Macklin and Crumrine 1973). Moreover, the study of a Spiritualist group in Jalapa, Mexico (Lagarriga Attias 1975), shows striking parallels to my observations of more than fifty *curanderos* working with El Niño Fidencio's spirit.

Fidencio's life and that of Mrs. A. follow a highly predictable pattern: both were rural, poor, unlettered, inclined to help others, egalitarian, and had the "gift" (*don*) to cure. Fidencio believed himself to have been elected by God to serve humanity; Mrs. A. regards herself as one of Fidencio's "chosen vessels." Both received a supernatural "call" to serve—which neither felt it possible to disregard—when they were ill, alone, and desperate. Fidencio never married and had no familial ties to demand his time and energy; Mrs. A. had only one daughter and was over forty years old when she began to serve El Niño. Being alone and unattached is not an uncommon circumstance among outstanding healers (Lagarriga Attias 1975; Macklin and Crumrine 1973).

As do most of the successful *curanderos*, Mrs. A. has separate rooms—a large one in Indiana and two in Mexican villages—that serve as *templos* or *centros* ("centers") devoted to healing sessions. Outside her building in Indiana, a plaster statue of the patron Virgin of Mexico, Our Lady of Guadalupe, welcomes the suppli- cant. Inside, the walls are adorned with framed testimonies to Fidencio's effectiveness. These are sometimes laboriously handwrit- ten, sometimes typed, framed, and often accompanied by before-and- after photographs. The power hierarchy is clear in these testi- monials, for the grateful, cured patient expresses his gratitude successively to God Almighty, La Virgen de Guadalupe, Fidencio, and then the *curandera* (sometimes called a *materia* or "medium"). Invariably, the testimonial asserts that the patient had been given up by a number of "doctors with title" before Fidencio and the *curandera* performed the miracle of curing, for which the under- signed always will be a grateful follower of Fidencio.

At the front of the room is a richly decorated altar on which icons of figures known for their curing miracles are prominent, e.g., the Virgin of Guadalupe, the Virgin of San Juan de los Lagos, La Purissima, and San Martín de Porres. Fresh and artificial flowers and fruit adorn the altar: many of these are used to divine the cause of the patient's problem as well as for curing. A statue of Jesus is at one side. Dominating the altar, however, are photographs of El Niño Fidencio appearing in various poses and costumes. The most favored one is of an androgynous Fidencio, wearing a long flowing gown and a blue cape similar to that of the Virgin of Guadalupe, with rays of light emanating from his head and body. Standing on a crescent moon above a solitary cherub's head, he has his right hand raised in priestly benediction while his left assumes the gesture portrayed by the image of the Sacred Heart of Jesus. The photograph, always referred to as El Niño Guadalupano, presents him as the embodiment of a unique, powerful trinity: the Christ figure; the highly revered, caring, compassionate Virgin of Guada- lupe; and El Niño Fidencio himself.

When the session begins, Mrs. A. crosses herself with holy water,

The *curandera*, Mrs. A., and her daughter (who also cures) pose next to their new altar dedicated to El Niño Fidencio. Note the painting of the Virgin of Guadalupe (left of altar, above votive candles), and that of El Niño Fidencio (near left of altar, over crucifix). *Dave Cole.*

she and the group of patients fall on their knees, and they sing in unison hymns of praise to El Niño, the Virgin, and God. The lyrics in praise of Fidencio recount much of the story of his early life, suffering, and "call" to become God's "doctor of doctors"; refer to him as the son of Joseph and Mary and as the son of God; reaffirm his ability to cure hopeless cases; and warn that he who is ungrateful to the Niño, or who doubts his power, deserves to be punished with illness.

The moment when Fidencio's spirit descends to take possession of Mrs. A. is recognized by some of her followers, who then assist her in donning a white robe. From then on she is no longer a humble, unlearned, powerless woman. She has been transformed into an effective, powerful, knowledgeable curer whom her patients now address as El Niño Fidencio.

Mrs. A. is regarded as being very skilled in treating those ailments that traditionally afflict only Mexicans and Mexican Americans: *mal de ojo* ("evil eye"), *susto* ("shock" or "fright"), *empacho* (food not passing properly through the stomach), and *caída de la mollera* ("fallen fontanel"). The author's observations corroborate the conclusions of Rubel (1960) that these illnesses "have remained firmly embedded in the sociocultural framework, despite the introduction of an alternative system of belief and competing healing ways." Where basic Mexican-American values are involved in illness—e.g., being the object of envy or having failed to be a good mother, wife, husband, or son—Mrs. A. often handles the healing publicly. Thus with each cure, the patient, and family, and the listening public are taught a moral lesson.

Although Mrs. A. feels that faith in El Niño Fidencio is the primary factor in assuring the success of a cure, she employs impressive ethnopharmacological skill in her prescription of medicinal plants. El Niño Fidencio himself always is referred to as having been a "great botanist" because of his reputed knowledge of over 200 plants. Geographer Clarissa Kimber reports that the folk medicine of the border area includes much empirical knowledge about plants with healing properties. "'Good' *curanderas* are often remarked upon as good because of their extensive knowledge of plants. Some medical doctors in Laredo and Brownsville actually prescribe these same herbs for their poor patients who cannot afford the cost of prescription drugs" (1974). Over 400 botanicals are in use along the border, and while the users of these plants conserve the

Mrs. A. "lends" her body to the spirit of El Niño
Fidencio. Curing in Espinzao, Nuevo León, Mexico.
June Macklin.

lore inherited from the past, they also test new species as these
come under observation. "Specialists of this experimental turn of
mind" appreciate the value of herbal medicine in curing and have
confidence in their own ability to cope with new ecological
situations, Kimber tells us, and adds that therefore "there is built
into the folk medicine the possibilities for change" (1974; cf. Kimber
1973).

But while the *curanderos* are open to innovation (some add
penicillin to a "sacred" pomade concocted from one of Fidencio's
recipes), many of their techniques are familiar and very old, some

being pre-Columbian in origin. For example, massage, using the hands or the feet (while walking over the patient) is very popular; ritual cleansing is performed with branches of healing bushes; infusions of teas are prescribed, and the sudden spitting of a liquid into the face or onto the chest of the patient is widely practiced. Most of the cases brought to the *curanderos* concern illnesses that are **chronic (and therefore suspected of having other-than-natural** origins); specific to Mexican Americans (and therefore not responsive to Western medicine); and usually reported to have been dismissed by physicians as hopeless or nonexistent.

Assured that miracles can still happen in an otherwise rational but threatening world, the patient encounters in the *templo* an ambience filled with comfortable, familiar, and legitimate supernatural healing figures. Healer and participant in these sessions share the same values, beliefs, aspirations, and problems. "No discontinuity in social contacts is required of participation. Little social distance separates the afflicted person from the 'expert'" (Rogler and Hollingshead 1961). That sharing extends to the possibility of the patient also becoming a medium, of being called to serve El Niño. Many people have become *curanderos* only after having been healed of a serious illness of supernatural origin. The patient enters into two new interpersonal contracts, one with the divinely gifted *curandera,* and the other with the charismatic, powerful Niño Fidencio. The patient willingly takes on these new obligations, and may begin to plan a pilgrimage to El Niño's Mexican village; at the same time, traditional Mexican values are being reemphasized and dependency on miraculous intervention as a problem-solving technique is being reinforced. As long as the social, economic, and emotional problems of her clientele do not change very much, Mrs. A. will continue to thrive as in the past. However, if the clients and the *curandera* find themselves facing a changing set of problems, the flexibility that permits the system to evolve becomes apparent, as shall be shown in the following case of a Spiritist medium.

The Spiritist Blueprint: The Teachings of Allan Kardec and Joaquin Trincado

Full understanding of the second practitioner, the Spiritist medium, requires some background information. Spiritism, like the folk healers' ideology, offers its followers control over illness. It differs from theirs, however, in its ability to make sense of the more complex problems faced by the urban Mexican and Mexican American.

Having originated in Europe, spiritism was exported in the nineteenth century to Latin America. The experiences and teachings of two men, Allan Kardec and Joaquin Trincado, conditioned the development of spiritism in the New World. Their theories, moreover, are still being applied today by Mexican-American Spiritists as they go about their "identity work" (Wallace 1967:67)— finding out who they are—within the structure of contemporary American society.

The views of Kardec (1875) and Trincado (1935, 1963) constituted a major departure from the tenets of Catholicism, the primary official religion of contemporary Latin America. Both men held that life is continuous and eternal, and that the spirit can be rein- carnated. At the transition called death, the spirit reenters the spaces from which it has come, and from which eventually it will enter upon a new material existence: free spirits can be reincarnated in either men or women, so most incarnated beings have been, or will be at some point or other, members of the opposite sex. Spirits remember the past and often foresee the future. They are able to communicate with one another, in this world and others, and are "incessantly in relations with men" (Blackwell 1975:xvi). While some of these ideas were exotic to the Catholic Latin American's understanding of the spiritual, others were compatible with folk Catholicism and permitted "a type of adaptation which makes the role of the human being intelligible to himself, both with reference to an articulated universe and to his fellow men" (Hallowell 1955:10). In the early part of the twentieth century, Mexicans on both sides of the Mexico–United States border had need of such adaptation. The collective search for a Mexican national identity had not yet begun (Hewes 1954). As several chapters in this volume have made clear, village and regional ties were more important than other traditional groupings. Most immigrants had come into the United States uprooted, and in many areas have continued to occupy a marginal position. Their language is distinct in that it contains elements of both Spanish and English, and as such it is the subject of criticism by both Mexicans and Anglo Americans. Catholics in a Protestant country, most had come from rural backgrounds, and those in cities remained "urban villagers" in some ways, valuing loyalty to family and kith and kin more than do most Anglo Americans (cf. Zarrugh Chapter 6). Moreover, the struggle that led to the territorial expansion of the United States by Mexican cession in 1848 bred mutual antipathies among Anglo Americans and Mexicans. At worst, Anglos regarded the Mexican as dangerous, dirty, drunken, ignorant, lazy, superstitious, backward, and immoral (Moore 1976:134). At best, the Mexican was romanticized, being seen as charmingly childlike and irresponsible, much given to fiestas and the *mañana* complex. Clearly, Mexican immigrants needed an ideology to locate themselves socially, culturally, and politically.

The Spiritist Blueprint Applied:
The Life of Juan Luís Martínez

A profile of the Spiritist medium, Juan Luís Martínez (a pseudonym), will illustrate the social, political, and psychic needs of many Mexican Americans. His story is typical of other Mexican immigrants who crossed the border in massive numbers between 1910 and 1930. Young and poor, having been born in the revolution-torn state of Coahuila, he emigrated alone, bringing less education and fewer skills than the average immigrant coming to America from other countries. In about 1912, he settled in a barrio on the West Side of San Antonio, where a concentration of Mexicans and Mexican Americans had lived since the 1870s, and where the Spanish street names, Mexican shops, and neighbors provided a familiar ambience. The barrio is still there today, as is the Spiritist school he established.

The product of a static, semifeudal, rural, social structure, Juan Luís encountered another kind of discrimination and structural rigidity in the United States—one that has persisted up to the present: consider the fact that 60 percent of the social interactions in which low-income Mexican Americans in San Antonio participate are exclusively with other Mexican Americans (Moore 1976:137). Disenfranchised by both the English literacy test and the discriminatory poll tax, Juan Luís nonetheless made many attempts to transcend the barriers that separated his community from that of Anglos. He and most of his compatriots belonged to one of the many mutual-aid societies that offered sickness and life insurance benefits that would protect him and his family[2] against the unknown elements of a world in which he was considered to be an alien. He became involved in several altruistic endeavors, joining a Masonic lodge[3] and assisting in attempts to organize a labor union among the Mexican pecan shellers in the city. An avid follower of the radical ideology of the Mexican anarchist, Ricardo Flores Magón, whose journal, *Regeneración*, offered a "socialist medicine for Mexico's ills" (Ireland 1971:23), Juan Luís and his friends learned the concepts of international socialism. Nonetheless, all of the efforts made by San Antonio's Mexican Americans to alter their political conditions were quashed effectively by the majority society.

Juan Luís soon found traditional Mexican patterns to be more rewarding than his continued attempts to enter or alter Anglo-American structures. He was beginning to enjoy considerable success as a *curandero,* was blessed with the "gift" of healing, and by 1919 had received a number of visions, the details of which he wrote down. A favorite daughter who had died communicated directly with him. Now literate, and eager to learn more about the world of spirits, he began to study Kardec's books. By the early 1920s, he was an active and powerful medium in the Kardecist Spiritist Center. As Juan Luís's fame had spread, Trincado heard of him, and forwarded to him his own books. Juan Luís came to consider Trincado—who prophesied that a utopian commune of the entire world, in which everyone would communicate in Spanish, could be expected by 1980—more progressive and "scientific" than Kardec. He was particularly attracted to Trincado's promise of equal and just treatment for all, including women, since this had been inaccessible to him and other Mexican Americans through more direct political and social efforts. He thus launched, in 1931, the first regional Trincado Spiritist school in the United States.[4] From Argentina, Trincado informed the San Antonio group that their two guides from the world of spirits would be Benjamin Franklin (who then began to communicate regularly through the mediumship of Juan Luís, sharing wisdom and advice) and St. John the Baptist (who in Trincado's system, is a great medium but not a saint). Consequently, Mexican-American Spiritists were able to establish very personal and direct relationships with a prestigious, scientific, Masonic, solid Anglo-American figure on the one hand, and, on the other, with a powerful prescient, erstwhile Catholic being. Juan Luís gave up his political struggle against the overwhelming system in which he found himself and commended himself and his followers to the care of these and other powerful and protecting spirits.

The Spiritist Blueprint Applied: The Spiritist School Today

With urbanization, the ideology of folk Catholicism and its attendant healing system appears to be adequate no longer (Edgerton et al. 1970). The roles one must play—within the family, at work, or as a citizen—in a complex and changing society are ill-defined and unpredictable; the traditional blueprint for decision making and action no longer works. For example, one long-time member of the Spiritist school founded by Martínez reported:

> Typically people came to Spiritism after considerable searching. Of course, since all of us are Mexicans, a large number of our members were brought up in the Roman Catholic Church; their disillusion-ment with the Church[5] started them asking questions. They then would try several of the Protestant groups, especially Pentecostalism, but find no satisfaction; many have studied Rosacrucianism also, before finding the school.

But Spiritism offers some Mexican Americans living in the United States today the means with which to cope with the strain of these uncertainties. Uncertainty about one's identity and purpose in life is resolved through Spiritist rituals. As the director of the school explained:

> After a child is born, he is presented at a . . . fiesta for children, held each April. At that time, a certificate of birth is filled out with the child's name and forwarded to Buenos Aires, where the central school is located. There the general director [today, Trincado's son], working through a medium, gets in touch with the spirit world. He finds out who the spirit guide is and who the spirit protector of the child is. He also learns what the individual's mission in life is to be.

The child's parents, as well as other members of the Spiritist community, socialize the child according to the medium's dictates, for they are duty bound to encourage and assist in fulfillment of the "mission" and, perhaps more important, the child is obligated to comply. The example provided by a young male Spiritist who works professionally as an occupational therapist in the state mental hospital demonstrates the impact of knowing about one's spirit guide, protector, and mission.

> The medium in Argentina had told my parents that my guide is

Giordano Bruno, and my protector is Elías, and although I never found out my mission, I try to think how these spirits are able to help me, and I gear myself to them almost unconsciously. Bruno[6] was considered a heretic by the Catholics, and Elías was a Jewish prophet who fought against idolatry. Trincado says that John the Baptist [the group's guide also] is the same spirit as the Prophet Elías, but with more power and wisdom . . . wisdom which is to be used fighting for human progress. . . . I think that has something to do with the work I'm doing today [he feels that his guide influenced him to become an official in the Spiritist school and devote much time to it].

One can see also how the belief in reincarnation figures in what has been called "typical" Latin-American fatalism; e.g., to a thirty-seven-year-old mother of thirteen children, Spiritism offers an explanation for the abuse she suffered at the hands of her husband, suffering she could not understand at first:

She appraised her own behavior as having been exemplary: she was a good mother and wife. However, it was revealed to her mediumistically that in a previous life she had been a man. As a burglar in *that* life, she had entered the house of her husband in *this* life and he apprehended her. In the ensuing struggle, she (the burglar) killed his wife of that earlier lifetime. Married in this existence to the man against whom she had offended, she now understood from spirit messages, that she must suffer at his hands in order to expiate the crime that her *same self* had committed in an earlier time and place.

Spiritists are prepared to accept with resignation the inequalities inherent in the social system since they believe that each person must acquiesce to his present station in order to atone for those "windows broken" in other times and places (Trincado 1963). It is not, however, a pessimistic view: the Spiritist is paying for all the missteps of an earlier life. With hard work and sufficient study, he will have a better life the next time around. It is a philosophy that makes it possible for the Spiritist to accept that which he cannot change, but apply himself to learning and every other undertaking with great optimism. In short, Spiritism provides a formula for success in this world as well as in the next.

The Spiritist, then, inhabits a complex world in which he interacts with a panoply of spirits, both incarnate and disincarnate, from all times and places, who are more educated, wiser, more developed, and more powerful than he. He can rely on their different specialized abilities and knowledge to assist him in coping with the multiple roles he has to play out in a fragmented, complex, urban, Anglo-dominated world. These diverse spirits sometimes provide dyadic relationships in which the Spiritist must be ingratiating; however, at other times and with other spirits he may practice dominance.

Finally, while both the *curanderismo* complex and Spiritism assist in the reconstruction of what Jules Henry has termed one's "personal community," or "the group of people on whom one can rely" (1958:827), Spiritism is especially effective in this process in urban areas. Fellow members are referred to by the kin terms "brother" and "sister," and, accordingly, can be counted on for family-like assistance. The personal community also includes those wiser, older, more experienced, more enlightened, and more powerful guiding and protecting spirits, who have been interested in one from birth; one knows that low, ineffectual spirits cannot assume these roles. And since the Spiritist has learned that life is eternal, his personal community is not diminished by the disincarnation (i.e., death) of a loved one: he can continue to seek the guidance and company of those who have made that transition into the spaces from which they came. It is clear that "social relations of the self when considered in its total environment [are] far more inclusive than ordinarily conceived" (Hallowell 1955:92). The Mexican-American Spiritists no longer have to feel that they are "forgotten people," or "strangers in their own land."

Conclusions

It would be difficult to determine whether the number of non-medical folk healers (both Mexican and non-Mexican) is increasing or decreasing, but their presence in the United States and Mexico is more and more apparent. It is possible that only these practitioners can offer healing for certain illnesses of certain kinds of patients. *Curanderos* and Spiritist mediums treat patients "whose expectations and conviction regarding the efficacy of the method of treatment" (Benson and Epstein 1975:1227) are high, and relief comes often enough to reinforce those expectations.

If more effective mental health care is to be made available, the beliefs and practices of *curanderismo* and Spiritism should be regarded as the products of particular historical, social, and cultural processes, as is Western scientific medicine. The *curandero* and Spiritist medium persist, although generally considered "illegitimate" and "marginal" because they (1) are flexible and heterodox within the context of a traditional system whose structure and content they tend to conserve; (2) apply considerable empirical medical knowledge; (3) offer pragmatic solutions to problems of health and poverty for those engendered by social and political impotence; and (4) treat an individual's specific case in the context of his family while providing him with either a new, caring, curing "saint" (El Niño Fidencio) or a new group of caring "brothers" and "sisters" (the Spiritist "school"). For urban migrants, Spiritism not only offers healing rituals but also constructs an extensive brotherhood of incarnate and disincarnate spirits that replace the kith and kin they often have had to leave behind, thus reducing some of the alienation engendered by a new environment.

However, because nonmedical practioners are "illegitimate," they usually are recruited from social groups depreciated by the dominant society. Tension between their naturally acquired charismatic authority and that *earned* by religious and medical professionals is omnipresent and makes cooperation between the two groups difficult. Such practitioners have persisted in part because of the vitality of the world view in which they are embedded, a view which "gracefully incorporate[s] the themes of historical persistence and recurrence, multiple identity, indeterminacy, and the interpenetration of the occult with the work-a-day world" (Morse 1974:493). Historian R. A. Morse conjectures that "in Latin America . . . the West may have kept alive some vital options for the future." It would appear that folk healers and Spiritist mediums are a part of that future.

Addendum

In 1975, Mrs. A. was able to build a handsome new *templo* as she had promised the Niño she would when she had amassed sufficient funds to do so. It is attached to her first curing room so that she now has two rooms and altars. She continues to see people every day during the migrant season, but her biggest crowds come on the weekends, when she treats an average of seventy-five to one hundred clients a day. Two young men of about thirty years of age come from Fort Wayne, Indiana, to assist her from time to time.

There is no question that in 1978 she is flourishing, affecting and serving more people than almost any single social agency, church, or Mexican-American voluntary association is able to reach. She says that nearly all of her clients are migrants, which corroborates the observations I have made intermittently since 1962 both in Mexico and Indiana.

More research will be necessary to determine whether or not *curanderos* are fading from the midwestern *urban* scene. The following case comes from my 1978 notes, and illustrates the viability of the complex of ideas as well as the strain between Texas-born and Ohio-born Mexican-American generations.

> The worried father of a twenty-four-year-old favorite daughter [my informant] traveled from his home in Toledo, Ohio, to San Antonio, Texas (he is a *tejano* who settled-out of the migrant stream), to locate a good *curandera* to help him handle his "wayward" girl. (He wanted something done to persuade her to marry the young man with whom she was living and by whom she had had two children.) He was told in San Antonio, "There is none here better than Mrs. A. of Indiana—and she's in your own back yard." He returned to the Midwest and hauled his daughter off to El Niño Fidencio's "selected vessel" for consultation. The daughter remains skeptical—and unmarried to her children's father. Her father and the *curandera* fault her for not believing in El Niño's power, but believe [El Niño] will prevail sooner or later.

Notes

1. The author first became aware of Trincado's spiritism in 1965 while involved in research on folk healing in Mexico and has since collected data for studies of the movement from groups in Monterrey, Mexico; Cabo Rojo, Puerto Rico; and San Antonio, Texas. Dr. Joan Koss, University of Puerto Rico, Rio Piedras, made available her field notes on a Trincado group in Cataño, Puerto Rico; newspapers published by Spiritists in both Caracas, Venezuela, and Mexico City (1966-1967) were consulted; and an interview was held with Sr. Juan Donato Trincado Riglos in 1968 in Buenos Aires, Argentina, where the movement started.

2. According to Kathleen M. Gonzalas, there were ten of these societies in San Antonio in 1928 and the largest had some 1,000 members and capital totalling $53,000 (1928).

3. Most scholars equate the higher grades of Freemasonry with Rosicrucianism. Certainly much of the content of Trincado's thought is

consistent with that movement. Frances Yates' admirable study states that Rosicrucianism "represents a phase in the history of European culture which is intermediate between the Renaissance and the so-called scientific revolution of the 17th century. It is a phase in which the Renaissance Hermetic-Cabalist tradition has received influx of another Hermetic tradition, that of alchemy. The 'Rosicrucian manifestos' are an expression of this phase representing . . . the combination of 'Magia, Cabala, and Alchemia' as the influence making for the new enlightenment" (1972:xi-xii). Both Kardec and Trincado were Masons at one time.

4. The smallest unit in the pyramidal organization is the *escuela* ("school") of a city; the provincial level is above that, while the regional group (which frequently represents an entire country) is next in the hierarchy. The court of last resort, of course, is the central *escuela* in Buenos Aires, seat of the founder and general director. The pyramidal hierarchy structure is a familiar one, whether one looks to the Masonic lodge or to the Roman Catholic Church. As Hobsbawm observes, "If there was a flourishing religion among the late 18th century elite, it was a rationalist, illuminist, and anti-clerical Freemasonry" (1962:259). He adds: "It is certainly evident that many, perhaps most, of the persistent revolutionaries and conspirators of the period from 1789 to 1830 had Masonic background, and continued to think, organizationally in something like Masonic terms" (1959:164).

5. To at least 90 percent of Mexican Americans, "church" means the Roman Catholic Church, and "back to the time of the first American settlement . . . whatever its desires or intensions, the church could do little to protect or help Mexicans" (Moore 1976:87). There was no bureau of Catholic Charities in San Antonio until 1941, according to Moore.

6. It is interesting to note that Frances Yates also wrote a book on Bruno and the Hermetic tradition, and believes that his influence can be detected in the Rosicrucian movement: "Bruno, the intensely Hermetic philosopher, who propagated throughout Europe in the late 16th century an esoteric movement which demanded a general reformation of the world in the form of a return to 'Egyptian' religion and good magic, may have formed a secret society . . ." (Yates 1972:216).

References

Benson, Henry, and Epstein, Mark D.
   1975   "The Placebo Effect: A Neglected Asset in the Care of Patients."
           Journal of the American Medical Association 232:1225-1227.
Blackwell, Anna, ed.
   1875   "Translator's Preface." In *The Spirits' Book*, by Allan Kardec.
           Boston: Colby & Rich.

Edgerton, Robert B.; Karno, Marvin; and Fernandez, Irma
   1970   *"Curanderismo* in the Metropolis." *American Journal of Psychotherapy* 24:124-134
Foster, George M.
   1960   *Culture and Conquest: America's Spanish Heritage.* Chicago: Quadrangle Books.
Gonzalas, Kathleen M.
   1928   *The Mexican Family in San Antonio, Texas.* Thesis, University of Texas. Reprinted by R.&E. Research Associates, San Francisco, 1971.
Hallowell, A. Irving
   1955   *Culture and Experience.* Philadelphia: University of Pennsylvania Press.
   1963   "The Objibwa World View and Disease." In *Man's Image in Medicine and Anthropology,* edited by I. Galston, pp. 258-315. New York: International Universities Press.
Henry, Jules
   1958   "The Personal Community and Its Invariant Properties." *American Anthropologist* 60:827-831.
Hewes, Gordon W.
   1954   "Mexicans in Search of the 'Mexican': Notes on Mexican National Character Studies." *American Journal of Economics and History* 13:219-223.
Hobsbawm, E. J.
   1959   *Primitive Rebels: Studies in Archaic Forms of Social Movement in the 19th and 20th Centuries.* New York: W. W. Norton & Co.
   1962   *The Age of Revolution 1789-1848.* New York: New American Library, Mentor Book.
Hopgood, James F.
   1976   *In the Mountains Shadow: Social and Economic Adaptation in a Monterrey, Mexico, Squatter Settlement.* Ph.D. dissertation, University of Kansas.
Ireland, Robert E.
   1971   "The Radical Community, Mexican and American Radicalism 1900-1910." *The Journal of Mexican American History* 2:22-32.
Kardec, Allan
   1875   *The Spirits' Book.* Boston: Colby & Rich.
Kelly, Isabel
   1961   "Mexican Spiritualism." *The Kroeber Anthropological Society Papers,* no. 25.
   1965   *Folk Practices in Northern Mexico.* Austin: University of Texas Press.
Kimber, Clarissa T.
   1973   "Plants in the Folk Medicine of the Texas-Mexico Borderlands."

Proceedings, Association of American Geographers, pp. 130-133.

1974   "Curing Mediums and Medicinal Plants in the Valley of Texas." Paper presented at the Seventy-third Annual Meeting of the American Anthropological Association, Mexico City, November 24, 1974.

Lagarríga Attias, Isabel

1975   *Medicína tradicionál y espiritismo: los espiritualistas trinitarios marianos de Jalapa, Veracruz.* Mexico, D.F.: Sep/Setentas.

Macklin, June

1974   "Folk Saints, Healers, and Spiritist Cults in Northern Mexico." *Revista/Review Interamericana* 3:351-376.

Macklin, June, and Crumrine, N. Ross

1973   "Three North Mexican Folk Saint Movements." *Comparative Studies in Society and History* 15:89-105.

Madsen, Claudia

1966   "A Study of Change in Mexican Folk Medicine." New Orleans: Tulane University, Middle American Research Institute, publication no. 25, pp. 89-138.

Madsen, William

1964   *The Mexican-Americans of South Texas.* New York: Holt, Rinehart & Winston.

Moore, Joan W., with Pachon, Harry

1976   *Mexican Americans.* 2nd ed. Englewood Cliffs, N.J.: Prentice-Hall.

Morse, Richard M.

1974   "The Claims of Tradition in Urban Latin America." In *Contemporary Cultures and Societies of Latin America,* edited by Dwight B. Heath, 2nd ed., pp. 480-494. New York: Random House.

Olson, Jon L.

1972   *Economic and Social Alternatives in a Northern Mexican Community.* Ph.D. dissertation, Michigan State University.

Rogler, Lloyd, and Hollingshead, August B.

1961   "The Spiritualist Medium as a Folk Psychotherapist." *American Journal of Sociology* 67:17-21.

Rubel, Arthur J.

1960   "Concepts of Disease in Mexican-American Culture." *American Anthropologist* 62:795-814.

1966   *Across the Tracks: Mexican-Americans in a Texas City.* Austin: University of Texas Press.

Shelley, E. G., et al.

1971   *Opinions and Reports of the Judicial Council: Including the Principles of Medical Ethics and Rules of the Judicial Council.* Chicago: American Medical Association.

Trincado, Joaquin
  1935   *Buscando a Dios.* Buenos Aires: privately published.
  1963   *El Espiritismo en su Asiento.* 4th ed. Mexico, D.F.: privately
          published.
Wallace, Anthony F. C.
  1967   "Identity Process in Personality and Culture." In *Cognition,
          Personality, and Clinical Psychology,* edited by R. Jessor and
          S. Feshback, pp. 62-89. San Francisco: Jossey-Bass.
Willems, Emilio
  1966   "Religious Mass Movements and Social Change in Brazil." In
          New Perspectives of Brazil, edited by Eric Baklanoff, pp. 205-231.
          Nashville, Tenn.: Vanderbilt University Press.
  1975   *Latin American Culture: An Anthropological Synthesis.* New
          York: Harper & Row.
Yates, Frances
  1972   *The Rosicrucian Enlightenment.* London: Routledge & Kegan
          Paul.

Part 3
Voluntary Associations
and Leadership

10
The Cultural Demography of Midwestern Chicano Communities

John R. Weeks and
Joseph Spielberg Benitez

Until very recently social scientists generally treated Mexican Americans, or Chicanos,[1] as a group of people whose cultural, social, and demographic structures could be viewed monolithically: as one undifferentiated mass. This perspective ignored the differences in the timing and patterning of the migration of Mexicans into and within the United States. It also ignored the social and cultural adaptive adjustments that any ethnic group makes to particular geographic areas and communities, adaptations that may introduce degrees of subcultural variation. Moore has noted that even at broad regional levels, Texas, California, and New Mexico each represents a different culture area for Chicanos (Moore 1970:11), and to that regional list should be added the Midwest. The purpose of this chapter is to demonstrate the effects of selective migration on population size and structure that, in turn, affect the patterns of organizational life in two broadly contrasting Chicano communities in the Midwest.

Mexican Americans in the Midwest

The ratio of Mexican Americans outside the Southwest to those in the Southwest has increased steadily since at least 1910; in 1970 the

The authors wish to gratefully acknowledge the financial assistance provided for this study by the Midwestern Regional Office, Division for the Spanish-speaking, United States Catholic Conference, under the direction of Mr. Ruben Alfaro.

Table 10.1 Total Spanish-Speaking Population in Selected States, 1970

State or Region	1970 Population
Great Lakes Region	658,802
Illinois	364,397
Indiana	67,188
Michigan	120,687
Ohio	95,128
Wisconsin	41,402
Southwest	6,188,349
Arizona	333,349
California	3,101,589
Colorado	286,467
New Mexico	407,286
Texas	2,059,671

Source: U.S. Bureau of the Census. 1970 Census of Population and Housing,
          Vol. PC (1) - D. Detailed Characteristics. Washington, D.C.:
          Government Printing Office, 1973.

Midwest had the greatest concentration of Chicanos outside of the Southwest. In that year, the 659,000 Spanish-speaking persons of the upper midwestern states of Illinois, Indiana, Michigan, Ohio, and Wisconsin represented a population one-eleventh the size of the Spanish-speaking in the Southwest (see Table 10.1). The lack of systematic data until the 1970 census has contributed to the disproportionately small amount of attention the Midwest has received.

The movement of Mexican nationals and Mexican Americans into the Midwest gained an early impetus from the passage of the Reed-Johnson Immigration Act in 1924, which limited the supply of European labor at a time when the general demand for relatively unskilled labor was still high, both in industry and in agriculture. Although good data do not exist for the first few decades of this century, it appears that relative to present-day trends, there was a considerable movement of migrants directly from Mexico into the Midwest, especially among middle- and upper-class Mexicans seeking refuge from the Mexican Revolution. Still, among migrants of Mexican descent moving into the Midwest, the highest proportion was from Texas, moving in an agricultural migrant stream that provided some relief for Chicanos from the competition of newly arriving immigrants from Mexico, which kept wages at very low levels throughout the Southwest.

The migration from Texas to the Midwest was enhanced in the 1930s, particularly in Michigan and Ohio, by the formation of an A.F.L.-sanctioned agricultural workers union among the European immigrants who had been working the sugar beet fields of that region (Moquin 1971:311). The threat of having to pay higher wages prompted midwestern growers to encourage the recruitment of Mexican-American fieldworkers. The Chicano workers were generally willing to work at the prevailing wage scales, especially since during this period the possibility of a "welfare repatriation" to Mexico existed for any indigent person of Mexican descent, whether or not he was a U.S. citizen.

After the depression, migration into the Midwest was spurred by the demand for industrial labor occasioned by World War II and the postwar economic boom. Of particular importance during this period was the movement of Mexican migrants (Mexican "nationals") and Mexican Americans directly into factory employment and construction work in the large industrial cities of the Great Lakes area, especially Detroit and Chicago. More recently, the midwestern Chicano population has grown as a consequence of migrants leaving the migratory farm labor stream and establishing permanent residence in the same areas where they previously sought seasonal farmwork. This "settling out" process, in turn, was in large measure caused by the increasing mechanization of agriculture and the sharp decline in farm labor demand that accompanied it. Additional inducements to "settling out" seem to be the generally higher wages paid in the Midwest, as well as the relative absence of open, ethnic discrimination of the kind they had experienced in their home communities in the Southwest. Urban areas were and are the primary sites for "settling out" and most midwestern cities, from small to large, have a growing number of Chicanos among their inhabitants.

From the foregoing it may be tentatively concluded that the pattern of migration of Mexican nationals and Mexican Americans (Chicanos) into the Midwest has had some significant variations or selective aspects. Generally speaking, Mexican-American migrants "settle out" in a broader range of large industrialized cities to small agriculturally based towns or small cities; Mexican nationals on the other hand, tend to concentrate in large heavily industrialized cities such as Detroit, Chicago, and Toledo. Thus, large industrialized cities are likely to have as many Mexican nationals as Mexican-

American exmigrants, whereas, in smaller, less-industrialized communities, the Spanish-speaking population is likely to be primarily if not exclusively Mexican-American exmigrants. It is our contention that such a selective pattern of migration and resettlement has important implications for the emergence of different patterns of sociocultural heterogeneity and social organization of Mexican-American communities in the Midwest.

In this preliminary study of Chicanos in the Midwest, we have chosen to contrast two Chicano communities that represent in most ways the sociocultural extremes among midwestern Mexican Americans.[2] The Chicano population in Detroit, Michigan, represents one of the oldest and largest Chicano communities in the Midwest. It is composed of a fairly high proportion of native Mexicans, and has been affected much less by the recent "settling out" of migrant farm laborers than has Fremont, Ohio. Fremont has a small, recently settled Chicano population dominated by former farmworkers from the Southwest. Our approach to the comparative study of these two communities is one we have chosen to call "cultural demography" for lack of a better term.

"Cultural Demography"

As we conceive of it, cultural demography is an attempt to view demographic processes and sociocultural processes as an interactive system, that is most amenable to observation at a local or community level. Population processes are usually viewed as products of the sociocultural system. In fact, this is the classic Malthusian approach. We also believe, however, that by investigating populations at the local level, one gains in detail of analysis at least as much as one loses in the ability to make inferences about larger populations. Anthropologists have been saying for a long time what Beshers noted with respect to general theories of fertility behavior: "Within any society there are quite different kinds of social situations. These are not randomly distributed over the society and are not shared by all individuals" (Beshers 1967:74). In this same vein, Keyfitz has recently lamented that "the weakness of population forecasts is due to our ignorance of the mechanisms by which populations grow and decline" (Keyfitz 1972:361). The implication in both cases is that we cannot understand the fertility of a population unless we understand the fertility of the population subparts. It may be that our ignorance will be abated only when we are willing to apply the ethnographer's microlevel cultural perspective to demographic problems.

But the study of population as an independent variable should also be of inherent interest to social scientists, since population size and structure can play significant roles in shaping the social, cultural, and economic structures of any group of people. A recent example of the latter approach is Uhlenberg's study showing that large family size among Mexican Americans acts as an impediment to social achievement for the ethnic group as a whole (Uhlenberg 1972). The importance of population size and growth in shaping or modifying social organizational forms has been important—albeit never adequately explored—in the thinking of some cultural anthropologists. George Foster (1960:177), for example, stressed the importance of population size as a contributing factor in the prevalence of hostility, suspicion, and distrust in peasant inter-personal relations that, in turn, creates an "informal dyadic contract" type of social structure in these communities. Cancian (1964) likewise attributed importance to the role of population pressure in bringing about significant structural change in the *cargo* system (positions in the civil and religious hierarchy) of a highland Mayan community in Mexico. Finally, Spielberg (1968) theorized that population size influenced the patterns of ritual coparent bonds (*compadrazgo*) in a Guatemalan peasant village.

Organizational life among Mexican Americans has received considerable attention from social scientists, particularly from those who contend that Chicano barrios tend to be "atomistic" in nature. Rubel (1966:239) defines the atomistic type society as "one in which the social system is characterized by an absence of cooperation between nuclear families." Elsewhere (Rubel and Kupferer 1968:89), the atomistic community is characterized as "a society in which the nuclear family represents the major structural unit and, indeed, *almost the only formalized social entity*" (emphasis ours). Other students of Mexican-American society have offered similar characterizations (Madsen 1964; Clark 1970). Such conclusions have typically been drawn without reference to demographic factors that might affect the potential for organized webs of social interaction beyond the family unit. The central assumption underlying these studies and the conclusions they have reached is that the underlying traditional or poverty-induced cultural values (established a priori) determine the behavior of Chicanos, their relations to each other and, consequently, the relative absence or paucity of formal organizational life. It is our contention, however, that the organizational life of any ethnic group in contemporary American society will be severely limited, modified, or rendered nonfunctional if the group is small in size and/or the group is sufficiently homogeneous (socially or economically) so that any formal organization would have to include most of the population in its definition of a member. In other words, in a small, socially undifferentiated ethnic community or population, formal organizations that set themselves and their members apart from the rest of the ethnic community do so by artificially defining differences for their members; therefore, they tend to factionalize the community unnecessarily. At the other extreme, a population that is large but culturally homogeneous (same ethnic group or stock) would tend to have within it greater social and economic variation (i.e., social and economic heterogeneity), and this heterogeneity would imply greater freedom for selective voluntary association within diverse types of formal organizations, established along preexisting or new, emergent normative lines.[3]

Two words of caution. First, in this study our interest is in making a preliminary and admittedly incomplete analysis of the relationship between demographic processes (i.e., population size and heterogeneity) and organizational life in two contrasting midwestern Chicano communities. The preliminary nature of our effort is stressed because we have not yet been able to undertake sufficient field work necessary for a more complete analysis. Secondly, it is not our contention (explicitly or implicitly) that demographic processes determine the social organizational forms of these or any other groups. We merely assert that demographic processes act as parameters to such forms; i.e., size and heterogeneity place limits on the types and/or functions of formal organizations that occur, regardless of the historical or cultural origins of these organizational forms. Let us now proceed to examine these two midwestern Chicano communities and discuss the organizational life of each within its demographic context.

Community Population Characteristics

Fremont, Ohio, is a small city southeast of Toledo. In 1970

Table 10.2   Age Distribution of Spanish-Speaking Persons in the City of Detroit, in the Detroit <u>Barrio</u> and in Fremont, by sex, 1970

Age	Males			Females		
	City of Detroit	Detroit Barrio	Fremont	City of Detroit	Detroit Barrio	Fremont
0-4	12.9%	10.3%	20.8%	13.4%	11.4%	21.3%
5-9	13.0	12.3	9.7	13.2	11.8	16.2
10-14	12.9	14.0	6.9	12.6	15.6	10.6
15-19	9.7	9.4	12.5	9.7	11.3	10.2
20-24	7.1	8.3	16.8	9.0	8.3	13.7
25-34	14.1	14.7	14.7	13.6	11.8	12.8
35-44	9.8	9.2	5.2	11.9	14.2	3.4
45-54	8.6	10.0	9.2	8.5	7.8	7.0
55-64	5.7	5.8	2.8	4.4	3.3	1.9
65-74	4.7	5.2	1.4	2.7	3.0	0.0
75+	1.5	0.8	0.0	1.0	1.5	2.9
Total	100.0%	100.0%	100.0%	100.0%	100.0%	100.0%
N	13,312	2,258	423	13,726	2,068	586

Source: U.S. Bureau of the Census.   1970 Census of Population and Housing, Vol. PC (1) - B. General Social and Economic Characteristics. Washington D.C.:   U.S. Government Printing Office, 1972.

there were 1009 Spanish-speaking persons included among the city's 18,490 inhabitants. Detroit, with a total metropolitan population of over four million people in 1970, had 56,301 Spanish-speaking persons in the entire standard metropolitan statistical area (SMSA), of whom 27,038 lived within the city limits of Detroit. Within those city limits, the core of the Chicano community (hereafter referred to as the barrio) is located directly to the southwest of downtown Detroit and numbered 4326 Spanish-speaking persons in 1970.[4]

Fremont is a young population by Detroit standards (see Table 10.2), and its age distribution is characteristic of a population that has recently experienced a heavy dose of in-migration, especially by family groups. In Fremont, for example, the ratio of children aged

0-4 to women aged 25-34 is 2.84, whereas that ratio is 1.91 for Spanish-speaking populations in both the city of Detroit and the barrio. These differences are probably accounted for by higher fertility and higher percentages of married women in Fremont than in Detroit. The age structure of Detroit is much more normal in appearance than that of Fremont, except for the decline in the proportion of children at the youngest age group in Detroit. This phenomenon may be indicative of some deliberate control of family size in that area, although it is perhaps explicable in terms of the movement of families out of the barrio and into the suburbs as a consequence of an abortive "urban industrial renewal" project begun in the heart of the Detroit Chicano community in the mid-sixties. This project resulted in a great deal of tearing down of residential areas and very little building of any kind save for the construction of an expressway through the middle of a previously densely settled Mexican residential area.

During this period, Detroit's barrio families and commercial enterprises relocated a few blocks to the west; the fact that urban renewal did not toll the death knell for this community is suggestive of the complexity of social interaction. However, there is evidence that the barrio lost a proportion of its young adults and young families to the process of suburbanization. The age distribution for the Spanish speaking in the Detroit SMSA, and even for the city of Detroit without the barrio shows higher proportions of children aged 0-4 than at ages 5-9. Since there is little evidence to suggest that those Chicanos who leave the barrio tend to cluster into Chicano enclaves, the implication is that young Mexican Americans are tending to assimilate into the Anglo suburbs.

An unusual feature of the population structures of both Fremont and Detroit is the age pattern of sex ratios. It can be seen in Table 10.3 that the sex ratios are generally higher than normal in Detroit, and at the younger ages are lower than normal in Fremont, but higher than normal at the older ages. Although it is not entirely clear at this point why the sex ratios are abnormal, the patterns appear to be related to differences in the timing of migration and the place of origin of the migrants into Detroit and Fremont (Weeks n.d.). Of particular importance is the fact that Detroit has been a reception area for Mexican Americans from Texas. In the city of Detroit in 1970, 20 percent of the Spanish-speaking population was foreign born whereas only 7 percent of the Fremont population was

Table 10.3   Number of Spanish-Speaking Males per 100 Females in the City of Detroit, in the Detroit <u>Barrio</u>, and in Fremont, by Broad Age Groups, 1970

Age	City of Detroit	Detroit Barrio	Fremont
0-14	96	103	56
15-59	92	105	86
60+	150	159	106
Total	97	109	72

Source: See Table 10.2.

foreign born. Furthermore, in Detroit, only 14 percent were natives of the U.S. South (which for Mexican Americans means almost exclusively Texas), whereas the percentage was 42 in Fremont. The recency of the migration into Fremont in comparison to Detroit is illustrated by the census data on residence five years prior to the census. In Fremont, 39 percent of the Spanish-speaking population had been living in Texas in 1965, while only 4 percent of the Spanish-speaking population of the city of Detroit and only 2 percent of the Detroit barrio had lived in the South in 1965. Looking at the same data from the opposite point of view, we find that whereas in the Detroit city and barrio virtually three-fourths of the population had lived in Detroit in 1965, only half of the 1970 population of Fremont had been living there five years earlier.

The differences in the timing and origin of the migration to these two communities are associated with differences in socioeconomic attributes of the two populations, with respect both to levels and to the distribution of these attributes. The census data permit us to make comparisons on three important characteristics: education, occupation, and income.[5]

In terms of educational level, Detroit has a much better educated Spanish-speaking population on the average than has Fremont. In the city of Detroit, the median level of educational attainment for those aged twenty-five or older was 11.0 years for males and 11.2

Table 10.4   Distribution of Spanish-Speaking Population of Detroit, Michigan
              and Fremont, Ohio by Educational Attainment for Males and Females
              Combined, Ages 25 and Over, 1970

Educational Attainment (In Years)	City of Detroit	Detroit Barrio	Fremont
None	6.5%	13.9%	5.6%
1-4	7.9	13.5	26.9
5-8	29.2	33.4	44.9
9-12	43.4	36.1	20.3
13+	13.0	3.1	2.3
Total	100.0%	100.0%	100.0%
N	24,140	1,895	305
x^2	50.5	40.3	47.9

Source: See Table 10.2.

years for females. In the barrio, a weighted average of the median attainments were 6.6 years for males and 6.7 for females. There are several ingredients to these educational differences, but most interesting is the fact that in the Detroit barrio, average levels of attainment are much lower than for the rest of the city and much closer to that attained by the population in Fremont. This is perhaps another piece of evidence suggesting that upwardly mobile Mexican Americans are the ones who are moving out of the barrio and into the more suburban areas of the city.

In order to examine heterogeneity, the data on educational attainment were grouped into categories as shown in Table 10.4, and it can be seen that there was little difference in variability of educational attainment between the city of Detroit and Fremont, although the slightly lower chi-square value for the Detroit barrio suggests that it might be more heterogeneous than Fremont.

On the other hand, if one makes the assumption that the most meaningful distinction in amount of educational attainment is between "some high school education" and "no high school educa-

Table 10.5 Distribution of Spanish-Speaking Populations of Detroit, Michigan and Fremont, Ohio by Attainment of Some High School Education or More and Eighth Grade Education or Less, for Males and Females Combined, Ages 25 and Over, 1970

Educational Attainment	City of Detroit	Detroit Barrio	Fremont
No High School (8 years or less)	43.6%	60.8%	77.4%
Some High School (9 years or more)	54.4	39.2	22.6
Total	100.0%	100.0%	100.0%
N	24,140	1,895	305

Source: See Table 10.2.

tion," then the Spanish-speaking population is more equally divided between these two categories. In Fremont, over three quarters of the adult Spanish-speaking population is to be found in the "no high school education" category. As can be seen in Table 10.5, the Detroit barrio occupies a position almost exactly midway between the extremes posed by the cities of Detroit and Fremont.

With respect to occupation, Detroit clearly has a population with greater proportions of Mexican Americans in high prestige occupations than Fremont. For example, in Fremont in 1970, there were only eight Chicano males in the professional category and none in the managerial occupation group, and those eight professionals accounted for only 4 percent of the total male labor force. In Detroit, on the other hand, there were 903 professional or managerial males constituting 15 percent of the male labor force. Almost two thirds of the labor force of Mexican Americans in Fremont is found among operatives, and most of these people work in the local sugar beet–processing factory. Since the 1930s Chicanos have been in the sugar beet fields, and as fieldwork becomes more and more mechanized, the Chicanos have moved into relatively unskilled positions in the processing plant, and thus have chosen to remain permanently in Fremont, rather than return to Texas at the end of the harvest season. In Detroit, only a third of the labor force is employed as

Table 10.6 Distribution of Spanish-Speaking Populations Aged 16 and Over of
          Detroit, Michigan and Fremont, Ohio by Occupation of Employed
          Males and Females Combined, 1970

Occupational Category	City of Detroit	Detroit Barrio	Fremont
1. Professional- Managerial	16.0%	5.8%	5.3%
2. Sales-Clerical	20.4	14.1	6.0
3. Craftsmen-Foremen	13.8	14.3	4.3
4. Operatives (Including Transportation)	30.1	35.6	62.4

5. Laborers (Including Farm),
   Service Workers, and
   Private Household Workers
	19.7	30.2	22.0

Total	100.0%	100.0%	100.0%
N	8,703	1,336	282
X^2	7.8	30.8	123.0

Source: See Table 10.2.

operatives, and most of these Chicanos work either for Great Lakes
Steel or at the nearby General Motors Cadillac plant.

There is then a much wider distribution of occupations among
Chicanos in Detroit than in Fremont, and this is reflected in the chi-
square test for heterogeneity. As can be seen in Table 10.6, there are
large differences in variability of occupation between these two
communities. It is interesting to note, however, that the Detroit
barrio area has far fewer professional and managerial people than
does the rest of the city, and many more persons, relatively, in the
laboring category. This is consistent with the fairly low average
level of education, and in fact highlights the extremely homogeneous nature of occupational attainment of Chicanos in Fremont
whose average level of educational attainment lagged behind that of
the Detroit barrio by only about a year.

Just as education is generally thought of as a primary determinant
of occupational level, so the latter is usually considered to be a
primary determinant of income level. In terms of median family in-

Table 10.7 Distribution of Spanish-Speaking Families in Detroit, Michigan and
Fremont, Ohio, by Total Family Income, 1970

Family Income	City of Detroit	Fremont
$ 0-2,999	8.9%	12.4%
3-5,999	13.6	32.1
6-8,999	21.5	30.7
12-000+	32.7	6.9
Total	100.0%	100.0%
N	5,697	225
x^2	16.9	24.7

Comparable data were not available for the Detroit barrio.

Source: See Table 10.2.

come in the city of Detroit, the family in the middle of the income
distribution made $9672, and in Fremont the median was $6261.
However, a weighted average of the median family incomes in the
census tracts that constitute the Detroit barrio was $9885 per year.
This apparent anomaly cannot be explained by differentials in
female employment (and the consequent additions to family
income) in the barrio, but may be explained by the fairly high wages
of auto and steelworkers, all of whom are unionized. Furthermore,
Chicano professionals and managerial level persons earn less money
on the average than their Anglo counterparts, and therefore
occupational level is not a completely accurate guide to income.

In terms of heterogeneity, it can be seen in Table 10.7 that the
distribution of income in Fremont is slightly more homogeneous
than the income distribution in the city of Detroit. Comparable data
were not available for the census tracts of the barrio.

Organizational Life

Having now placed these two communities into their respective
demographic settings, let us consider the organizational life that has
evolved in each milieu. The concept "organizational life," as we

have employed it in this study, has broader implications than when used in previous discussions of atomistic societies. Without repeating the previously given definitions of an atomistic society, such an hypothesis carries the implication or assumption that the formally structured groups of a community comprise the sum total of organizational life in those communities. Secondly, the atomistic hypotheses of Mexican-American social organization tends to be predicated not only on the relative absence of formally structured, voluntary associations, but furthermore on the absence of "overlapping, inclusive groups," to use Goldschmidt's terms (1959:71). In other words, such a concept is heavily weighted in favor of formal voluntary associations that, together, would involve the participation of most adult members of the circumscribed community.

In our view, however, the organizational life of these communities involves not only formal voluntary associations (with their attendant "membership" rolls, dues, or regularly scheduled meetings, etc.), but includes also all associations, organizations, institutions, or agencies whose activities involve the interests and participation of Mexican Americans, whether as founders, officials, members, affiliates, or clients. Our view of organizational life, we believe, is more useful and meaningful in analyzing significant variations in the level of sociocultural complexity of Chicano communities, as well as in analyzing the cultural and demographic factors that have brought about these variations.

Organizational Life in Detroit

Despite the disruption of the Detroit community by urban renewal, there is a wide diversity of organizations, associations, and agencies that function within the Chicano community of that city. Although the population of Mexican Americans is dispersed throughout Detroit, the area that we have identified as the barrio is the locus of most organizational activity, and is a location where Mexican Americans can and do "touch base" with Chicano culture, even if they do not live there.

In the earlier years of the community, the extant organizations were apparently tied quite strongly to the Catholicism of the Mexican Americans and especially to the receptivity, encouragement, and help of the Detroit archdiocese, which is physically located in what grew to be the city's barrio. These first organizations appeared during the 1920s at the time of initial immigration from

Mexico and were oriented toward the maintenance of the faith, as seen and practiced by Mexican immigrants. While the principal purpose of these groups was the manifestation and reinforcement of Mexican Catholicism, they very early on began to assume mutual self-help functions, especially as the barrio grew with new immigrants from Mexico, most of whom had virtually no experience in an industrial, English-speaking environment.

The growth of the barrio also apparently spawned other ethnic associations at least some of which were oriented more toward the maintenance of secular and patriotic aspects of the community's Mexican origin. Most of these latter types of groups, such as Comite Patriotico Mexicanidad and Los Restauradores de la Mexicanidad, are still functioning along with similar groups of more recent origin (such as El Imperio Azteca). Their activities are focused on keeping alive the knowledge of Mexican history and society.

It appears, then, that virtually all of the early groups were sponsored, at least initially, by the Catholic Church, which has remained as a fairly powerful social and political force in the Detroit community. However, a related element in the evolution of formal organizational activity in Detroit has been the appearance of an organized labor group composed almost entirely of Mexican-American steelworkers, all of whom are employed at the Great Lakes Steelworkers Union. It gained in membership as early Mexican employees of the steel company moved into supervisory ranks and began a practice of aiding in the hiring of the Spanish speaking. It is of interest to note that the employment of workers at the General Motors plant, although more numerous than at Great Lakes Steel, has thus far not been accompanied by a self-identification of Chicanos in their own shop of auto workers.

Athough we were unable to get much information on the history or development of the Mexican-American steelworkers organization, it is known that the group allied itself with the Catholic archdiocese to produce the most potent political force in the community. This alliance has been instrumental in the expansion of organizations whose explicit functions are social action and community service for the Spanish-speaking population of Detroit. One such product of the church-labor alliance was the formation in 1969 of a United Fund–supported agency called Latin Americans for Social and Economic Development (LASED), an agency that serves as a comprehensive coordinator of information, referral, and activity for the solution of local problems such as finding housing, employment, legal aid, medical assistance, etc. The emergence of this agency can probably be viewed, at least in part, as a response to the tremendous proliferation of organizations among Chicanos during the 1960s, the energy of which LASED is trying to channel into service to the community.

The proliferation of groups in Detroit is documented by our identification of at least forty-one active organizations, associations, and agencies within the Detroit barrio.[6] Of these forty-one groups, only eleven are primarily religious groups, despite the active role of the Catholic Church (and other religious groups) in the community. Furthermore, both religious and nonreligious organizations tend to perform a multiplicity of functions. Table 10.8 shows the distribution of organizations according to the major focuses of their activities. While the ethnic flavor of its origins has not diminished (many of these earliest organizations continue to function), the organizational life of Detroit has come to have a much expanded range of activities and professional orientation, especially in the area of community social action and services.

The origins of organizational life were rooted in the fact that the Detroit community very early received a fairly high proportion of native Mexican immigrants who sought to keep alive the observance of Mexican national celebrations and holidays. Furthermore, the social action nature of much of the more recent organizational life is possible only because in Detroit there is a population that is sufficiently well off to be able to provide services to others, yet heterogeneous enough that there are both people who need assistance and people who can provide it. Although the Catholic Church supplied the initial support organizationally, increased size and heterogeneity of the population have permitted a wide diversification of organizational activity in Detroit.

Organizational Life in Fremont

In 1969 Choldin and Trout interviewed Mexican Americans who had settled out of the migrant stream in Michigan and were impressed by the fact that "the local Catholic Church or Protestant sectarian church often seems to be the major source of support both physically and emotionally for in-coming migrants and continues to be the single focus of community participation" (Choldin and Trout 1969:5). The Mexican-American population of Fremont,

Table 10.8 Distribution of Organizations, Associations, and Agencies in the Detroit Chicano Community According to Major Areas of Activity (An Organization may thus be Entered More than Once), 1973

Area of Activity	Number of Groups
1. Community Service	12
2. Political Action	11
3. Recreational	10
4. Religious Observance	9
5. Schools and Education	6
6. Health	5
7. Patriotic	4
8. Labor/Occupational	2
Total	59

BASED ON LIST OF 41 GROUPS

NUMBER OF ACTIVITIES PER GROUP = 1.4

See text for data source.

Ohio, represents a case that fits this model well. Organizational life in Fremont exists at a more rudimentary level and currently revolves entirely around religious groups that are linguistically and culturally specific to the Spanish-speaking community. Of particular importance in Fremont is the role being played by Protestant sects in organizing Mexican Americans (Weeks n.d.). Such groups have a long history of proselytizing activity among Mexicans and Mexican Americans, but in general their impact has been minimal, being far overshadowed by the Catholic Church (see Grebler, Moore, and Guzmán 1970:487). Protestant sects exist in the Detroit barrio, but their community impact is negligible. Yet in Fremont an estimated 30 percent of all Chicano families have joined Protestant sectarian groups formed for the Spanish-speaking population. The reason here may be the fact, mentioned earlier, that approximately half of the 1970 Spanish-speaking population of Fremont has only lived there since 1965. Most of these recent immigrants were poorly educated, and many did not speak English. Under these conditions, it would not be surprising to find local church groups either unable or unwilling to provide organizational support for the Chicano community. In this regard it is significant to note that the Mexican-American sectarian groups have all been organized by Spanish-speaking migrants into the area, and that the impetus for the Catholic Church to establish a Cristo Rey ("Christ the King") Center for the Spanish-speaking in Fremont came from the mid-western Regional Office of the Division for the Spanish-speaking of the United States Catholic Conference. In other words, most of the initiative in organizing the Spanish-speaking community in Fremont has been imported from outside the community.

To date, virtually all of the social events and programs supported by the Catholic Church have been oriented toward either religion or the maintenance of Chicano culture, such as 16th of September celebrations commemorating Mexico's independence from Spain, dances, *kermeses* (bazaars), and holy day observances. The same can be said for the Protestant sects, although there is even less likelihood than with the Catholic Church that such groups will diversify their activity in the future. Protestant sectarian groups tend to be introspective and theologically conservative, and are rarely concerned with serving persons outside of their own congregations.

In general, the Catholic-Protestant competition seems to have arisen as a consequence of the pattern of growth of the Chicano population in Fremont, and it has factionalized the community into religious molecules that do not, and apparently never did, exist in Detroit. It is also unlikely that under current conditions of low levels of education and income and high degrees of occupational homogeneity, that the organizational life of the Fremont community could sustain much diversification.

Summary, Conclusions, and Implications

The growth of Mexican-American communities in the Midwest offers an excellent opportunity for a social scientific study of socio-cultural variation and adaptation of this, the second largest minority group in America. In this chapter we have endeavored to explore the relationship between demographic features and socio-cultural processes in two broadly contrasting communities: Detroit and Fremont. More specifically, we have attempted to demonstrate the effects of selective migration on population size and structure; and, in turn, the effects of population size and structure on the organizational life of Mexican Americans in these two communities.

In Detroit, it was found that the Mexican-American community has existed since at least the 1920s and has had a fairly high proportion of persons who migrated directly from Mexico, as well as Mexican Americans or Chicanos from Texas and the Southwest. Since that time the population within the Mexican-American community, including the barrio, has grown relatively large and is characterized by social and, especially, occupational heterogeneity. Also over this period of time there has developed a fairly complex network of organizational life that, in various ways, directly affects the lives of many persons in the Mexican-American community—as members, clients, functionaries, or supporters. From the limited information available on the evolution of organizational life of Mexican Americans in Detroit, it appears that this process has involved increasingly more diverse functions and more sophisticated and organized means of extracting attention and resources from the official structures and governing bodies of the larger Detroit social system. This process, furthermore, appears to have been marked by recombinations of associations, personnel, and resources of preexisting and less complex networks or levels of organization.

While the data on hand do not permit conclusions concerning causal relationships between size, socioeconomic heterogeneity, and the development of a more complex organizational framework, the data are at least consistent with our proposition that a relatively large population and a relatively high degree of social and economic heterogeneity is necessary to the process of evolving higher levels of formal organizational complexity. Implicitly, a corollary to this proposition is that a small, homogeneous population necessarily will not be complex in formal organizational terms. For example, Fremont, Ohio, is characterized by a population that has recently settled out of the migrant stream of agricultural laborers, principally from Texas and the Southwest. It is a small population, characterized by social, cultural, and economic homogeneity. In terms of its organizational life, there is little complexity. The principal forms of association above the level of familistic groupings found here are small pentecostal churches or congregations. These groups are essentially duplicates of each other and stress exclusiveness and separation, rather than sharing or recombining personnel and resources.

Given our tentative conclusions, two important but interrelated implications can be drawn. The degree of integration (in the sense of participation, involvement, and well-being within the larger social context) of Chicanos seems to be related to the community's ability to create, maintain, and expand its organizational life. One of the principal implications of this integration is its potential for changes in reproductive behavior among Chicanos, which in turn may affect the abilities of the Mexican American to advance economically. We might well expect then that the Chicano population of Detroit is already moving toward parity with Anglo fertility levels. Such a reduction in average family size, with its consequences for economic advancement, would only increase the organizational ability of the community through the social and occupational heterogeneity it would create in its wake.

On the other hand, Fremont represents a new migrant community with a great deal of homogeneity and it is likely that it will be some time before organizational life can diversify beyond the current stage of providing emotional and physical support for the Chicano population there. In the absence of delay of such organizational ability, the processes of social and economic advancement (with the concomitant effects on fertility levels) may take even longer to become manifest.

Notes

1. In this chapter the terms "Mexican American" and "Chicano" will be used interchangeably. It should be mentioned, however, that in recent years the term "Chicano" has come to have certain specialized aspects attached to its meaning and application. More specifically, the term "Chicanos" is often reserved for Mexican Americans actively involved or supportive of the Mexican-American civil rights movement. No such designation is intended by our use of the word here. Rather, it is intended merely to designate a person of Mexican descent.

2. The authors recognize that the census designation of "Spanish-speaking" is not synonymous with "Mexican American" or "Chicano." In the Midwest, especially in large cities such as Detroit, the "Spanish-speaking" would include persons of other than Mexican origin, particularly Puerto Ricans. Based on figures provided by the U.S. Commission on Civil

Rights (1976:23) we estimate that the optimum number of Puerto Ricans in the Detroit SMSA, 1970 census, was 8000 persons. If correct, this figure would represent only approximately 14 percent of the Spanish speaking in Detroit. In addition, no distinctive non-Mexican, Spanish-speaking organizations or agencies were revealed in our survey, either in Detroit or Fremont. Consequently, the authors feel justified in assuming that the overall demographic patterns in the 1970 census material are primarily reflective of Mexican-American social history.

3. This proposition finds some support in a number of social science studies. Lipset, Trow, and Colemen (1962:178-199), for example, find significant differences between large versus small shops of the International Typographers Union with respect to the types of associations found among the members. Spielberg (1973) theorizes that population size and heterogeneity influence the functioning of local level democratic government, even in widely contrasting cultures. Finally, Susan Tax Freeman (1970: 118-119) and Stanley Brandes (1973) call attention to the role population size plays in patterns of "nicknaming" social relations in Castilian peasant communities.

4. The Detroit barrio, as we call it, is comprised of Detroit census tracts 0005, 0007, 0008, 0067, and 0068, all of which had more than 20 percent representation of the Spanish-speaking in 1970 and which were included in the area identified by local informants as constituting the locus of Detroit's Mexican-American community.

5. In testing for heterogeneity, we have employed chi square as a goodness of fit model in which we assume that the heterogeneous population would be one in which there were equal proportions in each category of a particular attribute. This is, at best, only a very approximate test, but it should be capable of giving us an empirical sense of the contrast between these two populations.

6. The list of associations upon which our survey was based was compiled in early 1972 by a Mexican-American student organization (Chicano-Boricua) at Wayne State University's Montheith College, formerly under the direction of Dr. Gumecindo Salas. The original list contained fifty-two entries, but subsequent investigation eliminated fifteen duplicated and added four new organizations, bringing the revised total to forty-one active, predominately Mexican-American voluntary associations, organizations, or agencies.

References

Beshers, James
    1967   *Population Processes in Social Systems.* New York: Free Press.
Brandes, Stanley
    1973   "Nicknames and Social Structure in a Castilian Mountain

Village." Paper presented at the annual meeting of the Southwestern Anthropological Association, San Francisco. April.

Cancian, Frank
   1964   "Population Pressure and Social Structural Change in a Highland Mayan Community." Paper presented at the Sixty-third Annual Meeting of the American Anthropological Association, Detroit. November.

Choldin, Harvey, and Trout, Grafton
   1969   *Mexican Americans in Transition: Migration and Employment in Michigan Cities.* East Lansing: Michigan State University, Rural Manpower Center and Agricultural Experiment Station.

Clark, Margaret
   1970   *Health in the Mexican American Culture: A Community Study.* Berkeley: University of California Press.

Foster, George M.
   1960   "Interpersonal Relations in Peasant Society." *Human Organization* 19:174-178.

Freeman, Susan Tax
   1970   *Neighbors: The Social Contract in a Castilian Village.* Chicago: University of Chicago Press.

Goldschmidt, Walter
   1959   *Man's Way: A Preface to Understanding Human Society.* New York: Holt, Rinehart & Winston (paperback edition).

Grebler, Leo; Moore, Joan W.; and Guzmán, Ralph
   1970   *The Mexican American People: The Nation's Second Largest Minority.* New York: Free Press.

Keyfitz, Nathan
   1972   "On Future Populations." *Journal of the American Statistical Association* 67:347-363.

Lipset, Seymour; Trow, Martin; and Coleman, James
   1962   *Union Democracy.* Garden City, N.Y.: Anchor (Doubleday).

Madsen, William
   1964   *The Mexican Americans of South Texas.* New York: Holt, Rinehart & Winston.

Moore, Joan W.
   1970   *Mexican Americans.* Englewood Cliffs, N.J.: Prentice-Hall.

Moquin, Wayne, ed.
   1971   *A Documentary History of the Mexican Americans.* New York: Praeger.

Rubel, Arthur J.
   1966   *Across the Tracks: Mexican Americans in a Texas City.* Austin: University of Texas Press.

Rubel, Arthur J. and Kupferer, Harriet
  1968   "Perspectives on the Atomistic Society: Introduction." *Human Organization* 27:189-190.
Spielberg Benitez, Joseph
  1968   "Small Village Relations in Guatemala: A Case Study." *Human Organization* 27:205-211.
  1973   "Demographic Parameters to Local-Level Democracy: A Comparative Cross-Cultural Case Study." Paper presented to the Faculty/Graduate Colloquia Program, Department of Sociology and Anthropology, Western Michigan University, Kalamazoo. September.
Uhlenberg, Peter
  1972   "Demographic Correlates of Group Achievement: Contrasting Patterns of Mexican Americans and Japanese Americans." *Demography* 9:119-128.
U.S. Commission on Civil Rights
  1976   *Puerto Ricans in the United States: An Uncertain Future.* Washington, D.C. October.
Weeks, John R.
  n.d.   "Ethno-Religious Factionalism Among the Spanish-speaking in a Midwestern Community." Manuscript, Department of Sociology, San Diego State University.

11
To Join or Not to Join: Chicano Agency Activity in Two Michigan Cities

Jane B. Haney

Introduction

When Alexis de Tocqueville visited the United States in the 1800s he described America as a nation of volunteers (de Tocqueville 1966 [1835]). Ever since that time popular opinion has held that one way to exercise power in the United States is through the creation of voluntarily recruited groups that can elect representatives who share their views or pressure other elected representatives to support their special interests. There is a stereotype of Chicanos[1] that portrays them as unable to organize long-lasting, effective voluntary associations (groups voluntarily joined by persons with common interests who tend not to be paid for that involvement).[2] This suggests, therefore, that the Chicano population lacks effective political power and representation because it is unable to develop such voluntary associations.

The above-mentioned stereotype has been both reinforced and questioned by the work of social scientists. A number of studies were carried out in the 1960s to examine patterns of Chicano associational behavior and to search for their causes. It was found that lower class Chicanos showed little associational involvement while association leaders tended to be middle class (Barbosa-DaSilva 1968; Lane 1968; and Officer 1964). Chicanos were and still are found disproportionately among the poor and working classes, so the logical prediction of the findings cited would be that few Chicanos anywhere will be involved in voluntary associations. Other social

253

scientists had already suggested that there are certain values in the traditional Mexican cultural heritage of Chicanos that seem to conflict with involvement in groups organized according to principles other than kinship (Brown reviews and critiques this perspective [1971:9-18]). This viewpoint supported the popular stereotype that Mexicans and Mexican-Americans are docile nonjoiners.

This chapter describes the evolution of the Chicano agency—an organization designed to serve selected social and physical needs of a specific local population—as part of the total pattern of Chicano associational behavior in Flint and Lansing, Michigan.[3] Although the two cities are separated geographically by a distance of only fifty miles, they have quite different histories and politico-economic bases. Chicano agency development has been distinctive within each city as well, in spite of similar government guidelines. This paper is addressed to an examination of the proposition that the distinctive local nature of Chicano agency evolution is a result of differences in (1) funding sources and (2) vertical political ties available to these agencies;[4] these two interrelated factors further appear to reflect a basic variable influencing minority association behavior: the politicoeconomic base of each city.

Early Chicano Association History in the Two Cities

Flint and Lansing are both medium-sized cities within the automobile-manufacturing realm that is centered at Detroit, Michigan. Both cities are the sites of several major manufacturing and assembly plants of the General Motors Corporation (GM), the world's foremost automaker.[5] The high visibility of the auto industry in both cities tends to obscure some important differences in the economic base and resultant political tenor that has developed in each over time. These differences have had considerable influence on the organization of their minority populations.[6]

Flint is now and has always been far more industrial than Lansing. It is also more geared to a single industry and a single company. The city developed as a fur-trading and transport center, became a sawmill town during the lumbering days near the end of the nineteenth century, branched into wagon and carriage construction, and with little effort made the transition into horseless carriage production during the first decade of the twentieth century. Most important in Flint's history was the organization of the

General Motors Corporation there in 1908. Population growth and decline in the twentieth century has been a reflection of the economic health of the auto industry, as even service industries exist by virtue of the needs of the GM plants and their employees. Even public schools and the local housing market have received direct assistance from GM or the Mott Foundation, a private organization begun by a former GM executive and three-term mayor of the city. Flint's dependence on GM has led some to consider the city a "company town" (Fine 1969, Chapter 4; Haney 1978, Chapter 3).

In contrast, Lansing owes its development to a series of accidents. The capital of the state was moved from Detroit to Lansing in 1847 although Lansing was then only a small farming village. In 1855 the state board of agriculture established what was to become Michigan State University a few miles away. Then in 1896 R. E. Olds successfully adapted a gasoline motor to a horseless carriage in his father's Lansing steam-engine shop. From the start, therefore, the Lansing economy included more than one component. Agriculture and government shared the local political and economic scene with the auto industry. These combined to create a context in Lansing to which Chicano associational behavior has had to adapt that is quite different from that in Flint.

Chicanos from south-central Texas, the border region, and northern Mexico first began to settle in Lansing and Flint during the 1920s and 1930s. The earliest Chicano settlers had been actively recruited for hand labor in the sugar beet fields and refineries of the area (Haney 1977). Many of these early settlers were poorly educated, had few occupational skills, and spoke only Spanish. There was considerable hostility to their permanent residence in these cities, particularly in Lansing. In response, Chicanos in both cities developed mutual aid societies and ethnic associations—associations devoted to promoting Mexicanness (Kerri 1976:24)—which served as support group, informal credit union, and promoter of selected aspects of Mexican culture. The Comisión de Mexicanidad,[7] formed in Lansing in the early 1940s, still existed in the 1970s. By the 1970s, most recent Chicano migrants to Flint were U.S. born with at least some high school education, and most adult males were veterans of the armed services. In contrast, Lansing still enjoys a migration of poorly educated, lesser skilled Chicanos, many of whom are young adults recently arrived from Mexico. This difference is largely due to the fact that Lansing-area agriculture still employs hundreds of field hand laborers every summer while most of the hinterlands around Flint have become industrial city suburbs.

Within the first decade of Chicano settlement in Flint, many had secured jobs at the expanding auto factories and were thereby exposed to immigrant workers of different ethnic backgrounds who had similar occupations in the factories. Flint Chicanos sought help from the same organizations as did other newcomers to the city. For example, they went to the International Institute—first established to aid European immigrants—for English-language lessons and citizenship assistance. Flint Chicanos were also involved with workers of other ethnic groups in the forty-four-day sit-down strike against General Motors factories during the winter of 1936-1937. This strike was a milestone in national labor union history since various fringe benefits, previously unavailable to factory workers, were among the rights finally agreed upon. Many Chicanos were employed at those factories and therefore knew firsthand of such things as the long hours, lack of medical attention, and difficulties in attaining raises and promotions common in the plants. Therefore most were sympathetic to these issues even if they were not personally involved in the strike.

Therefore, in spite of similarities in early Chicano associational behavior in Flint and Lansing, by the 1930s an important difference had begun to develop. In Lansing, banding together as a distinct ethnic group was stressed, while in Flint awareness of similarities with other ethnic groups developed because of shared working-class life-styles. To summarize, this difference appears to be a reflection of the fact that Flint is the center of a major multinational corporation and is essentially a one-industry, one-company city, while Lansing is the center of an agricultural region, as well as serving industrial, educational, and administrative functions.

Church, State, and Chicano Associations in the Two Cities

In the 1950s various associations devoted to Catholic religious interests—altar societies, church-organized service clubs, religious study and spiritual self-improvement circles—were added to the Chicano support groups in both cities. These were outgrowths of the Catholic missionizing effort among Chicano migratory farmworkers. Since the 1930s Chicanos have been the principal hand laborers in mid-Michigan fields (Haney 1977) and Catholic missionaries were sent out to the labor camps. The number of camps grew during the 1940s and 1950s—particularly during the mid-1950s—with the bracero labor recruitment program. This was especially true in the Lansing area. Religious associations were set up among the seasonal migratory farmworkers. Some members remained behind in the city while seeking, and after obtaining, regular employment, and as they settled out of the migrant stream they took these church-related associations into the city.

The Chicano community of faith was able to obtain a church building in Flint that was abandoned as a result of a tornado in 1953. By 1957 the Chicano Catholic parish at Flint was formally operating at the site and the men's religious fraternity—which remained large and influential in the mid-1970s—was founded. Most Flint Chicanos are at least nominally Catholic although there are some who are Protestants. In the early 1970s Flint Chicano Catholics achieved the near impossible: they built a new church and now maintain it and support their own priest autonomously. They do not receive diocesan funds and therefore feel free of diocesan decision making on mundane affairs such as bake sales and use of the building.

It was not until the early 1960s that Lansing Catholic Chicanos were able to establish a separate parish. There was a distinct Chicano neighborhood by that time, and although the Chicano parish was first located outside it there was considerable involvement by large numbers of Chicanos in celebrations, social work outreach for the parish, and religious programs. Lansing Chicanos who recall this era describe it as a "paradise lost." In 1965 the priest of the Chicano parish and the bishop decided to replace the parish with a social service center prepared to serve a multiethnic population although specializing in the needs of Chicanos. Their rationale was that the Chicano population was a "problem" population with both social and spiritual needs; a freeway was about to pass through the location of their parish, and transformation to a social service center could be accomplished easily when the move was forced. Documents do not indicate the reason for the shift to serving multiple ethnic groups but it is probable that it was assumed that the Chicano population would stop growing since the bracero program had ended[8] and would show more natural increase than growth from immigration. This organizational change appears to have been an attempt to deal with the Chicano population as an assimilating immigrant group and to encourage that assimilation. Some Chicanos turned to Protestant churches at this time, but the vast majority remained Catholic.[9] The building that housed the Chicano parish was sold to the state highway department and the money was used to purchase land in the barrio (Chicano neighborhood) upon which the new center for social services was erected. The latter was opened in 1967 as Chicano Social Services.

To summarize, during the 1950s and early 1960s—the bracero era—Chicanos in both cities were able to establish their own separate Catholic parishes. There was an array of associations devoted to religious interests organized at each parish. However, just as was noted for earlier Chicano associational behavior in the two cities, the evolution of the parishes and their associations in the two cities was different. In Lansing, the Church hierarchy reorganized the Chicano parish at the close of the bracero era, converting it into a social service agency. In Flint, Chicanos were able to raise enough money to build a new building and support their priest without having to accept funds (and the control of purse strings) from the diocese.

The Chicano Agency

The late 1960s was a time when minority population membership was suddenly "in"—not necessarily acceptable, but a possible road toward more equal distribution of resources. Affirmative action guidelines to hire minorities began to be applied. Government funding opened up new jobs for minorities. Government grants were available for minority businesses and minority-run service associations. In this climate, Lansing, the capital of Michigan, was a center for a number of pilot programs for minority and "disadvantaged" populations and for the collection and redistribution of grants from various national and state-level departments of government. Flint was less central for the government organization of disadvantaged populations, and, as will be demonstrated, the pattern of Chicano agency development—like earlier association behavior—was different.

By the 1970s there was a sizable permanent Chicano population in both cities: at least 7000 in Flint and 8000 in Lansing (Michigan Civil Rights Commission 1973), cities with respective populations of 193,317 and 179,169 (U.S. Bureau of the Census 1971a and b). Chicanos in Flint lived dispersed throughout the city while many poor, elderly, or recent arrivals and their kin lived in the Lansing barrio. In addition, Flint had a segregated black population twice as large as that of Lansing. Lansing blacks were less visible due to their smaller population size and closer approximation to the socio-economic norm of the city. Chicanos in the mid-1970s in both cities had developed associations ranging from patriotic associations, sports and religious clubs, local chapters of a Chicano veterans' club, to formal social service agencies. In both cities, the associations best known to Chicanos and others alike were the agencies—by-products of the federal-level interest in local-level minority organization of the 1960s era, particularly the War on Poverty declared by President Johnson in 1964.

In 1975 Lansing enjoyed five such Chicano agencies, each of which had a membership, a separate funding source or sources, and employed workers to provide some sort of service to the Chicano population. All of these agencies had offices in the heart of the barrio. Each specialized in a particular aspect of information or social services. For example, Chicano Social Services provided religious and mental health counseling; emergency food, clothing, and medical help; and crisis intervention for the newcomer and the chronically poor. Michigan Migrant Agency, a state-level organization, had a Lansing office devoted to incoming seasonal farm-workers: to their immediate needs, the education of their children, and future employment. El Grito de Michigan published a regular newsletter and provided job training in clerical and publishing fields. Finally, Aztlán del Norte directed its efforts toward drug and alcohol abuse among Chicanos while its parent agency, La Patria Aztlán, operated a separate program for Chicano former prisoners returning to the city. All of the agencies provided services through funding from local, state, or federal sources. In addition to the agencies, several other associations in Lansing with nonprofit status also competed for funding. These were clubs that had sought and obtained the legal status required to apply for funds that could permit them exclusive control of some aspect of services to Chicanos.

At least one and possibly three of the existing agencies were actually splinters from already-established agencies that had originally been such clubs. For example, several organizers and/or current staff members of La Patria Aztlán and El Grito de Michigan had at one time been employed at Chicano Social Services and originally founded these agencies as simple clubs. In this manner Chicano Social Services had served as the "parent" for numerous offshoot associations. It also served as a training ground for relatively unskilled Chicanos who moved from clerical and casework positions there into city and state government positions at far higher salaries. By the time of my investigation the newer agencies were also performing these functions. The membership of one of the current clubs includes many persons who were previously board members of one of the already-established agencies and shows potential to become yet another agency. There was a tendency for every Chicano club of any size to draw up legal nonprofit corporation papers in Lansing. The reasons for this were: (1) such legal status meant a club could apply in its own right for funds not only from private but also from public sector sources, and (2) models existed that indicated that associations could successfully evolve from clubs, through incorporation, to agency status.

All of these Chicano associations were parties in the nearly constant quarrelling, competition, charges, countercharges, and political factionalism[10] that formed the pattern of agency *"envidia,"* loosely translated as "envy and distrust," in Lansing. Parties to the discord could see that their struggles were sometimes counter-productive, yet they would explain, "Chicanos simply can't work to-gether." The folk explanation given—i.e., the reason offered by the individuals involved—was that Chicanos are by nature full of *envidia*. An important figure at Chicano Social Services brushed off criticism of a program at that agency by a leader of La Patria Aztlán with the comment, "Oh, he's just suffering from *envidia* of my agency." Agency *envidia* was generally carried out in the following ways: (1) attempts by an agency or club to "steal" a social service program already funded or in the process of being funded from another agency by submitting a proposal to the same funding source and applying pressure through the news media or pickets; (2) charging the administrator of some program or agency with corruption, simple mismanagement, or lack of concern for Chi-canos; and (3) constant gossiping.

The Chicano population of Lansing was by no means an interacting social community and yet the two spoken symbols most frequently called upon in these power struggles were "the Chicano barrio" and "the Chicano community." It is not difficult to understand the importance of the first. The barrio was visible, large, and an economic resource because local programs administered with money from the Community Development Agency—the 1975 descendant of the Model Cities Program—were based on target neighborhoods, of which the barrio was one. In regard to the second, there appears to have been a tacit assumption between both Chicanos and interested outsiders, particularly funding sources, that the two were coterminous, i.e., that those Chicanos who had a stake in the agencies and their programs lived in the barrio. Yet although most of the agency clients did indeed live there, less than half of the professionals or leaders did. Their interest in the barrio appears to have been due to the facts that agency funding was dependent upon the barrio and that the agencies were a source of power. Barrio residents were well aware of the fact that their clientship was a route to upward mobility to the agency leaders. However, they often looked at the agencies as giant patrons and referred to each agency by the name of its director (e.g., the migrant agency was "La oficina de José"). When a client's request of the agency was not forthcoming, then, "José no lo me quiso dar" ("José didn't want to give it to me"). Agency as patron therefore maintained vertical integration between the clients and professionals within an agency, cementing them into a faction with mutual interests.

In contrast, in Flint there was a Chicano agency bloc. In 1969 a group of eighteen local Chicanos had met with an interested local sociologist, a grant was obtained from the Model Cities Program, and the Raza Services and Referral Group (Razas) opened its doors the following year. By the mid-1970s Razas had a twenty-member board of directors that included both at-large board-appointed individuals and elected representatives from Chicano clubs. All the board members were Chicanos[11] but few had expertise in urban planning, social services, grantsmanship, or administration. Most of the staff members were recent high school graduates on their first jobs, and they had little complementary experience. The Razas staff and board had, however, carefully developed other associations linked to them. In 1973 Parents and Teachers for Education was formed to raise money for Chicano scholarships, and although few Chicanos were ever involved, members were recruited from the various Chicano associations in the city. The Comisión de Mexicanidad, active intermittently for ten to fifteen years, was reorganized so that it also included delegates from all the Chicano associations in the city. Finally, Chicanos for Youth Development was organized in 1974 as a separate agency with the same board of directors as Razas to serve recreation and counseling, particularly substance abuse counseling, needs of young people.

There was no proliferation of Chicano agencies in Flint. When new clubs formed they did not immediately seek private nonprofit status as did clubs in Lansing. The only associations that could have formed the bases of factions or entered into competition with each other were the two agencies (one of which was planned offspring of the other), and the Chicano parish. Although there was tension between the agencies and the parish, it was largely confined to two spheres: (1) competition for support from the "whole community," and (2) conflict over ideals. The parish and the agencies alike not only desired but also needed support—emotional and financial—from the total Chicano population. Both were keenly aware that most of the time they were taken for granted, but many claimed them in a crisis. Likewise, at fiesta time, both the agencies and the parish appealed to the Chicano population that was normally uninvolved in their affairs for support.

The parish and Razas were centers of two broad camps among Flint Chicanos. These two camps were acknowledged by all my informants, one of whom called them *"los cristianos y los diablos"* ("the Christians and the devils"). These camps were potential factions, but had not crystallized into that pattern. The calm was due to (1) strong leadership, (2) overlap in membership among most of the Flint Chicano associations in both camps, and (3) demographic variables. Both the agency director and priest worked to defuse potential problems between their respective factions, largely through discussion of the situation with persons involved in both camps. The demographic variables included the balance in numbers between regularly involved members of both camps, and Chicanos' relative unimportance numerically and situationally in Flint. The latter factor led to attempts by some Chicano leaders to establish vertical ties to higher levels of power not only through brokers such as politicians but also through alignment with black associations. The Flint black population had been the major target of the local War on Poverty and later government programs, so some Chicanos were attempting to make their voices heard through representation in black agencies as well as in "mainstream" ones.

Differences in Chicano agency development and general outlines of Chicano association behavior in general in Flint and Lansing have been detailed above. Chicano agencies in Lansing were in competition with each other over funding and supporters within the barrio, while Flint's agency bloc cooperated with the religious associations centered at the Catholic parish to present a united front to the outside. The following section presents the pattern of funding sources and vertical ties available to Chicano agencies in both cities and suggests that these influence the pattern of cooperation or competition noted above. It is also suggested that the availability of funding and political ties is part of the local politicoeconomic structure.

Funding Sources and Vertical Political Ties

Tables 11.1 and 11.2 show the overlap in funding sources of agencies in the Lansing barrio yet quite different vertical ties available to the diverse associations. For example, La Patria Aztlán, Aztlán del Norte, Michigan Migrant Agency, and Chicano Social Services had city and county funds and several had turned in competing proposals for exactly the same funds in the past. Most of the agencies received direct federal funds as well as local ones. Chicano Social Services, however, remained more closely tied to its local barrio base: its highest level funding sources were the county and the diocese. The clubs depended largely on member donations but also tapped the Chicano population and area people for funds through fiestas, raffles, dinners, and dances. From time to time the agencies would also have dances or raffles, which put them in direct competition with the less powerful clubs for the same resources—a constant source of irritation to the clubs. Members of the latter, however, did not think the agencies should be annoyed if they then competed for grant money.

As a result of the differences in funding sources and of the personal friendships among some of the leaders in the agencies, these associations had access to different sources of political power. All the agencies except Chicano Social Services had "friends" on the city council, at city agencies, on the county commission, in county agencies, in the state legislature, at state governmental offices, and in Washington. The bestowers of such political power had something to gain from the Chicano associations just as the associations had something to gain from them. For example, one

Table 11.1   Funding Sources for Lansing Chicano Associations

| | ASSOCIATION | | | | | |
FUNDING SOURCE	Sports & Veterans Clubs, Comisión de Mexicanidad	Religious Clubs	Chicano Social Services	Patria Aztlán-Aztlán del Norte	El Grito del Michigan	Michigan Migrant Society
Membership	X	X	X		X	
Chicano Population	X	X	X		X	
City & Area Population	X		X		X	
Private Organization		X	X			
City Funds			X	X		X
County Funds			X	X		X
State Funds						X
Federal Funds				X	X	X

state official had obtained his office through initial success in a county election in which he carried the barrio vote in spite of the opposition of two Chicano candidates in the primary. He provided an important vertical tie in his own right and was a broker with access to even more powerful persons and groups. He owed much of his success in the barrio to friends from the Aztlán del Norte–Patria Aztlán alliance, so he could be counted on to support these associations.

Table 11.3 shows that Flint Chicano associations were almost totally dependent upon local sources of funds while, as noted above, a number of Lansing Chicano organizations received funds from more powerful governmental levels. Not only were sports, religious and veterans' clubs dependent upon membership dues, contributions, and fundraisers among the Chicano and city populations, but so were the agencies. This competition for the same funds may have bolstered existing antagonisms along the lines of the two broad camps outlined above. However, leaders of both camps attempted to understate their differences when it became clear that resources might be withheld from any one of the associations by an outside funding source. Thus conflict was limited both by circumstances and by design to squabbles between the two camps not evident to outsiders.

Table 11.2   Vertical Political Ties for Lansing Chicano Associations

Association		Tie	Association	
Chicano Social Services	Comisión de Mexicanidad		Patria Aztlán—Aztlán del Norte—Michigan Migrant Agency	El Grito de Michigan
X		Private Agency		
X		City Agency	X	X
X	X	City Official	X	X
X		County Agency	X	X
X		County Official	X	X
		State Agency	X	X
		State Official	X	X
		National Agency	X	
		National Official	X	X

Vertical ties (see Table 11.4) to sources of political power, like funding sources, were largely local. Although the agency bloc had state- and federal-level ties, they were with individuals, not departments. Since such individuals were mostly elected officials, they were able to command only very loose coalitions at their respective levels. In contrast, certain Lansing agencies had contacts with administrators in state and federal bureaucracies that could place the power of their own organizations behind their Chicano dependents. The vertical ties for the agency and church-centered camps in Flint were different: the agency bloc had allies at supralocal levels in the public sector. The church-centered network was limited to the hierarchy within the Catholic Church itself. Those contacts were somewhat circumscribed since the Chicano parish was not funded by, therefore not completely within the control of, the diocese but instead was dependent upon the Chicano parishioners themselves for support.

Discussion

Chicano agencies in Lansing competed with each other for funds,

Table 11.3   Funding Sources for Flint Chicano Associations

		ASSOCIATION			
FUNDING SOURCE	Sports Clubs	Veterans & Ethnic Associations	Catholic Associations	Protestant Associations	Razas et al.
Membership	X	X	X	X	
Chicano Population		X	X	X	X
City & Area Population			X	X	X
Private Organizations				X	
City Funds					X
County Funds					X
State Funds					
Federal Funds					

supporters, and programs while in Flint there was a Chicano agency bloc. Some Lansing Chicanos indicated that this factionalism could be expected since Chicanos are by nature invidious, yet only fifty miles away Flint Chicanos—who also tended to indicate they consider Chicanos naturally invidious—were able to keep factionalism low key. Lansing Chicano leaders indicated that they have heard either that their counterparts in Flint "have their stuff together" or that they are not organized *as Chicanos* there at all. Flint Chicano leaders indicated they are aware of Lansing Chicano factionalism, and several base their observations on personal experience with Lansing associations. Their observations of each other therefore tend to support the above description. It has been suggested here that differences in the availability of funding sources and vertical political ties to local, regional, state, and federal levels has explanatory value. Although agencies were incorporated into each distinctive associational pattern, in neither city was the development of the Chicano agency really a "natural" outgrowth of Chicano association behavior. That is, Chicanos did not unilaterally decide that the 1970s was the appropriate time to develop a number of such agencies to serve their population. Instead, the Chicano agency can be viewed in much the same manner as Roberts (1973) has described associations of the poor in Guatemala City: they are structures designed by outsiders (in this case, according to the rules of the government funding source) as an

Table 11.4 Vertical Political Ties for Flint Chicano Associations

Association	Tie	Association
Agency Bloc		Chicano Parish & Non-Agency Associations
X	Private Agency	X
X	City Agency	
X	City Official	
	County Agency	
X	County Official	
	State Agency	
X	State Official	
	National Agency	
X	National Official	

attempt to provide a formal means by which the more powerful can deal with the less powerful. However, these structures were added by Chicanos to their already-existent range of associations in Flint and Lansing. They were accepted because they served useful purposes (serving as training grounds for professional positions, providing emergency needs to the poor, offering a chance for political mobility to the leadership), but they were added to the range of associations differently in the two cities because local contexts placed constraints upon the manner in which Chicano agencies could develop.

In Lansing, the barrio was the focus and location of the agencies. The segregation of poor Chicanos, including recent farmworkers and recent Mexican immigrants, into a separate neighborhood in a transitional section of the city (Burgess termed "transitional" those areas changing from residential to industrial land use [1929]) made them a "problem" population easily visible to the various funding sources. Although there were many diverse funding sources from different levels of government and many interest groups available in this capital city, money for Chicano social service needs was in fact more limited than it seemed. As a result of the limitations, Chicano agencies were kept constantly in search of new funding sources, and in addition, the amount of money available for Chicano projects was not proportional to the needs of either the Chicano agencies or the Chicano population. The real limitations were hidden, however, by the location in the capital of multiple resource bases and political ties to many others.

Several factors impinged on Chicano agency development in Flint that stemmed from the primary dependence of those Chicano associations on local funding and political links. First of all, demography was even more crucial for Flint Chicano associations than for Lansing ones. Their dispersed settlement pattern meant that it was difficult to obtain funds from the local administration of Community Development Agency money, which is tied to target neighborhoods. Their numerical minority vis-à-vis blacks meant that organizations of the latter were far more visible and effective as pressure groups. Their class similarity to the majority of Flintites—blue-collar factory workers—made any demand for more Chicano-run or Chicano-staffed social service agencies appear unjustified. The Flint Chicano agency bloc was fighting a battle on two fronts simultaneously. Not only was it fighting external constraints but it was also trying to undo several decades of acculturation: Chicanos in Flint were far more Anglicized in language, kinship, and identification than their Lansing counterparts. They were also better integrated socially (through intermarriage), economically (as fellow factory workers), and politically (as regular voters). Another important factor stemming from the locality of Flint Chicanos' power base was the need to work within the local system, i.e., to operate effectively in a company town. Flint was not the center for divergent interest groups as was Lansing, and Flint Chicanos found it necessary to adapt their interests to those of the city.

Summary and Conclusions

The incorporation of Chicano agencies, organizations that are by-products of the national-level War on Poverty, into the range of Chicano associations in Flint and Lansing has been different. From the earliest decades of Chicano settlement there, Flint Chicanos have been identified with others who share their predominantly working-class life-style more than they have been identified as a distinctive ethnic group. In contrast, Lansing Chicanos are known as an ethnic group. Whereas Flint Chicanos are mostly U.S. born and fit the general socioeconomic average for working-class Flint, many Lansing Chicanos are recent immigrants from Mexico and/or have recently settled out of the stream of migratory agricultural laborers and are generally considered "problem" people from a social services standpoint. Therefore, socioeconomic or class differences between the Chicano populations of the two cities have impact upon the type and number of agencies that can be added to the range of Chicano associations. In addition, however, during the decades that Chicanos have been migrating into and settling in Flint and Lansing the local politicoeconomic base of each city has also conditioned not only Chicano associational behavior but even the class differences between the two Chicano populations noted above. The local politicoeconomic base continues to mold local adaptation of the agency structure into the range of associations through differential availability of funding and political power sources.

Chicano adaptation of the agency structure into their overall association behavior in the Michigan cities examined, although conditioned by the locality of funds and power brokers, appears to call into question the stereotype of Chicanos as ineffective organizers. Flint Chicanos are maintaining the new agency structure against formidable odds, while Lansing Chicanos seem to have learned quickly what type of association is the most effective tool in the competitive context of a capital city. Whether or not these behavior patterns will be adaptive in the long run is open to question, but at this point both patterns are effective given the context. Based upon this research, I suggest that if local constraints on resources available for the support of Chicano associations are greater than what appears to be the case, then factionalism or competition between Chicano associations will be encouraged. Conversely, where local resources appear quite limited Chicano association cooperation will be encouraged.

Notes

1. I use the term "Chicano" to refer to persons of Mexican heritage, regardless of their place of birth or origin. Most persons of Mexican heritage in Lansing and Flint refer to themselves as "Mexican" and occasionally as "Mexican American." Those involved in the agencies discussed herein, however, use the term "Chicano," which is acknowledged to be a political term.

2. Voluntary associations have been described as private groups joined

voluntarily and maintained by members pursuing a common interest by means of part-time, unpaid activities (Kerri 1972, 1976).

3. The element of common interest appears to be a more important feature than "voluntary recruitment" or "unpaid activities." I will refer to the entire range of Chicano clubs through social service agencies as associations. Even if they are not true "ethnic associations" devoted to promoting Chicano culture, using Kerri's term (Kerri 1976), all the associations considered in this paper share a common interest in the Chicano population.

4. This chapter is based on data from a variety of sources including a sample survey of Chicano households in both cities and historiographic techniques. Most important for the ensuing discussion was participant observation among the associations examined. This study was made possible by a grant from the U.S. Department of Housing and Urban Development.

5. According to the *World Almanac*, General Motors Corporation had the highest gross revenues and largest net profit of any automaker in the world in 1977 and the second highest gross revenues and second highest net profit of any world corporation of any type that same year. The gross revenues of General Motors were better than half the gross national product of the country of Mexico (*World Almanac and Book of Facts* 1978:83, 557).

6. See Haney 1978, Chapter 3, for details of the politicoeconomic differences in the two cities.

7. Pseudonyms have been given to all associations discussed.

8. The bracero program was terminated in 1964.

9. Ninety-one-and-one-half percent of Lansing Chicano household heads sampled in a survey conducted by the author in 1976 indicated that they were Catholic (Haney 1978:165).

10. Factionalism is conflict between factions. A faction is a coalition of followers recruited along different lines on behalf of a person in conflict with someone with whom he was formerly united, over honor or the control of resources (Nicholas 1965:27-29; Boissevain 1974:192).

11. One of them was actually Puerto Rican but had been raised in a predominantly Mexican-American neighborhood and closely identified himself with Chicanos.

References

Barbosa-DaSilva, J. F.
   1968   "Participation of Mexican-Americans in Voluntary Associa-
           tions." *Research Reports in the Social Sciences* 2:33-43.
Boissevain, Jeremy
   1974   *Friends of Friends: Networks, Manipulators, and Coalitions.*
           New York: St. Martin's Press.

Brown, Jerold Berry
 1971   "The United Farm Workers Grape Strike and Boycott, 1970-1976:
         An Evaluation of the Culture of Poverty Theory." Ph.D. disserta-
         tion, Cornell University.

Burgess, Ernest W.
 1929   "Urban Areas." In *Chicago: An Experiment in Social Science
         Research*, edited by Thomas V. Smith and Leonard D. White
         pp. 113-138. Chicago: University of Chicago Press.

de Tocqueville, Alexis
 1966   *Democracy in America.* New York: Harper & Row.
 (1835)

Fine, Sidney
 1969   *Sit-down: The General Motors Strike of 1936-1937.* Ann Arbor:
         University of Michigan Press.

Haney, Jane B.
 1977   "Formal and Informal Labor Recruitment Mechanisms: Stages
         in Mexican Migration into Michigan Agriculture." Paper pre-
         sented at the annual meeting of the American Anthropological
         Association, Houston, Texas.
 1978   "Migration, Settlement Pattern, and Social Organization: A
         Midwest Mexican-American Case Study." Ph.D. dissertation,
         Michigan State University.

Kerri, James N.
 1972   "An Inductive Examination of Voluntary Association Functions
         in a Single-enterprise Based Community." *Journal of Voluntary
         Action Research* 1:43-51.
 1976   "Studying Voluntary Associations as Adaptive Mechanisms: A
         Review of Anthropological Perspectives." *Current Anthropology*
         17, no. 1:23-47.

Lane, John Hart Jr.
 1968   "Voluntary Associations Among Mexican Americans in San
         Antonio, Texas: Organizational and Leadership Characteris-
         tics." Ph.D. dissertation, University of Texas.

Michigan Civil Rights Commission
 1973   "Michigan Community Profiles." Unpublished memorandum of
         the commission.

Nicholas, Ralph W.
 1965   "Factions: A Comparative Analysis." In *Political Systems and
         the Distribution of Power*, edited by Michael Banton, pp. 21-61.
         London: Tavistock Publications.

Officer, James E.
 1964   "Sodalities and Systematic Linkage: The Joining Habits of
         Urban Mexican-Americans." Ph.D. dissertation, University of
         Arizona.

Roberts, Bryan
  1973   *Organizing Strangers: Poor Families in Guatemala City.* Austin:
            University of Texas Press.
U.S. Bureau of the Census
  1971a   "1970 Census of Population and Housing." PHC(1)-70, Census
            Tracts, Flint, Michigan, SMSA.
  1971b   "1970 Census of Population and Housing." PHC(1)-70, Census
            Tracts, Lansing, Michigan, SMSA.
World Almanac and Book of Facts
  1978   New York: Newspaper Enterprise Association, Inc.

12

Homogeneous Mexican-American Leadership and Heterogeneous Problems in a Midwestern Community

Alfredo H. Benavides

"Donde hay tres mexicanos, siempre hay cuatro opiniones," goes an old Mexican *dicho* ("saying"). "Wherever you find three Mexicans, you will find four opinions," one of my informants reminded me when discussing the diversity he believed to exist among the Mexican Americans living in Port City, Michigan (as I shall call the city of my study). It is the purpose of this chapter (1) to describe this heterogeneity and its origins; (2) to show that Port City's Mexican-American leaders are homogeneous in background, in their definition of the community's problems, and in the solutions they suggest, and therefore cannot adequately represent or solve these problems; and (3) to argue that even if leaders do emerge to represent the community's various factions and problems, the complex interactions between informal Mexican-American kin and social networks and the social structure of the city in which they now live compel the nonconforming leaders to adopt the modus operandi of the present homogeneous leadership.

Research Methods

The research on which this programmatic report is based was carried out between June 1974 and June 1976 (Benavides 1978). Three principal methods of investigation were employed, namely, (1) interviewing key informants; (2) participant observation; and (3) the collection of survey data by means of an open-ended questionnaire. These three methods together provide a fairly accurate description of the various facets of Port City's Mexican-American community. Because I intend to present the past, present, and future of the community from the points of view of many of its members, I shall rely heavily on case materials and anecdotal, qualitative data to support my analyses. The propositions my data suggest are tentative and await considerably more research in this and other comparable communities.

Community History

A brief look at the history of the Mexican-American community can provide some insights into the heterogeneity found there today. Although voter registration files show some "voting-age" Spanish-surnamed individuals in Port City as early as the 1890s, their first substantive immigration into the area began in the late 1930s and persisted through World War II. Although many Anglos assume that these early settlers were agricultural fieldworkers, they actually were skilled and semiskilled industrial workers, having come from a variety of places, including Monterrey and Torreón, Mexico; Texas; and some from New Mexico. Many had been educated formally in Spanish, and took pride in being Mexicans, speaking good Spanish and knowing something of Mexican history and culture. They were employed in factories and foundries in or near Port City, according to Jesús Garcia, a retired factory worker and resident for over forty-five years.

Garcia and other older community residents agree that language was often a positive factor in acquiring factory jobs. By the time World War II had broken out, they report, there were several bilingual Mexican Americans working in the foundries and factories. Therefore, Garcia pointed out, if a *mexicano* were both skilled and bilingual, it was not difficult for him to become a foreman. The companies then could recruit Mexican and Mexican-American laborers and assign them to bilingual foremen. In this manner, the companies were able to meet their labor demands without regard to language barriers. Accordingly, socioeconomic heterogeneity was beginning to develop, based on the Mexican-American foremen's skill, bilingualism (read "acculturation"), and higher income.

Immigrant Diversity: Urban and Rural Origins

When World War II came to an end, American soldiers returned to Port City, as elsewhere, to reclaim the jobs in the factories they had given up to do military service. As older Mexican-American residents there perceive it, this influx of returning service men created a surplus labor market, and as a consequence, many Mexican Americans lost their jobs. They then could return to Mexico or the Southwest; or begin life anew as agricultural fieldworkers, but with lower status. However, a "significant" number of Mexican Americans remained in what were considered to be "good-paying jobs" in the factories, many as foremen.

Although Port City is predominantly an industrial community, it is surrounded by large counties that are almost excusively agricultural and at the same time (in the 1940s) that Mexican Americans were being recruited to work in factories, unskilled agricultural laborers were beginning to migrate seasonally into the adjacent counties to harvest the asparagus, pickle, apple, and cherry crops. Although these latter workers also came mainly from northern Mexico and southern Texas, they were rural in origin and largely unskilled. However, some of these migrant families also were able to secure jobs in factories and foundries, so aside from the earlier immigrants who were recruited specifically for industry, by the middle to late 1940s, a gradual "settling-out" process began among migrant workers in the area also. This "settling-out" process was hastened during the 1950s as farmers began using mechanical equipment to replace field workers. By 1968, several federal and state agencies, such as United Migrants for Opportunity, Inc. (UMOI), began to make concerted efforts to "settle out" migrant families in order to provide more stability within the migrants' lives as well as to decrease the numbers of people forced to follow a migrating way of life. Therefore, social concern for migrant workers, added to technological changes, resulted in a rapid influx of Mexican Americans into Port City, and created the need for more jobs as well as for social agencies to care for the diverse needs presented by the jobless families.

Thus, the incipient division between the "older" and "younger" populations within the Mexican-American community was widened and deepened. Equally important was the concomitant creation of jobs for Mexican Americans (especially for women) in the social service agencies themselves, positions that now are considered important to leadership, as I shall show later.

The two populations differed in several significant ways. First, the "older" group was for the most part skilled or semiskilled and held factory jobs, while the "younger" group was unskilled for the most part and had come to the area as migrant agricultural workers. Second, the "older" Mexican American considered himself to be middle class, having attained some measure of economic security and success through stable factory employment. Third, the factory-employed Mexican and Mexican American's self-image was that of being "above" the migrant, socially as well as economically. In effect, class differences were becoming pronounced. Fourth, although the "older" population was fast becoming assimilated and acculturated to the Anglo life-style, they nonetheless considered their Spanish and knowledge of Mexican culture to be superior to that of the recent Texas agricultural migrants. Their social disdain for "settled-out" field workers was observed in several ways, including casual conversations when members of the "older" population at times referred to *"esa gente corriente"* ("those common people"). They also made comments about "how vulgar and crude those people" were because "they cannot even speak correct Spanish"—a reference to the migrants' use of colloquial "Tex-Mex" Spanish. The apparent discomfort suffered by these "older" residents during and after the influx of the "younger" population appears to have been a reaction to the disturbance of the status quo, and their hard-earned middle-class respectability. Many told me that what these "older" generation Mexican Americans feared most was that their status would be diminished in the eyes of the Anglo community if "those people" did not conduct themselves in the "proper" manner (even as European immigrants worried about the "greenhorns" among their late-arriving immigrant cousins). A fifth difference between the two groups can be seen in their different orientations to the Anglo community. The "older" population does not believe that there is much discrimination against them, and want to maintain the status conferred upon them by the Anglos; the "younger" population believes that there is discrimination and often think of themselves as "Chicanos." The "older" population rejects that term and feels depreciated by it.

Diversity and Community Settlement Patterns

The differences outlined above, distinguishing the "older" from the "younger" population, originally were expressed spatially. Each settled into a distinct geographical area of Port City. The "older" population settled into an area that is referred to as "La Colonia," which, according to community sources, began as company housing projects in the early forties. The projects, according to one of the men who did much of the recruiting in the Southwest, were "very adequate," by which he meant that they had all of the city services. La Colonia was located in the northeast section of Port City (see Figure 12.1), bordered by an Italian neighborhood and a highway. I was told that black laborers were placed in company housing across the highway. It is of considerable interest that there still is marked separation between these two groups, the Mexican-American leaders seeing themselves as being in competition with black leaders for a "fair share" of the federal dollar. They have not considered forming a coalition with this other minority group, which might give them some leverage in the voting booth, nor do they use the black agencies as models, even though these latter seem to have been more successful in justifying and attracting more federal aid.

Even though the older population was segregated in La Colonia, they were in a middle-class neighborhood, and even today the housing appears sturdy, parks have been developed, and businesses have expanded into the area. However, by the 1970s, most of the "older" population had dispersed to other middle-class neighborhoods. By contrast, the "younger" population of mainly "settled-out" migrants found homes in the southeast section of Port City (see Figure 12.1). Their neighbors in this area of town are lower-socioeconomic-class Anglos "from the South," according to a local educator who has been in the area for over eighteen years. Known as "El Barrio," this area of town always has been an eyesore, according to both Anglo and Mexican-American residents. One would have to agree that El Barrio has a rather shabby appearance, many of its streets being unpaved and the majority of houses old and in need of general repair. There are no parks or major businesses there, and it also is the low-rent district of town.

Although the visual differences between La Colonia and El Barrio are striking, they are merely extensions of the social, economic, and problem differences that separate the two groups. But the size of the Mexican-American community also is directly related to the kind of power bases available to their leaders.

Size of Community and Leadership

The actual size of the Mexican-American community in Port City has been disputed by community leaders in recent years. The

Figure 12.1
Division of Zones in Port City

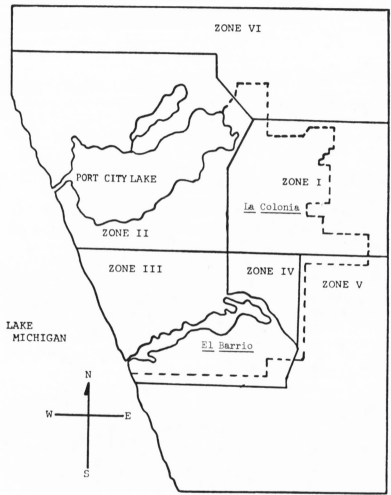

consensus among them is that Mexican Americans have been greatly
undercounted. Therefore, their leaders contend, too few social and
public aid programs have been provided to their community because
these are funded on the basis of population size. Although the claims
of these community leaders are not totally without foundation (the

U.S. Commission on Civil Rights acknowledged in 1974 that the census bureau "did not pay sufficient attention to methodology"), my survey data do not support their claim for Port City.

The total population for the county in which Port City is located is reported by the U.S. Bureau of the Census to be 157,426 and the population of metropolitan Port City to be 61,935 (U.S. Bureau of the Census 1972:1). The census bureau also calculated the size of Port City's Mexican-American population from two categories—"Spanish surname" and "Spanish mother tongue"—and found a total of 3,770 ("Spanish surname": 2,221; "Spanish mother tongue": 1,549). Using lists of Spanish surnames assembled from various sources (telephone and city directories; voter registration and agency files; social clubs; churches; and older residents' knowledge), I compiled a list of 620 households of persons potentially of Spanish or Mexican-American descent, and made 620 contacts during the survey. I was able to complete interviews in 364 households (which identified 1,537 residents); another sixteen refused to be interviewed; and twenty-seven were located but unavailable. The final 213 households (of my original 620) were not available for diverse reasons. Using 4.2 as the average number of persons per household (Benavides 1978), a conservative estimate of Mexican Americans in the county is as high as 2,226, far less than the figure of 3,770 published by the U.S. Bureau of the Census. Therefore, although the true size of the Mexican-American population of Port City is very difficult to determine, my research suggests that community leaders' concerns about under-counting by the census bureau are unjustified, although such concerns may be appropriate in other U.S. cities and regions. However, important to my argument is the fact that numerically Mexican Americans in Port City are of no significance to Anglo politicians; there simply are not enough of them, so their leaders have to rely on tactics other than the ballot box to achieve either recognition or results, and these tactics do not give sufficient consideration to the heterogeneity discussed above. My survey data support key informants' opinions as well as qualitative impressions of the "older" and "younger" groups: two thirds of all Mexican Americans can be classified, objectively, as generally economically depressed and their problems vary accordingly.

Socioeconomic Conditions

The heterogeneity discussed above can be seen most easily in housing, income, employment, and welfare statistics. For purposes of my research, I divided the metropolitan area of Port City into four zones (see Figure 12.1), each representing differences in each of the above characteristics. Zone I includes La Colonia and the inner-city area. Zone IV includes El Barrio almost exclusively. These two zones were generally the poorest in all socioeconomic categories. Zones II and III are more suburban areas; both of them border on resort lakes, are well developed for recreational purposes, and many upper-middle-class professionals live there. Some of the "older" Mexican Americans have moved into these areas, as I mentioned above, although most are there marginally, both geographically and socially.

Although annual incomes also vary among Mexican Americans in Port City, one can see that the differences probably are not great enough alone to account for the heterogeneity found in community attitudes. The total annual income reported by 334 Mexican-American households shows that (in recession year 1975) about one third (34.4 percent) earned $5,900 or less, one third (32 percent) earned between $6,000 and $10,000, while the remaining third earned "above $10,000," at a time when Port City Mexican Americans suffered an unusually high unemployment rate. According to the Michigan Employment Security Commission, the unemployment rate in Port City as a whole reached a recession-level high of just under 18 percent in 1975, while the overall unemployment rate for Mexican Americans during that same period was over 26 percent. (This rate applies only to Mexican-American heads of households.) In Zone IV (including El Barrio), the rate was just over 36 percent. Even in the supposedly more affluent zones (II and III), the rate for Mexican Americans was just over 23 and 28 percent respectively. Therefore, it is not surprising to learn that many Mexican-American households needed and were receiving public services. Sixty percent—216 out of 356 households—reported having received one form of assistance or another, the range being over 50 percent in Zone I to just over 70 percent in Zone IV. Small wonder that leadership and power is seen to reside in those individuals who are in positions to provide the services so sorely needed by over two thirds of the population: and small wonder that the other one third who does not need such services sees themselves as a distinct population.

Kinship, *Compadrazgo, Personalismo,* and the Latin American Club

Regardless of other sources of power, there are two interrelated and very important factors with which any potential Mexican-American leader must reckon. First, there are four very influential "older" families that are interrelated by kinship, marriage, *compadrazgo* (ritual coparenthood), and friendship; their power originates in their numbers, length of residence, and relative economic success. If any one leader can influence enough of these families, their *compadres*, and friends to see things his or her way on an issue, their backing gives that particular leader a sufficient basis for proclaiming "community support." If, however, these families cannot be won over, a leader's political strategy has to be one of caution and compromise. This is an example of what Rubel (1966) describes as *"personalismo"* in the border town he studied: his analysis of Mexican-American political behavior asserts that Mexican Americans tend to vote for the person and not the issues involved, and that political power also functions through whom you know, rather than for what you stand. Therefore, Mexican Americans' political decisions are based primarily on how well they know someone and his values, rather than on the issues concerned (Rubel 1966:138-139). While *compadrazgo* and *personalismo* are important in Port City, both are complex and are influenced by other historical and structural factors so that their functioning is not as simple as it appears to have been in Mexiquito, the community Rubel studied.

The second important variable affecting any given leader's success is the Latin American Club. Historically, the club has enjoyed periods of prosperity when the membership exceeded 300 people. It also has experienced lean years when the membership was down to only a couple of board members. Nevertheless, the Latin American Club functions not only like a private social club, but also as both a sounding board and a springboard for its politically inclined members. In order to understand the sociopolitical connection between the community and its leadership, it is necessary to understand first the composition of the Latin American Club. The leaders of the club are mainly composed of "older"-population Mexican Americans, and every "older" community leader also is a member of the Latin American Club. Most of these leaders have been residents of Port City for over twenty-five years. Some were born and reared there; many have known each other most of their lives and share numerous early experiences, which sometimes complicates the functioning of the *compadrazgo* and kinship systems; i.e., friendship ties, based on these shared experiences may take precedence over familial ties.

Almost without exception, "younger" aspiring leaders are not members of the club, although membership is open to all; therefore, one must infer that their failure to join is a conscious choice, reflecting political and value differences with the "older" population. This greatly reduces the impact of the "younger" leadership, however, because most community residents *are* members of the club. When a problem arises in the community, "older" leaders have an advantage because they can go straight to the club membership and discuss it. By doing this, they can claim to have consulted the community; whether or not they follow the sentiments expressed by the community members in the club is of less political importance than the appearance of having listened. "Younger" leaders do not have any avenues for giving the impression of such consultation with the community; and the constituents to whom they do listen are among that economically depressed two thirds of the population who are receiving welfare assistance. People within the club share many attitudes that reflect their middle-class orientation, regardless of real differences in their incomes. Most often-mentioned opinions one heard in the club, which reflected mainly "older" male statements—although many "younger" males also expressed the same ideas—can be summarized as the following:

- Discrimination against Mexican Americans does not exist in Port City.
- Welfare is wrong because ultimately all pay for it.
- We want our children to succeed in life, and a good education is an important part of that success.
- The club members have a deep pride in being Mexican or Mexican American, but not in being Chicano, and feel that the Mexican-American population has to take some of the blame for being "where they are."

In short, the informal power structures represented by the four influential families, their *compadres* and personal networks, along with public opinion formed and expressed by "older" males in the Latin American Club established the tactics and set the limits within which potential Mexican-American leaders can work.

Mexican-American Leaders

Although some distinct political differences among the Mexican-American leaders do surface when one listens to them, it is the investigator's opinion that the outcome of any political action by Mexican Americans in Port City is predictable. Individual leaders may approach the solution to problems in different ways, but the result is usually the same, because they (1) must deal with the traditional networks and attitudes in the Mexican-American community described above; (2) share a common base of power, that is, occupying positions in social service agencies; and also (3) must deal with the agency structures themselves, which are supposedly there to create employment opportunities and upgrade the standard of living within the entire community. Nonetheless, once an agency is initiated, high priority is given to its own survival. Much time is spent on creating a rationale for the agency's continued existence, which does not always coincide with the needs of the community; it does, however, keep the agency staff employed, including those members of Mexican descent.

Homogeneity among the leaders, then, is the result of the several factors mentioned above. The majority of those actively involved in these politics are women who take jobs with the several social service programs and thus come into direct contact with the Mexican-American population; these positions, along with membership and activity in the Latin American Club, gives rise to the present leaders.[1] The social service agencies themselves often foster ineptness among these leaders. The agency does not necessarily hire Mexican Americans who are equipped to do the job or for qualities of leadership; they are hired occasionally in order to make that particular agency look good both in the eyes of the Mexican-American community and in the eyes of their own funding sources. This is a disservice to the Mexican Americans, because, as my data show (Benavides 1978), comparatively few households receive services, and also because the agencies may be pushing an unqualified Mexican American into a position of leadership. Whether intentional or not, such hiring practices on the part of social agencies help keep Port City Mexican Americans relatively powerless, vis-à-vis other factions in the community.

There also are too few Mexican-American leaders in Port City with specialized knowledge. Community leaders who attempt to articulate the "needs" of their constituents to more powerful Anglo leaders are able to draw only upon lay knowledge of the community, rather than on empirical research. Because they and the Anglo leaders alike also are interested in keeping their agencies and institutions going, as I suggested above, the articulated needs voiced by community leaders often are based primarily on these latter considerations. For example, Mexican-American leaders understand clearly that bilingual education programs will need bilingual directors, teachers, and teacher aides. My impression (in this particular case) was that education was merely a political and economic arena with the improvement of education a secondary concern. This seems to be true of other areas of concern, also. Therefore, the Mexican-American community's apparent lack of knowledge or expertise in such fields as education, law, and social services truly hampers the community's development.

In order to illustrate the points made above about the backgrounds and functioning of leaders in Port City, I shall profile three typical but different kinds of leadership in the community. All names have been changed to provide confidentiality to my informants.

Juanita Rodriguez

Juanita Rodriguez is a fifty-nine-year-old "older" Mexican American who has been involved in community affairs for over twenty-five years. Although she was born in San Antonio, Texas, Juanita was reared and educated in Mexico. Over the years she also has completed two years of study at a local community college. She has served the Mexican-American community in several capacities, such as legal assistant at court hearings involving Mexican-American community members; school board member for several years; city council member for eight years; former social service employee working for agricultural fieldworkers (UMOI); board member (and president) on several community agency boards of directors; and employee of the Michigan Department of Civil Rights as a specialist in Mexican-American affairs.

Through her involvement in community agencies and local-level politics, Rodriguez has gained statewide visibility, and some national recognition as well. Ms. Rodriguez has been awarded numerous citations for community service by both Mexican-American and Anglo organizations. She has been recognized by other Mexican-American community leaders and members as "having the power" in Port City. Anglo Americans also seek her opinion as the spokesperson for the Mexican-American community. Rodriguez's long tenure in the community, her long years in the Latin American Club, and her staff position in the Michigan Department of Civil Rights add considerable clout to her political activities.

The twenty-five years that she has spent in Port City have helped solidify her political constituency better than that of any other single community leader. Her kin and friendship networks are extensive, and she is *comadre* to various members of the four influential "older" families mentioned above. She also has shared experiences with many of the "older" residents; therefore, it is easy for them to identify with her. Although Rodriguez is admired and respected by many Mexican Americans in the community, she is despised by many others. Those who do not regard her very highly are usually members of the "younger" population. She is sometimes radical in her approach to problems, yet sophisticated enough to be extremely diplomatic in seeking her way. For example, when school officials were contemplating the implementation of a bilingual curriculum at a nearby school, Rodriguez privately cursed (among Mexican-American friends) each administrator's knowledge and competence, but flattered them at successive meetings. Finally, the administrators acted as if the original idea for a bilingual program had been theirs alone, even though the manpower program run by Mexican-American interests had initiated the action.

One of the main assets in Rodriguez's political behavior is her astuteness; she plays both sides of an issue well. Although her "fence-straddling" has enabled her to be consistently on the "winning" side, other community leaders and members interpret her "straddling" as noncooperation with them and accuse her of using devious means to achieve her goals.

In her many conversations with me, Rodriguez often talked of "retiring," but not before she felt there was someone who could take her place. She consistently spoke of developing younger leadership so that she could "rest." Others see this as a leadership that she could continue to manipulate and control.

Ben Garza

Ben Garza is a community leader who is somewhat of an enigma to the community. He is in his late thirties, was born and reared in Port City, and is a "charter" member of one of the four influential Mexican-American families. Garza is a prime example of the second-generation Mexican American who speaks little Spanish and rarely mixes socially with the Mexican-American community although he is a Latin American Club member. He worked his way up through union activities at a local factory. He quit his factory job and took a position as a "community organizer" with a religiously affiliated regional agency. Few, if any, community members know what his position or role is in the community.

On several occasions, I noted that Garza's political behavior was impulsive and characterized by what others considered to be "grandstanding." One such incident involved the local school board. The Mexican-American community for some time had been pressuring the local school administrators to implement a bilingual program at an elementary school with a sizable Mexican-American population. The negotiations had been long and delicate. Finally, the Mexican-American community had its chance to go before the school board to make its formal request. Garza, who was in the audience at the meeting, rose and told the Board of Education that if a bilingual program were not implemented immediately, all Mexican-American children would boycott the schools before the fourth Friday count could be taken. Garza felt that the Port City schools would lose a lot of state funding if Mexican-American students were not included in this enrollment count. This statement enraged many Mexican-American parents and also stiffened opposition by several board members.

Several agency personnel felt that Garza was trying to establish himself as a bona fide community leader. He was generally considered to be very close to Juanita Rodriguez, although many thought him to be merely an instrument for her use. Nonetheless Garza actually held some power of his own that did not come from the Mexican-American community, but from his position on the Manpower Advisory Board. This board had great influence on the County Board of Commissioners who in turn decided the financial fate of many social service agencies in Port City. Garza was the only Mexican American on this advisory board and thus was the voice of the Mexican-American community interests. Therefore, my opinion is that while Garza did not have as much grass-roots support as Rodriguez, his powerful position on the Manpower Advisory Board forced other community leaders to take him seriously.

Jane Garcia

Jane Garcia is a direct contrast to either Rodriguez or Garza. She is a member of the "younger" population, having lived in Port City for only ten years. She is a native of Mission, Texas, where she finished her high school studies, and her subsequent arrival in Port City was by the migrant stream. Garcia has been employed as a nutrition aide for six years by a county agency. Her efforts in the community are helped somewhat by her work at a local radio station: she is well known because she has a one-hour show that she devotes to Mexican music and news items in Spanish for the community. Her leadership has its support base in El Barrio and is composed almost exclusively of social service or welfare clients. These people see Garcia not as an employee of an agency but rather as a "neighbor who cares," a *person* who is able to provide services rather than an *employee* of an agency providing services.

Garcia felt that Rodriguez was selfish and only wanted the recognition of being a community spokesperson. To my knowledge, Garcia never received any community awards or formal recognition. This does not mean, however, that she was not active or deserving of community recognition. I know personally that the initial funding for a Mexican-American agency in the community came about largely due to her efforts. Garcia's accomplishment not only was unrecognized, but Juanita Rodriguez took credit for the agency's establishment.

In spite of Garcia's efforts, her base of support is limited to her employer, one or two service-agency personnel, and her direct service recipients. She is unknown to the educational administrators and has never appeared to be active in community educational reform. Garcia's effectiveness as a leader is diminished by her not being a member of the Latin American Club since much of the social and political events are tied to the club membership.

Discussion

In summary, these vignettes, typifying three kinds of leadership, reveal the power structures at work among Mexican Americans in

Port City. Most leaders are women, and come from the "older" community: they occupy positions in social agencies (although these are not policymaking positions) from which they articulate the needs they know to be acceptable to the Anglo establishment (including federal, state, and local funding groups) and that will secure simultaneously career longevity for the agency and for themselves.

New programs and ideas must be tried out in the Latin American Club where "older" males discuss and validate them (the community has been "consulted"), while the approval and support of the four powerful, interrelated, "older" families must be obtained before the new plans can be implemented.

One is impressed by the limits on personal power created through the complex interaction of factors such as those described for Mexican-American leadership in Port City. The problem is epitomized in the case of Juanita Rodriguez, whose power was not institutionalized; it is doubtful that she could have handed it over to any other Mexican American (even if she could have overcome her reluctance to do so). Each aspiring leader must begin anew.

Further, as the case of Ben Garza demonstrates, if one can obtain a truly powerful position in the Anglo power structure (with discretionary control over funds that support other agencies), this obviates the necessity for him/her to have much grass-roots support among Mexican Americans at all. However, he does maintain his all-important membership in the Latin American Club. At the same time, Garza's power reinforces the ranking system of the "older" and "younger" populations: he is "old" family, second-generation Port City; acculturated; secure economically, his income originally having been factory based; and his organizational skills have been acquired and honed through union activities outside the Mexican-American community.

Finally, the case of Jane Garcia makes it clear why Mexican-American leaders are homogeneous. Her attempts to give voice to a segment of the community not presently well represented have been slow and difficult, and credit for some of her more effective efforts has gone to others. She has not found community support or recognition, and will no doubt either give up or modify her tactics in the direction of those used by the others. Meantime, the heterogeneous problems of the community persist and remain

Summary and Conclusions

Perhaps the most important factor involving the Mexican-American leaders in Port City, is their homogeneity. These leaders have been representing the community for many years, but it is a heterogeneous population, comprising "older" and "younger" segments each of which exhibits heterogeneous problems. *Compadrazgo* and *personalismo* continue to be important, but one cannot make the assumption that these concepts are simple in nature and accurate predictors of all Mexican-American social and political behavior because they are extremely complex and involve several variables. The development of a more diverse leadership is necessary to insure proper community representation.

Another lack on the part of Mexican-American leadership in Port City is that once community political and economic goals are achieved, the leaders fail to carry out the responsibility they share with community agencies and institutions to insure that programs actually work as intended. Further, the community itself must bear much of the responsibility for developing a knowledgeable leadership. But the larger community's established agencies and institutions also must assist in developing existing potential leaders and in attracting Mexican-American professionals (if necessary from the Southwest) to Port City. Both actions would benefit the entire community by helping its constituents meet their diverse needs: the more diverse the leadership becomes, the more capable it will be of understanding the needs and developing and executing plans for solving diverse problems.

In summation, social, political, educational, and economic goals in this community can be achieved only if a diverse leadership emerges. It would be desirable for these leaders to have knowledge in different fields and be prepared to work with community agencies and institutions. When a number of diversely qualified residents are given a share of the responsibility for bettering their community, the individuals, the institutions, and the entire community will benefit.

Note

1. Editors' note: Dr. Benavides' data parallel precisely those found in

John Soto's 1974 study of Mexican-American leadership in Toledo, Ohio. Dr. Soto found that community informants consider "community involvement" and "the position the individual holds and his ability to deliver a wide range of services to people in the community" to be the two most important characteristics of leaders (Soto 1974:76-77).

References

Benavides, Alfredo H.
  1978   *Mexican Americans and Public Service Institutions in a Midwestern Community: An Analysis of Mutual Images and Interactions.* Ph.D. dissertation, Michigan State University.
Rubel, Arthur J.
  1966   *Across the Tracks: Mexican Americans in a Texas City.* Austin: University of Texas Press.
Soto, John A.
  1974   *Mexican American Community Leadership for Education.* Ph.D. dissertation, The University of Michigan.
U.S. Bureau of the Census
  1972   *Census of Population and Housing: 1970, Census Tracts.* Final Report PHC(1)-138 "Port City," Michigan SMSA. Washington, D.C.: U.S. Government Printing Office.
U.S. Commission on Civil Rights
  1974   *Counting the Forgotten, the 1970 Census Count of Persons of Spanish Speaking Background in the United States.* Washington, D.C.: U.S. Government Printing Office.

13
Chicano Organizations in the Midwest: Past, Present, and Possibilities

Ricardo Parra, Victor Rios,
and Armando Gutiérrez

This chapter is designed to present an analysis of the development of Chicano organizations in the Midwest. A focus will be placed on the significance of the organizational activities of the late 1960s and early 1970s and the historical actions and events that unfolded in the Midwest during this period. The chapter will cover urban and rural, migrant and nonmigrant, and state and regional organizing efforts. The analysis will deal with the successes and failures of these organizing efforts as well as suggest possible organizing strategies for the future.

Chicanos in the Midwest

Few people are aware that there are over a million Chicanos in the Midwest (Cardenas 1974b:16). Rarely have discussions about Chicanos included the people who live in this area. This neglect is not due to a lack of organizational efforts in the Midwest. Instead, it appears that the common misconception that Chicanos are only a regional minority, confined to the Southwest, has prevailed in discourses concerning the nation's second largest minority.

There are important demographic differences among Chicanos in the Midwest. The central states area (Kansas, Iowa, Missouri, and Nebraska) is largely made up of rural communities, small and

Reprinted from *Aztlán: International Journal of Chicano Studies Research* 7 (summer 1976):235-253, with permission of the authors and *Aztlán*.

medium size towns, and only a few large cities. In contrast, the Great Lakes area (Minnesota, Wisconsin, Illinois, Indiana, Michigan, and Ohio) is composed of large industrial and urbanized communities. In this region, Chicago, Milwaukee, Gary, Detroit, Cleveland, Toledo, and Lansing have sizable Chicano populations (Cardenas 1974b:16). Moreover, the latter region also has a large agricultural sector requiring a greater amount of farm labor than the central states. For example, the state of Michigan has an estimated migrant labor population of over 90,000 annually, as compared to some 40,000 to 50,000 for the entire central states area (Reno 1971; Cardenas 1974a).

The way in which Chicanos came to the Midwest is also varied. The first and largest wave of Chicanos to the region came at the start of the Mexican Revolution in 1910 when many Mexicans fled their country and settled in the industrial and railroad areas of the Midwest. These people found jobs as track hands for the railroad, in steel mills, packing houses, and in industrial factory work in such cities as Chicago, East Chicago, Detroit, and Kansas City (Taylor 1932; Gamio 1931; Humphrey 1943).

Years later, large groups of Chicanos from Texas settled in the region. Many settled out of the migrant stream into permanent occupations. Michigan became the prime state for this kind of settlement activity due to its high utilization rate of migrant farm labor (Choldin and Trout 1969).

Theoretical Framework

Oppression in our society occurs in various forms, from the crude and violent to the less direct and more sophisticated methods of manipulation and domination. The discrimination and degradation that dominated people suffer in the areas of justice, socioeconomic and political conditions, cultural and linguistic expression, and general well-being should be understood as tactics that are carried out for the maintenance and development of the process of oppression—a process in which an elite profits from the domination, exploitation, and dehumanization of others. To further the course of this domination, the elite wages a campaign of degrading the oppressed's culture, so that it may be considered inferior to their own. This cultural action on the oppressor's part is a systematic and deliberate form of action that operates upon the social structure with the objective of preserving that structure. It is this notion of cultural action, both as it is used by the elite to maintain the status quo and as it can be used by the dominated to transform it, that will be used here to critically examine the organizational efforts of Chicanos in the Midwest.

Cultural action on the part of the oppressors takes the form of cultural invasion. If cultural invasion is successful, those dominated become convinced of their inferiority and of the superiority of the dominators. The oppressed incorporate the values of the oppressors. "In cultural invasion it is essential that those who are invaded come to see their reality with the outlook of the invaders rather than their own: for the more they mimic the invaders, the more stable the position of the latter becomes" (Freire 1972:151). In cultural invasion, the world view of the invaders is imposed upon the invaded, and this inhibits their creativity by curbing their expression.

To confront this dominant and alienating culture, cultural action is also needed on the part of the dominated. This cultural action takes the form of a cultural synthesis that serves the liberation instead of the domination of people. In cultural synthesis, the actors who come from "another world" to the world of the oppressed become integrated with the oppressed; they act "with" the people instead of "for" the people. There are no models imposed on the people. The leaders and the people together create the guidelines of their action. The contradiction between the world view of the leaders and that of the people is resolved to the enrichment of both. Cultural synthesis is a way for leaders to avoid organizing themselves apart from the people. Thus, there are no models imposed on the oppressed; there is no other culture they have to mimic. Expression is found within the context of their culture because it is not portrayed as inferior. In this way, group consciousness is strengthened and the potential for liberating action enhanced.

Organizations

Sociedades Mexicanas

Some of the first organizing efforts in the Midwest centered around churches and the *sociedades mexicanas* ("Mexican societies"), both of which attempted to fulfill the need for fellowship, community, and identity. Particularly between the years of 1900 to 1940, the *sociedades* organized as social and fraternal mutual aid societies assisting in burial insurance programs, credit unions, social events, fiestas patrias, etc. (Duncan and Alonzo 1972). The larger industrial sectors of the Midwest (Chicago, Kansas City, Detroit, Gary) saw many such organizations form and provide a significant social and cultural function in the community of Mexicans.

The membership of the *sociedades* was largely composed of newly arrived Mexican workers with low paying, back-breaking jobs as railroad hands, and laborers in the packing houses, steel mills, and other industrial work. The names of the organizations reflected not only the Mexican background of the membership but also the cooperative spirit of the union (Taylor 1932:131-143). Such groups as the Sociedad Mutualista, Sociedad Union Cultural Mexicana, Comite de Beneficiencia Mexicana, and Union Civica Mexicana were quite active throughout the Midwest. Occasionally, the *sociedades* became involved in social action activity. For example, the Union Cultural Mexicana in Kansas City pressed for improved health care in the 1930s (Duncan and Alonzo 1972:13). Some of these organizations have managed to survive to the present. Some own buildings and dance halls, some operate bars and credit unions and are an important force in the Fiestas Patrias annual celebrations (national holidays celebrating Mexico's independence from Spain).

LULAC

The League of United Latin American Citizens (LULAC) was founded in 1929 in Corpus Christi, Texas (Tirado 1974). It was one of the first, and probably the most prominent, Chicano organizations to adopt an overtly assimilationist position as a solution to improving the plight of the Mexican American. LULAC soon found its way to the Midwest and has been a prominent, if conservative, institution since. Not only did LULAC restrict membership to native born or naturalized citizens, but also it made English its official language and stated in its constitution that "each member must pledge himself to learn, speak and teach same [English] to our children."

Traditionally, the organization has appealed almost solely to middle-class Mexican Americans. Its image has been that of a Mexican-American social fraternal group that conducts queen contests, picnics, socials, and raises money for small scholarships. However, with the advent of the Chicano movement in the last decade or so, some LULAC members have sought to keep stride with current developments by passing resolutions in support of the farmworkers, on education, and other Mexican-American concerns.

With the initiation of the federal War on Poverty, the organization has collaborated with the American G.I. Forum in the implementation of the Operation Service, Employment, Redevelopment (SER) Manpower Programs in addition to operating federally funded education centers in those states where LULAC has been most prominent.

In the Midwest, LULAC organizations are located in Topeka, Kansas; Davenport, Iowa; Racine, Wisconsin; Chicago and East Chicago; and South Bend and Kokomo, Indiana.

American G.I. Forum

The American G.I. Forum paralleled LULAC in several ways. Not only was it founded in Texas and then transplanted to the Midwest but it also adopted an overtly accommodationist position (Tirado 1974). Formed to protect the rights of returning war veterans, its focus soon branched off into a general demand of civil rights for all Mexican Americans. Though more aggressive in their demands for opportunity and systematic participation than LULAC, they not only required citizenship but they also required that the organization had to be composed of 75 percent veterans.

If LULAC sought to soften its image through the use of the phrase "Latin American," the forum erased any obvious reference to ethnicity altogether. While it is probably true that even the aggressive demands that the organization made for its rights as "Americans" may have been a militant action for the times, it is perhaps equally true that its exaggerated conformity and overly dramatized patriotic posture did serious damage to the consciousness of the organization's membership. Implicit in this accommodationist posture was the notion that if Chicanos were to achieve equality in the United States, they would have to change and integrate into the dominant society.

As a rule, the organization appears to be less conservative on the national level than on the local level. This is especially true for the chapters in the Midwest. In the late 1960s, for example, the national office of the forum called for a boycott of the Coors Beer Company because of discriminatory employment practices against Chicanos. Yet, one of the Kansas chapters continued to sell the beer at its headquarters. On other occasions, the use of the term "Chicano" had been of concern to the forum. Not until Vicente Ximenes, a noted national leader of the organization, gave the word his blessings did it gain some respectability among forum members. In the last decade, the forum newspaper, *Forumeer*, has given the group a bolder image than it undoubtedly deserves. Its policies have undergone no substantial revisions.

Like LULAC, the American G.I. Forum now essentially engages in such activities as awarding scholarships, holding dances, socials, queen contests, picnics, and so on. Such events are quite common in Kansas, Nebraska, Illinois, Michigan, and Indiana. In a more specific political vein, the forum has encouraged involvement in civic and political affairs. On the national level, the forum has advocated for government programs and the appointment of more Spanish-speaking people to government posts. It too sponsors SER Manpower Programs in various cities within the aforementioned states.

The Chicano Movement

It is important to preface a discussion of the more specific political and contemporary organizations in the Midwest with a brief explanation of some of the factors that gave rise to them. For if the modern organizations are a result of what is loosely called the "Chicano Movement," it is helpful to understand what gave rise to this movement.

Although many historical occurrences such as World War II, the American G.I. Forum Movement, the Civil Rights Movement, and others can be related to the gradual groundswell that has become the Chicano Movement, it was probably the United Farm Workers (UFW) led by César Chávez that gave the movement its most vital and forceful thrust. For not only did the UFW point to the shameful treatment of Chicano farmworkers, and by extension to its cause, corporate capitalism, but it also gave a ready avenue of involvement for other Chicanos, namely the boycott (Kushner 1975).

It was the boycott called by the UFW that spread rapidly throughout all of the states in the Midwest. Soon, acts of defiance and resistance by Chicanos as *Chicanos* began to surface vis-à-vis other issues. The government and nation soon began to be conscious of this, the nation's second largest minority. As a result, a White House conference on the problems of Mexican Americans was called in El Paso in 1967.[1]

As might have been expected, none of the more militant leaders of the Chicano Movement were invited to the conference. This prompted a walkout by a large number of Chicanos who held an alternative conference at another site in the city.[2] In the end, this new conference was probably more important historically than the officially planned one. The meeting, chaired by Dr. Ernesto Galarza, saw many ideas exchanged, the most important and far reaching was the surfacing of the concept of *"la raza unida,"* (literally, "the united race"). This concept was to reappear later throughout the nation and be the single most significant development in the modern Chicano Movement.

La Raza Unida

Unlike its southwestern counterpart, La Raza Unida in the Midwest developed as an organized pressure group rather than as a political party. Chicano leadership in the Midwest felt that La Raza Unida would be more effective in obtaining reforms and benefits as an organization rather than a political party. A party, they felt, would risk exposing voter weaknesses among Chicanos.

Initial La Raza Unida efforts began in Michigan under the leadership of Ruben Alfaro (*La Raza Unida* 1971). Because of the large farmworker population in this state, initial organizing efforts concentrated on their issues. Marches were held at the state capital, highlighting the plight of the farmworkers. As more and more people began to identify with Raza Unida's efforts, chapters soon spread throughout the state. State conventions, which were widely attended, were soon held. Raza Unida began to develop a communication network throughout the state. Demands began to be made for state agencies to provide more services to Chicano districts. Results soon began to be seen, not all of which were positive.

Chicanos were soon placed in key areas with command over a variety of resources. However, just as some of these people applied their power to building Raza Unida efforts, others did not. The internal strife caused by these defections quickly weakened the solidarity of the organization, which also reduced the number of volunteers who had done much of the street-level organizing. A proposal to the Ford Foundation for funding the organization on a statewide basis was rejected (Rios 1972). Raza Unida continued but with much less impact than before.

Meanwhile, Ruben Alfaro was encouraging others in the Midwest to organize. He introduced the Raza Unida concept in Ohio, Iowa, and Wisconsin. In Ohio, the organization was successful in obtaining funds to operate a migrant program, a move that had the counteracting effect of weakening its efforts in other important social action areas for fear of losing the migrant money.

In Wisconsin, the Raza Unida effort was headed by Eugenio Lara of Kenosha. The organization ran into difficulties from the start, first in securing funds, and second because the Chicano statewide organizing efforts were already centered under the United Migrant Opportunities Services (UMOS) in Milwaukee. Raza Unida in Iowa also met with organizational difficulties. In Nebraska, a statewide organizing drive, similar to the one conducted by Raza Unida in Michigan, was started. This effort, headed by the Reverend Robert Navarro, was called the Nebraska Statewide La Raza Coalition.

Labor and Civil Rights Organizations

The Midwest has also witnessed numerous groups develop around issues related to labor, particularly farm labor, as well as around a variety of civil rights issues. These organizations developed through all sections of the Midwest, and their successes and failures were quite varied.

In Wisconsin, for example, such organizations as the Obreros Unidos (Michigan State Department of Labor n.d.), the United Migrant Opportunities Services (UMOS),[3] and the Latin American Union for Civil Rights, all developed in the later 1960s to serve various needs within the Chicano communities.

In Ohio, farm labor organizing was undertaken through the Farm Labor Organizing Committee (FLOC), while in Indiana, similar activities were sponsored by the United Mexican Americans (UMA), the Midwest Council for La Raza, and the Farm Labor Aid Committee (FLAC).[4]

United Mexican Americans was formed in South Bend, Indiana, in August 1969. The membership consisted mostly of blue-collar Chicano factory workers.[5] An attempt was made at statewide organization, and chapters were soon established in Fort Wayne, Decatur, and Marion.[6] Like Raza Unida in Michigan, UMA was an advocacy organization and not a political one. It was issue oriented and marches and leafletting in support of the farm workers' huelga ("strike") were carried out. In South Bend, one of the projects undertaken was to gain control of the then Anglo-controlled El Centro Migrant Program. UMA was successful in this drive and the first Chicano director, Mr. Guadalupe Gonzalez, was installed.

Another effort by South Bend UMA was to advocate for a Chicano social service center to be funded by the local poverty program ACTION, Inc., which had always ignored Chicanos. The group was successful in obtaining a Spanish-speaking department within the Catholic diocesan structure. Within a period of time, in the absence of relatable issues, UMA deteriorated and disappeared.[7]

The Midwest Council of La Raza (MWCLR) grew out of a conference sponsored by the Urban Studies Institute of Notre Dame in 1970. The meeting had been called to highlight Mexican Americans in the Midwest and bring together leadership from the Southwest, Washington, D.C., and states surrounding Indiana to discuss a plan to merge all Mexican Americans into one national group (*South Bend Tribune* 1970). The Midwest Council is a self-determination organization. Its purpose is to give greater cohesion to the efforts of Spanish-speaking groups to advocate their own interest and to focus attention on the presence of Spanish-speaking people in the Midwest. Its activities include conferences, community development, communications, education, research, and training. Among the Midwest Council's numerous projects have been three major conferences held over a period of four years. The first of the conferences, titled Mi Raza Primero, was held in Muskegon, Michigan, in January 1972. The purpose of the conference was to educate the people—a promotion of self-identity and political awareness. Two philosophies emerged from this conference: one group thought Chicanos should work within the Democratic Party, another group wanted to support La Raza Unida Party. A resolution was passed "to support LRUP and urge people to organize chapters in their areas"(*The Militant* 1972). Bert Corona and Jose Angel Gutiérrez were the keynote speakers. The conference was important in that it was an indication of the new political movement in the Midwest (Corona 1972).

In June 1972, MWCLR sponsored a Chicano conference titled "Adelante Mujer." The idea for this conference came out of the Mi Raza Primero conference. The conference was held at the United Auto Workers hall in South Bend. The nearly one hundred women present unanimously passed a resolution calling for a national commission of Spanish-speaking women to plan and implement bilingual and bicultural day-care and education programs for children of Spanish-speaking families. Plans were made to organize and politicize Spanish-speaking women of the Midwest.[8] A board of eleven women from the states of Illinois, Michigan, Indiana, Kansas, and Ohio were appointed to organize conferences in each state and another regional conference in the following year.

In April 1975, the Midwest council held a symposium on "Human Rights and Social Justice and the Church."[9] Addressing the conference were Archbishop Robert Sanchez from Santa Fe, New Mexico, Bishop Gilberto Chavez from San Diego, California, and Bishop Patricio Flores from San Antonio, Texas. The responsiveness, or lack of responsiveness, of the Catholic Church to the needs of the barrio was the constant theme of discussion. Noting that the Catholic Church had appointed five Chicano bishops since 1970 (after having none for the previous 120 years), Archbishop Robert Sanchez said that involvement would have to come at all levels to make the church more responsive. Catholic leaders do recognize Chicanos, Sanchez said, but they tend to see them as a problem. The bishops agreed to send a telegram questioning the airlift of South Vietnamese to the United States; at the same time, Mexicans were being deported and calling for amnesty for all residents without documents.[10]

Youth Organizations

Probably the heart of most organizational activity in the late 1960s and nearly 1970s was youth. The high levels of energy and commitment displayed by youth manifested itself in the creation of a multitude of organizations that were essentially youth oriented. Like its southwestern counterpart, the Midwest created a plethora of such groups.

Undoubtedly the best known of the youth organizations was the California-founded Brown Berets. The concept of the Brown Berets caught on in many cities in the Midwest, even prior to the formal communication with official Brown Berets headquarters for authorization. The organization of the Brown Berets was based on a foundation of cultural nationalism (Mi Raza Primero) ideology. Brown Beret activity took place in the following locations of the Midwest: Kansas (Wichita and Topeka), Missouri (Kansas City),

Illinois (Chicago), Wisconsin (Milwaukee), Michigan (Detroit, Kala-mazoo, Grand Rapids, Lansing, Muskegon), Ohio (Toledo), and Indiana (East Chicago). The transitory state of youth eventually weakened the group's influence. They did serve, however, to realign the positions of other organizations to a more militant and compatible position in terms of *la causa* ("the cause").

Other youth-oriented programs developed around storefront organizations.[11] Started with the purpose of providing community services and information for the raising of political consciousness, most of these organizations waxed and waned as money to pay rent and other expenses was less available. In addition, some of these storefronts soon became little more than substitute "hangouts" with little purpose other than providing a locale for camaraderie. The vast majority of these operations have now become defunct.

An important area of youth activity revolved around student groups. Inspired by the actions of the student movement in the Southwest, Chicano student organizations in the Midwest prolif-erated rapidly and soon began to press their demands and concerns. Many of the once mild social and fraternal type of Mexican-American student organizations began to change their style, tactics, and even names. For example, the Mexican American Student Association at Wichita State University (MASA) soon become Movimiento Estudiantil Chicano de Aztlán (MECHA). In Kansas City, the United Mexican American Student Association (UMAS) surfaced; in Topeka it was the Latin American Student Service Organization (LASSO); at Kansas University it was the Association of Mexican American Students, which eventually became MECHA; at Kansas State the organization that surfaced was MECHA; in Chicago it was the Organization of Latin American Students; in St. Paul it was the Latin Liberation Front; in Iowa it was the Chicano-Indian American Student Union; and at the University of Notre Dame it was MECHA on the undergraduate level and the Centro de Estudio Chicanos e Investigaciones Sociales at the graduate level.

These organizations pressed for more recruitment efforts aimed at Chicanos, employment opportunities at the staff and faculty levels, relevant cultural studies programs, and counseling and supportive services.[12] They sponsored cultural awareness events that sought to bring people together with leaders and activists of the Chicano Movement and thereby provide important forums for giving voice and expression to the Chicano struggle. *Teatro* ("theatre") groups were particularly active in not only providing entertainment but also in providing an ideological message "between the lines" of the acts.[13]

Unique among the student organizations was the Centro de Estudios Chicanos e Investigaciones Sociales at the University of Notre Dame. Established in September 1972, to sponsor and promote social action and research within the Chicano community, the *centro* ("center") began as an outgrowth of the community activities of Chicano graduate students and was later organized into an active force for task-oriented community development. Centro de Estudios Chicanos was significant in that it was the first project of its kind to be initiated in the Midwest and indeed may be the first and only such project to be initiated outside the Southwest and East Coast. The *centro* was proposed to benefit Chicanos in the Midwest by programmatic social action activities and scholarly research. It would fulfill a need for regional and national advocacy, for historical documentation and broader private, public, and scholarly attention to the plight of Chicanos in the Midwest (Cardenas 1975).

Among the *centro*'s projects was the Midwest Conference on Raza Studies held in South Bend on April 23-25, 1974, and sponsored in conjunction with the Midwest Council of La Raza and the National Concilio for Chicano Studies Administrative Institute in Boulder, Colorado. The conference brought together Chicano professionals to develop strategies to cope with the issues that challenge the existence of Chicano studies as viable, academic disciplines (Centro de Estudios Chicanos 1974). In August 1974, the *centro* completed a study of the social and economic conditions of the Spanish-origin population of South Bend (Faught 1974). There was also a study of Chicanos in the Midwest and the Great Lakes region completed in January 1973. A recent effort has been to publish manuscripts based on the research studies of graduate students. Included in these oral histories are a compilation of newspaper articles dealing with Chicanos and Chicano activities in the Midwest (Leininger 1975). Unfortunately, the level of consciousness and commitment of newly recruited students may not be as strong as that of students at the turn of the decade.

An important organization founded by youth, but providing essential social services for Chicago's Eighteenth Street barrio has been the Centro de la Causa. In the past, it has housed a community mental health training project, a youth project, English classes for the Spanish-speaking program, and a drug abuse project along with other projects aimed at serving the needs of barrio residents. This organization has struggled to maintain its commitment to *la causa* while at the same time meeting essential program responsibilities.[14]

Centro de Accion Social Autonomo (CASA), formerly Illinois Raza Unida Party or El Enfoque, is also based in the Eighteenth Street barrio of Chicago and is also interested in promoting political education and awareness among Mexicans. This group has continued to provide a forum for the dissemination of ideas and the creation and sophistication of a truly revolutionary ideology. They conduct popular forums where they involve the community in political dialogue and discussion groups.[15]

Critical Analysis

By taking a critical look at some of the actions and dynamics of the Chicano organizations metioned, we can observe patterns of development similar to those found in organizations outside the Midwest, as well as some patterns unique to the midwestern organizations themselves. A critical reflection of these actions and their significance is important in determining the direction and emphasis of future organizing efforts. What follows is an attempt to develop a critical analysis of the aforementioned Chicano organizations within the framework of cultural action explicated earlier.

One of the most important conclusions that can be reached from the preceding discussion of midwestern organizations is that, contrary to popular belief, and like their southwestern counterparts, Chicanos in the Midwest have a long history of organizational activity. Indeed, it appears that just as Chicanos in Texas, California, and elsewhere displayed a highly dynamic culture, capable of creating and developing institutions to meet the needs created by an everchanging environment, so too did Chicanos in the Midwest.

From a theoretical perspective, the preceding descriptions essentially pinpoint at least two broad categories of institutions that have developed within the Chicano midwestern communities. On the one hand, we find those organizations that are a result of cultural action (cultural invasion) on the part of the dominant society. These institutions essentially operated for maintenance of the status quo. We can call these organizations parallel institutions, for they parallel or mimic the larger society. On the other hand, we are able to discern alternative institutions. These organizations resulted from a counteracting cultural action (cultural synthesis) on the part of the dominated society. These provided Chicanos with services that were essential to the community, and most importantly, within a cultural perspective that was not alien to the clientele.

Parallel Institutions

Chicano institutions that are parallel to those of the larger society tend to be the most accommodationist. The simple fact that they pattern themselves after Anglo institutions reveals the extent to which the larger society exists as a reference group for the creators of these institutions. Such organizations as LULAC and the American G.I. Forum are particularly indicative of these kinds of institutions. Both sought to be as much like Anglo institutions and to make their members as Anglo as possible. Thus, their names, by-laws, language, style, and so on were closely paralleled by similar Anglo social institutions. The formal dances, sweetheart contests, and scholarship benefits all found their origin in Anglo society.

Curiously enough, however, a most interesting paradox existed within these organizations. While the members of the organizations sought the acceptance of members of the larger society, it was precisely because Chicanos were unacceptable to Anglos that the organizations existed. That is, had there not been racism by the Anglo toward the Chicano and had Chicanos been accepted as equals, the institutions of Anglo society would have been open to all, thus negating the need for LULAC and the G.I. Forum.

The existence of these organizations in the Midwest was soon enough used by the larger society as a mechanism for coopting Chicanos and defusing and delegitimizing other, more radical institutions. As the ideological lines between the more conservative (LULAC, etc.) and the more radical (United Farm Workers, CASA, etc.) Chicano organizations crystallized, so too did the groups with which the Anglos were willing to work solidify. Through the dispensing of local, state, and national monies to programs such as SER and an American G.I. Forum–sponsored Veterans Outreach Program, Anglo authorities were performing various functions. First, the appropriation of money to the more conservative, parallel institutions served to legitimize these as working the hardest for the betterment of the Chicano community and by extension to de-legitimize the more radical organizations as nonpragmatic, exceedingly idealistic, uncompromising, and dysfunctional to Chicano advancement. Secondly, the dependency that was created by having programs at the mercy of Anglo funding, was to be used as a leverage time after time. Fearing the loss of monies, LULAC and forum leaders were often forced into a position of attacking further-left groups as well as endorsing Democratic and/or Republican party candidates at all levels. The existence of these institutions essentially as hostages of the larger society has severely curtailed the extent to which any strong challenge could be made to the Anglo power structure both by moderate and radical groups. In the Midwest, as in the Southwest, parallel institutions have more often hindered rather than fostered Chicano advancement.[16]

Alternative Institutions

As was argued elsewhere in the chapter, Chicanos have a long history of creating a vast array of institutions to deal with needs ranging from health to recreation. It is probably safe to say that all cultures engaged in such institutions, both formal and informal, have often operated from a completely different perspective than those of other groups. *Mutualistas* (mutual aid societies), for example, were normally nonprofit organizations run cooperatively with few formal rules and regulations governing behavior. Unlike the formal-legal nature of Anglo lending institutions with emphasis on legal contracts and sanctions, the *mutualistas* relied on peer group cooperation and mutual respect. This normally sufficed to compel participants not to take unfair advantage of the organization. They were not, therefore, Anglo lending institutions with brown faces; they were true alternatives to the values and processes of these alien institutional arrangements. As such, they looked not at the larger society for a reference point, indeed they turned their back on it. They, instead, focused on Chicano and/or Mexican culture as the basis for their operation.

Within this framework of alternative institutions, we find two variations. On the one hand, there existed the more passive, withdrawal-oriented groups. These kept Chicanos away from Anglos as much as possible. On the other hand, there also existed the action-oriented, more aggressive institutions. Both have played an important historic as well as contemporary role.

At the more passive level of resistance, we found the *sociedades mexicanas*. These organizations essentially created a sense of belonging and fellowship among Mexicans living in the United States, while providing a number of essential services. They performed the important function of preserving Mexican culture in an area physically far removed from the homeland. Although it is difficult to speculate, one can surmise that Chicano culture might not be as strong today in the Midwest had it not been for these early resistance efforts.

At the other end of the alternative institution spectrum, we find Chicano organizations that engaged in active resistance efforts. These institutions were much more aggressive and assertive not only in the demands they made on the larger society but also in their efforts to recruit, support, and raise consciousness among the Chicano community. The Midwest saw these organizations flourish historically and continue into the present.

As the prior discussion illustrated, particularly in the areas of farmworkers and/or labor organizing, all of the midwestern states saw organizations develop time and time again. In fact, a good number of strikes, boycotts, etc. have been reported throughout this region.

In the years after World War II, some of the most active of the alternative institutions revolved around the youth and a growing youth rebellion. A rigid and oppressive social structure necessarily influences the institutions of child rearing and education within that structure. These institutions pattern their action after the style of the structure, and transmit the myths of the latter. The parent-child relationship in the home usually reflects the objective cultural conditions of the surrounding social structure. If the conditions that penetrate the home are authoritarian, rigid, and dominating, the home will increase the climate of oppression. Young people increasingly view parent and teacher authoritarianism as inimical to their own freedom. For this reason, they increasingly oppose forms of action that minimize their expressiveness and hinder their self-affirmation. Thus, we cannot see youth rebellion as a mere example of traditional differences between generations. Something deeper is involved. Young people in their rebellion are denouncing and condemning the unjust model of a society of domination. If children reared in an atmosphere of oppression—children whose potency has been frustrated—do not manage during their youth to take the path of authentic rebellion, they will either drift into total indifference, alienated from reality by the authorities and their myths, or they may engage in forms of destructive action. During and just after the World War II era, many Chicano youths reacted against the oppressive social structure by incorporating the *pachuco* (a pejorative term for hip behavior; synonymous with the Anglo term "zoot-suiter") life-style. Although the values, behavior, and general life-style of this group marked a sharp departure from "Mexican" patterns—and much of their activity centered in areas that were illegitimate and/or illegal—they showed a clear tendency to avoid assimilation and accommodation. In fact, their strong antisystemic orientation often led to outright violent attacks upon them by law enforcement officials. These groups provided a haven for urban Chicano youth from both the attacks of the larger society and the assimilationist efforts of many Mexican-American groups such as LULAC.

More recently, Chicano youth have taken the path of authentic rebellion. Primary among these groups have been the Brown Berets, storefront organizations, and social action agencies such as CASA, along with some student organizations. The program of action of these groups has been one of providing community services, raising political consciousness, and denouncing the lack of justice in society.This change is a manifestation of the change in the cultural action taken by the oppressed against the oppressor.

Conclusion

This consideration of midwestern Chicano organizations sought to demonstrate several important points. In the first place, it was illustrated that the nation's second largest minority is not a regional minority but a national one. Focusing on the Midwest, we saw that large and significant Chicano populations reside in this nation's heartland. Future considerations of Chicanos, academic and political, must never lose sight of the million-plus inhabitants of Mexican background in this region. In addition, it was demonstrated that since Chicanos first came to the Midwest they have been a dynamic population giving rise to numerous institutions, many of which have persisted to the present. Like their southwestern counterparts, midwestern Chicanos have exhibited a culture that is alive and vibrant and constantly changing.

This chapter also examined the many Chicano institutions in the Midwest with an eye in finding unique as well as common strands. What emerged was an analysis that found that essentially two kinds of institutions have existed throughout time: parallel and alternative. The former institutions have been modeled after Anglo patterns. While they have been more successful in an economic sense, this "success" has been a function of their willingness to accommodate to Anglo wishes. Thus, the monies that they have received have served the larger society by making hostages of these institutions and delegitimizing those alternative Chicano institutions that sought fundamental change. These alternative institutions on the other hand, have survived in spite of efforts to destroy them. To be sure, many have come and gone as was illustrated in this chapter. But almost as quickly as one disappeared, another emerged. These have offered Chicanos in the Midwest true alternatives to the institutions of the larger society. The fact that they have continued to develop is testimony enough to the need and desire of Chicanos to be offered this alternative.

While it would be easy enough to conclude from the preceding picture that the future will probably be little more than a repeat of the past, the reality is likely to be much more complicated. Even though there has been a great amount of effort and resources expended by the dominant society to destroy Chicano alternatives— most of these efforts have been successful—each of these expenditures involves an even greater risk that Chicanos will come to see the repression forced upon them. Indeed, the central focus of many of these organizations' efforts has been precisely to expose the repressive nature of American society. A clear manifestation of such repression can be more illustrative than countless talks and newspapers. It appears, then, that what is unclear is the potential success of these institutions. What is clear is that any amount of effort by the larger society is not likely to permanently erase alternative Chicano institutions in the Midwest or elsewhere.

Notes

1. Few Chicanos from the Midwest were invited to the meetings; Roy Fuentes from Michigan was one of the few persons invited and who participated.

2. Sacred Heart Church in *Barrio Secundo.*

3. The United Migrant Opportunities Service (UMOS) of Michigan, the Agricultural Migrant Opportunities Services (AMOS) of Indiana, etc., were originally established under the auspices of the Migrant Division of Organization of Economic Opportunity (OEO) Act, known as Title 3-B programs. These statewide organizations in the early 1970s provided a source of resource mobilization among Chicano activists in the rural sectors of these states.

4. FLOC in Ohio was organized by Baldemar Velasquez. FLAC in Indiana was organized by David Cormier, Gilbert Cardenas, and Delfina Landeros.

5. Membership in this organization consisted of former migrants who had settled out of the migrant stream. For the most part they were from the lower Rio Grande valley of Texas. Ethnic and class consciousness among the UMA membership was intense during the formative stage of the organization.

6. Raul Carrasco and Manuel Garcia of South Bend, and Benny Lopez of Marion were among the leaders of the United Migrants' Association (UMA) movement in Indiana.

7. One possible explanation for the decline of UMA was offered by a former member: "Once UMA was successful in forcing concessions from established agencies and programs, some of the leaders assumed the positions that were opened, yet created a leadership vacuum that could not be filled. Many of the struggles normally waged by UMA were carried out under the banner of Chicano-controlled agency programs and many of the issues eventually ceased to be raised. Although the former leaders maintained a militant and persistent posture, the change could be described as a systematic form of cooptation where the conditions of cooptation are not necessarily reducible to an individual level."

8. The conference was organized by Olga Villa, Jane Gonzales, Cordelia Candelaria, and Betty Samora. Resolutions were compiled by the MWCLR.

9. Prior to this conference, the bishop's committee on the Spanish speaking attempted to gain more attention to the social and pastoral needs of the Spanish speaking throughout the Midwest. The conference in part, was a further step in this direction, yet it was organized primarily by an independent (non–church related) coalition of Chicano groups.

10. The entire conference was videotaped by the MWCLR, Notre Dame.

11. Examples of storefront organizations include: Aztlán Center (Kansas City, Missouri), Centro de Los Barrios (Chicago), Quinto Sol (Lansing, Michigan), and Chicanos United (Minnesota).

12. Activities of student organizations varied from location to location. Included were recruitment and minority cultural programs.

13. The Teatro del Barrio, led by Jesús Negrete, although based in South

Chicago has travelled throughout the Midwest, Southwest, and Mexico carrying a message of cultural awareness in the Midwest. The Teatro Campesino has also made numerous visits to the Midwest.

14. The Centro de la Causa has been the major catalyst in the Chicago West Side, Pilsen area, particularly along the Eighteenth Street vicinity.

15. Despite the numerical importance of the Chicago area and despite the strategic importance of Chicago-based Chicano organizations, a "Chicago" influence on Chicano movement activities in the Midwest has been minimal. The Chicano movement in the Chicago area failed to serve as a catalyst in other areas or as a central coordinating base for the Midwest. This emergence of a regional consciousness was more prevalent in the small- and medium-sized cities throughout the Midwest. The relative isolation there was, in part, a major variable in the development of a regional consciousness. An exception is the Teatro del Barrio.

16. Similar developments occurred with respect to many of the Midwest migrant programs initially established as Title 3-B migrant programs.

References

Cardenas, Gilbert
1974a "The Status of Agricultural Farmworkers in the Midwest." Notre Dame, Ind.: University of Notre Dame, Centro de Estudios Chicanos e Investigaciones, Inc. Mimeo.
1974b "The Spanish Origin Population in the Midwest." Notre Dame, Ind.: University of Notre Dame, Centro de Estudios Chicanos e Investigaciones, Inc. Mimeo.
1975 "Research and Documentation Project on La Raza in the Midwest: History and Accomplishments of a Social Action Research Strategy." Notre Dame, Ind.: University of Notre Dame, Centro de Estudios Chicanos e Investigaciones Sociales, Inc. Mimeo.
Centro de Estudios Chicanos e Investigaciones Sociales, Inc.
1974 *Midwest Raza Study Conference.* Notre Dame, Ind.: University of Notre Dame. Mimeo.
Cholden, Harvey, and Trout, Grafton
1969 *Mexican Americans in Transition: Migration and Employment in Michigan Cities.* East Lansing, Mich.: Michigan State University, Rural Manpower Center.
Corona, Bert
1972 *Bert Corona Speaks on La Raza Unida Party and the Illegal Alien Scare.* New York: Pathfinder Press.
Driscoll, Barbara
1976 *Documentary History of Chicanos in South Bend: Newspaper*

Sources. Notre Dame, Ind.: University of Notre Dame, Centro de Estudios Chicanos e Investigaciones Sociales, Inc. Mimeo.

Duncan, John T., and Alonzo, Severiano
1972 "Guadalupe Church—50 Years Service." Kansas City, Missouri. Mimeo.

Faught, Jim
1974 *Social and Economic Conditions of the Spanish Origin Population in South Bend, Indiana.* Notre Dame, Ind.: University of Notre Dame, Centro de Estudios Chicanos e Investigaciones Sociales, Inc., Census of the Population, Report no. 1.

Freire, Paulo
1972 *Pedagogy of the Oppressed.* New York: Herdor & Herdor.

Gamio, Manuel
1931 *The Mexican Immigrant: His Life Story.* Chicago: University of Chicago Press.

Humphrey, Norman D.
1943 "The Migration and Settlement of Detroit Mexicans." *Economic Geography* 19:358-361.

Kushner, Sam
1975 *Long Road to Delano.* New York: International Publishers.

La Raza Unida
1971 Lansing, Mich.: La Raza Unida of Michigan.

Leininger, Julie
1975 *Chicano Community in South Bend: Oral Histories.* Notre Dame, Ind.: University of Notre Dame, Centro de Estudios Chicanos e Investigaciones Sociales, Inc. Mimeo.

Michigan State Department of Labor
n.d. "Obreros Unidos." *Bureau of Labor Statistics.* Lansing: Michigan State Department of Labor.

The Militant
1972 February 4. Quoted by Richard Santillan in *La Raza Unida,* Los Angeles, 1973.

Reno, L.
1971 *Pieces and Scraps.* Washington, D.C.: Rural Housing Alliance.

Rios, Santiago
1972 *Proposal for La Raza Unida of Michigan.* Lansing, Michigan. September. Mimeo.

South Bend Tribune
1970 April 23.
1971 December.

Taylor, Paul S.
1932 *Mexican Labor in the United States: Chicago and the Calumet Region.* Berkeley: University of California Publications in Economics.

Tirado, Miguel

    1974   "Mexican American Community Political Organization: The Key to Chicano Power." In *La Causa Politica*, edited by F. C. Garcia, pp. 105-127. Notre Dame, Ind.: University of Notre Dame Press.

Index